ANNA JONES

a modern way to eat

200+ satisfying vegetarian recipes
(that will make you feel amazing)

Ten Speed Press
Berkeley

For John
no words suffice, how lucky I am

Published in the United States by Ten Speed Press, an
imprint of the Crown Publishing Group, a division of
Random House LLC, a Penguin Random House Company,
New York.
www.crownpublishing.com
www.tenspeed.com

Originally published in slightly different form in hardcover
in Great Britain by Fourth Estate, an imprint of
HarperCollinsPublishers, London, in 2014.

Ten Speed Press and the Ten Speed Press colophon are
registered trademarks of Random House LLC.

Library of Congress Cataloging-in-Publication Data is on
file with the publisher

Hardcover ISBN: 978-1-60774-803-8
eBook ISBN: 978-1-60774-804-5

Printed in China

10 9 8 7 6 5 4 3 2 1

First United States Edition

Foreword by Jamie Oliver

It gives me great pleasure and pride to write this foreword for dear Anna, one of my first-year students at Fifteen in London. Here she is, eleven years later, publishing her very own, beautiful, well-thought-out cookbook. This book deserves a home in any cookbook collection because it shows you how to celebrate vegetables, something we should all be doing. It has a clear sensibility about eating well, eating in balance, and embracing the seasons, all of which gives you, the reader, a real sense of how Anna puts delicious, simple, doable meals together. You're going to get lots of opportunities to see the family tree of how you can take something from the same humble beginning to all sorts of totally different endings, and that's what cooking is all about—responding to what's around you, what's in season, how you feel, and who you've got to feed. It's all very well saying that, but you need someone to explain it and get you to visualize how you can tweak, evolve, and perfect any recipe, just like Anna's done so effortlessly in these pages. Well done, Anna—this is a great cookbook, and I'm super proud.

a modern way to eat

I'd like to make a few promises about the food in this book:
- It is indulgent and delicious.
- It will make you feel good and look good.
- It will leave you feeling light yet satisfied.
- It will help you lighten your footprint on the planet.
- It is quick and easy to make and won't cost the earth.
- And it'll impress your family and friends.

The way we eat is changing

We demand so much of our food nowadays that the idea of meat and two vegetables every night for dinner seems prehistoric. We want food to be delicious, healthy, local, fast, cheap, and good for the planet. This book shows you how to make easy meals that will impress and, more importantly, nourish your friends and family, quickly and simply.

Today, almost everyone you meet, of any age, is becoming super-conscious of what they eat and the effect on their health. They also understand the importance of a home-cooked meal more than a couple of nights a week to stay healthy and on budget. Alongside that, our awareness of provenance, quality, and sustainability has come so far that if we look back at what supermarkets sold ten years ago and what we can buy now, the change is astounding. Interesting varieties of vegetable are the norm, and more unusual herbs, interesting and different grains, spices, and ingredients from afar now line the aisles. So with all this choice available to us, where do we go now?

All my friends, whether or not they are vegetarian, want to eat more simple, seasonal, vegetable-led food. As the number of vegetarians in the US slowly creeps up, the number of people reducing the amount of meat in their diet is sky-rocketing. We all know that eating lots of meat may not be the best for our bodies or the planet. For me being vegetarian is easy and how I live; for you it might be different, a few nights a week without meat maybe. However it works for you, I think we all need some new ideas.

6

We are reaching a middle ground, bridging the gap between heavy cheese- and carb-laden vegetarian restaurant offerings and the nutrition-led green juice diets. We want the best of both worlds, mind-blowing flavor that does us good: a stacked-high burger that is super tasty but also healthy, a brownie that is devilishly chocolaty but boosts our energy too, a breakfast pancake that leaves us satisfied but is packed with nutrition.

But I also believe that eating should be joyful, and as soon as rules, pressure, and diets are linked to eating, we lose track of that joy. While I eat healthily almost always, I also feel strongly that eating is one part of our fallible humanness. So there is a place for the odd too-good-to-pass-up chewy salted caramel brownie alongside a clean bowl of grains and greens.

I want to eat in a way that satisfies but leaves me feeling light and happy at the same time. Too much healthy food leaves me miserably hungry, but equally, I don't like to rely on a lot of heavy carbs or dairy to fill the gaps. I use spice, texture, flavor, and easy grains to satisfy without heaviness.

So in this book I have tried to bring together a type of food where clean and healthy meets delicious, where sustainable meets affordable, where quick and easy meets hearty. These recipes will make you and the planet healthier; they will make you richer and won't have you spending hours in the kitchen. This is a new way of eating, the way I eat, the way my friends want to eat, and, I believe, how we will all move toward eating in the future.

A change in how I cook

My cooking changed when I became vegetarian—all of a sudden I had to look at cooking in a completely different way. The building blocks that I had grown up with and the rules I had learned as a chef didn't quite fit anymore. So the challenge to find new ways to add texture, interest, and flavor to my food have meant using a new palate of ingredients and some new techniques in the kitchen.

I am led by the things that got me so excited about cooking in the first place: the haze of citrus oils spritzing off the skin of a freshly zested orange; the deep purple brilliance when you slice into an earthy beet; the warming scent of ginger and brown sugar baking into a crumble; the Willy Wonka magic of melting chocolate over a bain-marie, and so many more moments when my taste buds start dancing and my heart beats a little faster.

When I write a recipe or cobble something together for dinner, I always have three things in the back of my mind that shape my cooking: How will this taste? How can I make it more interesting to eat by layering up the textures? And how can I make it look the most beautiful on the plate?

Taste for me is about making the most of the ingredient I am cooking. Sometimes that means a little scatter of Anglesey sea salt and nothing else. Other times it means balancing herbs, spices, sweet, and sour, backing up the natural character of a deep dense caramely piece of roasted squash with warming spices, or spiking a tomato sauce with a hit of vinegar.

Textures are often forgotten in cooking, but to me they are just as key to a good plate of food as flavor, particularly in vegetarian food. I think about how children respond to food—we are tuned in to texture just as much as flavor. Toasted seeds tossed into a salad, charred, oil-drizzled bread next to a bowl of soup, the crunch of some peppery radishes inside a soft taco: it's texture, just as much as flavor, that hits the taste buds and tells your brain that this is delicious and helps you feel satisfied.

The beauty bit comes from my day job as a food stylist. For the last ten years I have been making food jump off the plate and getting you to want to eat what is on the page at that exact moment: the slick of chocolate drooling out of a chocolate fondant; the drops of water on a freshly washed leaf of the freshest, crispest salad; the melting cheese and crumble of perfect flaky pastry around the edge of a tart. I know that when I cook for friends, the simplest salad put on a plate with a bit of thought, or an easy bowl of pasta topped with some bright herbs and a flash of red chile, means we start eating before we've even got a fork in our hands. But even when I'm just making a quick breakfast or hurried lunch, I take a few extra seconds to make the food I have cooked the very best it can be.

My final consideration is a top note, a finishing touch. I almost always finish a plate with a final spoonful of something. A slick of yogurt to top a chile-spiked dahl, a drizzle of quick herb oil on a bowl of chili, some toasted hazelnuts strewn on a bowl of soup. To me, it's these final considerations that set a good meal apart from a great plate of food. Usually the quickest thing to do, these finishing touches layer flavor, add color, and create a contrast of hot and cold. These top notes make food look more thought out, they give a final boost of taste, and they make you look like a damn good cook without your really having done anything at all.

A new set of ingredients

As I started cooking in this lighter and healthier way, I started to understand more and more the importance of variety, such as using toasted nut butters in place of butter in cookies, coconut oil for buttering toast, and quinoa or millet in my morning oatmeal. Using an ingredient where it fits and tastes amazing, not solely for its nutrients, makes me push myself to step outside the reliable old recipes.

In my kitchen I look to more unusual, exciting, and flavorsome ingredients to add depth and interest to my cooking. The spelt flour in my ginger and molasses cake adds structure and a deep toasted malty flavor and is naturally easier for us to digest. The almond milk in my morning coffee, which tastes incredible, boosts my protein intake for the day and provides the healthy fats my body needs. Or the coconut butter that I use to temper spices for curries, which can be taken to a higher heat than olive oil, is perfect for releasing the flavor of the spices, with the added bonus of the subtle coconut flavor working beautifully in a south Indian dal or a dosa potato cake.

That said, flavor, above anything else, informs my cooking, so if I think butter will do a better job, I say so; if a cake needs a little sugar, I go for it. But on the whole, I keep my recipes whole-food focused.

I have, as much as possible, used different and interesting grains, as I believe that all these grains deserve a place in our diets and are often easier on our bodies. Just as with fruits and vegetables, it's important to vary the grains you eat too. Each grain has a different flavor and texture and provides your body with different sorts of vitamins and nutrients. Along with the rainbow of fresh produce in my fridge and fruit bowl, the bottom shelf in my kitchen, below the plates and platters, is a colorful spectrum of jars containing red quinoa, black rice, yellow millet, golden amaranth, and dusky pearl barley. Alongside them are jars of good pasta and spelt bread flour too, but for those trying to eat less gluten, my recipes have suggestions and ideas for delicious ways to sidestep them, and the gluten they contain, if you prefer.

A couple of extra things

Though I cook for a living, I am also pretty impatient and want my dinner on the table in less than half an hour most nights, especially after having spent a day behind the stove already. So I cook under the same constraints as most people I know. I don't want too much bother or dirty dishes at the end, a skill that harks back to my training with Jamie Oliver. So rest assured, with only a couple of special exceptions in this book, my recipes are quick and won't use every pan in the cupboard.

Another amazing kickback of these recipes is that they are easy on the pocket. Vegetables are affordable, so I make sure that I buy the best stuff I can afford and buy local and organic produce where I can. I buy heritage carrots when they are in season as I love their russets, yellows, and deep purples, and with their rainbow of colors comes a spectrum of nutrients. I buy purple kale or dinosaur kale when it's around and use it where I might use a more run-of-the-mill spinach or cabbage. I also love to use the underdog vegetables that rarely get a starring role: a violet-crowned rutabaga makes a mighty french fry; a bag of frozen peas boiled and mashed with some mint is great to stir into pasta or pile on hot toast.

When I think about how to sum up how I look at food, I am always drawn back to Michael Pollan's super-simplified equation: "Eat food, not too much, mostly plants." This is my notebook of a discovery of a new and modern way to eat and cook, one that considers our bodies and tastebuds alike. Insanely delicious, joyful food brings new possibilities and flavors that make me excited to cook and eat it for all the right reasons.

Gluten free and vegan

Gluten-free diets have become increasingly popular as a way to overall wellness. Many of the recipes in this book are naturally gluten free or can easily be adapted to make them so. While I personally eat bread and pasta from time to time, I too like eating this way as it leaves me feeling lighter and happier. I like to use gluten-free pastas, such as brown rice and quinoa pasta. I also have friends who have celiac disease, for whom eating gluten is much more than a dietary choice.

I should point out that you don't get exactly the same results by substituting a gluten-free flour for a wheat one. Using gluten-free flours in baking recipes does sometimes give a slightly crumblier texture but a deeper flavor than if you used regular flour. When I'm baking cakes, I like to add ground nuts, which can help add richness and structure.

You can use gluten-free oats (which won't have come into contact with any wheat) in place of normal oats. Some people with gluten intolerances may prefer not to eat even gluten-free oats, in which case quinoa flakes can be used instead. Some of the staple ingredients I use may have hidden gluten and if you are sensitive to it, then watch out for soy sauce or tamari (you can find gluten-free versions in health food stores), miso pastes (use naturally gluten-free white miso paste), tofu and tempeh (use plain rather than smoked or flavored and check the label carefully), and baking powder (a gluten-free version can be bought in supermarkets). I don't specify to use gluten-free bouillon, but you can buy these easily in supermarkets. I use 100 percent corn, authentic tortillas in place of flatbreads.

Many of my recipes are naturally vegan, as I often cook for my vegan brother and sister. I've included a lot of egg and dairy alternatives in my recipes as it's becoming more and more a way of life for people who want to lighten the load on their bodies and the planet.

Where I do use cheese, eggs, or butter, I have given alternatives if I can. Coconut yogurt is a favorite in place of regular or Greek yogurt, almond milk is my milk of choice for baking, and most of the dishes in this book can be made really easily without the cheese (you may want to add a little more salt, though).

On pages 350–351 is a list of recipes that are either entirely gluten free or vegan, or need only simple tweaking.

HOW I PUT A
RECIPE TOGETHER

This is what goes through my head when I'm writing a recipe. If you're anything like me, then sometimes you like the confines of a recipe and sometimes you like to freestyle. This is a guide for those freer days, which will help you layer up flavors and textures into a killer plate of food. I've used kale as an example here, but use this process for any vegetable.

1	2	3	4
HERO INGREDIENT	**HOW SHALL I COOK IT?**	**SUPPORTING ROLE?**	**ADD AN ACCENT**
↓	↓	↓	↓
CURLY KALE	BLANCH	QUINOA	AVOCADO
DINOSAUR KALE	ROAST	FARRO	FENNEL
GREENS	SAUTÉ	ROASTED SQUASH	FETA
	BLEND	SPINACH	ROASTED CORN
	RAW SCRUNCH	SWEET POTATO	PRESERVED LEMON

5

ADD A FLAVOR

↓

GARLIC

/

CHILE

/

COCONUT

/

YOGURT

/

PARMESAN

6

ADD AN HERB

↓

BASIL

/

CILANTRO

/

PARSLEY

/

MINT

/

FENNEL TOPS

7

ADD SOME CRUNCH

↓

CROUTONS

/

TOASTED
PUMPKIN SEEDS

/

ALMONDS

/

PISTACHIOS

8

SEASON AND FINISH

↓

LEMON

/

LIME

/

ORANGE

/

SALT

/

PEPPER

what gets me up
in the morning

I've never been very good at early mornings, and for years, breakfast wasn't part of my routine. But a few years back, I told myself that I deserved a real breakfast every morning. Whether that's sitting on my back doorstep, enjoying a cup of coffee and watching the early sun break through the mimosa tree or hurriedly eating a delicious bowl of granola before rushing out the door, breakfast for me is setting out my intention of how I want the day to be. Because you need different breakfasts for these different types of days, the recipes in this chapter progress from quick to slow, with the slow recipes starting on page 32.

blueberry pie oatmeal · overnight oats with peaches · turkish fried eggs · morning smoothies—a few ways · lemon maple granola · ten ways with avocado on toast · herbed parisian scrambled eggs · my morning fruit · a new eggs benedict · huevos rancheros · lemon ricotta cloud pancakes · banana, blueberry, and pecan pancakes · cherry poppy seed waffles · dosa-spiced potato cakes with quick cucumber pickle · whole-grain sunday brunch

Blueberry pie oatmeal

This is a whole-hearted, good-for-you start to the morning, as the quick maple blueberries lift this oatmeal from standard morning fare to shout-from-the-rooftops delicious.

I use a mixture of amaranth and oats here (and you could use gluten-free ones), as I love the deep nutty taste of amaranth. The way it holds its bite and then pops in your mouth makes a welcome change from the uniform texture of most oatmeals. You could leave out the amaranth and replace it with more oats, millet, or some quinoa flakes—just remember, though, that these will cook much faster, so keep an eye on them.

I vary the fruit here according to the season—apples work in winter, strawberries and cherries in spring and summer, and plums in autumn.

....

First get the oatmeal going. Put the amaranth and oats into a pan with half the milk and bring to a gentle simmer. Leave to bubble away for 20 minutes, topping up with the rest of the milk when needed and some extra hot water if the oatmeal starts to look a bit too dry.

While your oatmeal is cooking, put the blueberries into another pan with the maple syrup, cinnamon, and lemon juice and cook over a medium heat. Use a wooden spoon to mash up some of the blueberries and release their deep violet juices, leaving a few whole. They are ready when most of the liquid has reduced to a jammy texture, like a pie filling.

Your oatmeal is ready when the amaranth grains have softened and been absorbed into the creamy oats but still have a little bite.

To serve, pile the oatmeal into bowls and top with the blueberries and more maple syrup, if you like. It's dessert for breakfast.

SERVES 2

2 handfuls of amaranth
(see above for alternatives)

2 handfuls of oats

2 cups/500 ml milk of your choice
(I like to use coconut milk; see
page 39)

1⅓ cups/200 g blueberries

1 tablespoon maple syrup

1 teaspoon ground cinnamon

juice of ½ lemon

Overnight oats with peaches

Weekday breakfasts for me are usually two bleary minutes before I run out the door. If you take time over breakfast, good for you. I certainly do when time is on my side. When it's not, I get clever and make this super-quick muesli the night before.

I add chia seeds because they give a rich creaminess—if you don't want to add chia, just don't add as much milk. As good peaches aren't around all year, I often swap them out for other fruits.

A note on chia seeds: these amazing little seeds boost the nutritional value of the breakfast tenfold. They look a bit like poppy seeds and come in a variety of colors: black, white, and gray. I use the white ones here. You'll find them in health food stores and in big supermarkets beside the nuts and seeds. Chia seeds were the food of choice of Aztec and Mayan warriors, and a single tablespoon would keep them going for 24 hours. They are high in protein, so they're perfect for breakfast time. I use them in smoothies and in baking.

SERVES 2

1 cup/100 g oats
2 tablespoons white chia seeds
1 tablespoon pumpkin seeds
1½ cups/350 ml milk of your choice (I use almond or coconut)
1 tablespoon maple syrup
a dash of pure vanilla extract
a little squeeze of lemon juice
2 ripe peaches

SERVE WITH
Spring · chopped strawberries
Summer · peaches, as in recipe
Autumn · chopped sweet, ripe pear
Winter · a couple of handfuls of chopped dried peaches or pears

The night before, put the oats, chia seeds, and pumpkin seeds into a bowl or container, pour over the milk, and add the maple syrup, vanilla, and lemon juice. Mix well, then cover and pop into the fridge overnight.

In the morning, chop the peaches into little chunks, squeeze over a little more lemon, and either layer them up with the oats and seeds in a glass or bowl or just run out the door with everything in a little container.

Turkish fried eggs

This is a really good weekend breakfast, easily quick enough to squeeze in on weekdays too. It's filling, fresh, and perky from the chile and will start your day off properly. I use *pul biber*—Turkish chile pepper flakes—here. They are easy to find in Turkish shops. If you can't get them, use a chopped fresh red chile or a tiny pinch of dried, crushed red pepper flakes instead.

Pul biber, or Aleppo chile, makes its way into a lot of my cooking these days. I love the gentle heat and sweetness. I guess it's closest to an ancho chile. It's got a sweet fruity character, smells of really good sun-dried tomatoes, and still packs a chile punch. I use it in place of the searingly hot crushed chiles we find in the UK.

....

Mix the yogurt and salt in a bowl and set aside.

Heat the butter in a large nonstick frying pan over medium heat. Allow it to begin to brown, then crack in the eggs and turn the heat down, spooning the butter over the eggs until they are cooked exactly how you like them. I like my fried eggs to be just set, with a super-runny middle and just starting to crisp up around the edges. If you are having problems getting your eggs perfect, a lid over the pan can help keep in the heat so that the top and the bottom cook evenly.

Once your eggs are ready, quickly toast your pitas, then top with a good spoonful of yogurt and the fried eggs. Sprinkle over the chile, sumac, and herbs and season with a little salt if needed.

Try these with the Turkish coffee on page 330.

SERVES 2

4 tablespoons Greek yogurt

a good pinch of sea salt

a good pat of butter

4 organic or free-range eggs

2 whole wheat pitas or flatbreads

1 teaspoon Turkish chile flakes

a good pinch of sumac

a few sprigs of fresh mint, parsley, and dill leaves, picked and chopped

MORNING SMOOTHIES— A FEW WAYS

These smoothies are a glassful of everything you need to start the day off right. I am always in a rush in the morning and find it hard to make time to eat: a 2-minute smoothie helps me walk out the door with a healthy glow and boosts my protein and nutrient levels sky high. These smoothies are also great to have straight after exercising.

Smoothies are great, as they are so flexible—you can make them with whatever fruits and milk or juice you have on hand, and in the winter, you can delve into the freezer for handfuls of frozen berries. But for smoothies to be a generous alternative to a couple of pieces of toast or some perfectly scrambled eggs, they need a little bit of consideration. The flavors need to be balanced, there needs to be some protein to keep you satisfied, and there needs to be a boost of morning nutrients to start your day properly.

I have included a couple of smoothies with greens here. Green smoothies can be a new experience, but I hope these blends will win over even the more skeptical. Ounce for ounce, dark leafy greens are some of the most nutrient-dense foods on the planet, and blending greens this way breaks them down and makes it much easier for your body to take in all the goodness.

I have included some notes here on some of the things I like to add to my smoothies for an extra nutrient kick, but they will be delicious without too.

Each of these four recipes makes one giant smoothie that keeps me going until lunchtime. If you can't skip your cereal or toast, then split this between two people for a little morning kick-start.

Put all the ingredients for your smoothie, apart from the ice cubes but including any extra powders you want to use, into the blender. Blend on low to start, then turn it up to high for a minute or so. You may need to turn off the blender, take the top off, and use a spoon to get everything moving. Blend until smooth and a vivid green.

Add a few ice cubes and blend again until completely smooth. If you have added a lot of powders, you may need to water the smoothie down with a little cold water.

EASY WAYS TO ADD PROTEIN
A super easy and delicious way to boost the protein in your smoothies is to add a tablespoon of a nut or seed butter. Almond butter and tahini are my favorites, and they add a depth, richness, and creaminess to smoothies too.

Oats are a surprisingly good source of protein as well as fiber—a couple of tablespoons in your smoothie will add a lush creaminess. Instant oats work best but rolled oats work well too; I just soak mine first for a few minutes in some of the milk I will use for my smoothie.

LUCUMA   This super fruit comes from Peru, where it's known as "the gold of the Incas." It's a golden-hued pulpy fruit that is utterly delicious, and it is sold as a powder. Lucuma has a sweet, fresh kind of caramel flavor, so it's a great option for people with a sweet tooth who are trying to cut down on sugar. Perfect for sprinkling on your oatmeal or spooning into a smoothie, it's high in antioxidants, minerals, and beta-carotene. You'll find it in any health food shop. Add between a teaspoon and a tablespoon to your morning smoothie, depending on how sweet you like things.

MACA   Maca is another amazing Peruvian root, which comes from the same family as cabbage and broccoli. It comes in powdered form and has an almost malty sweet flavor. It is thought to calm the nervous system, balance hormones, and help our bodies cope with stress. Look for 100 percent maca root when you are buying it—start with a teaspoon of maca a day in your smoothie and work up to a tablespoon if you like.

HEMP   Hemp comes in seed and powder form and both are perfect for adding to smoothies. Hemp is one of the only complete plant sources of protein, making it great for vegetarians or vegans. It is also high in omega-3s and -6s, and in fiber, and delivers a solid dose of vitamins, minerals, and the super-green chlorophyll.

A tablespoon a day in your smoothie or on your yogurt and granola every day is just right.

BEE POLLEN   This isn't the stuff that floats around in summer and causes sneezing. Bee pollen is the pollen that bees collect from flowers and take back to store in their hives. They go from flower to flower collecting the stuff and packaging it into little golden granules. It may seem a bit out there to be eating this stuff, but it's an incredible whole food in the truest sense, as it provides our body with almost every nutrient, vitamin, and mineral we need as well as being super-high in protein and digestion-boosting enzymes. You can buy raw bee pollen in granules (not blocks) from your local health food store. If you are able to buy local bee pollen, it can help protect against allergies and hayfever. Bee pollen is powerful stuff, so start off with a teaspoon a day for adults, working your way up to a tablespoon, and for kids, just a few grains, working up to half a teaspoon.

SPIRULINA AND CHLORELLA   Spirulina and chlorella are two types of algae that are insanely rich in nutrients and protein. When I put either in my morning smoothie, I feel so full of energy. The stuff is like natural green caffeine. The taste of both spirulina and chlorella is quite strong, so start with half a teaspoon and work your way up to couple a of teaspoons.

GO-TO GREEN
•
1 small banana, peeled
2 apples, cored and chopped
2 large handfuls of greens (spinach or kale)
juice of ½ a lemon
1 tablespoon hemp seeds
a good pinch of ground cinnamon
1 cup/250 ml milk of your choice (I use almond)

AVOCADO AND TOASTED COCONUT
•
½ an avocado
1 banana, peeled
juice of ½ lemon or lime
1 tablespoon chia seeds
1⅔ cups/375 ml coconut water or milk
1 tablespoon toasted coconut
2 dates
a few ice cubes

SESAME AND DATE
•
1 banana
2 persimmons or ½ a mango
1 tablespoon tahini
1¼ cups/300 ml milk of your choice (I use almond)
a small handful of oats
a drizzle of honey
the juice of ½ an orange
2 dates

BERRY AND BASIL
•
1 large handful of berries (blueberries, blackberries, or strawberries)
1 large handful of greens
1 banana
5 fresh basil leaves
1 tablespoon almond butter
2 tablespoons hemp seeds
⅞ cup/200 ml milk of your choice (I use almond)
a few ice cubes

Lemon maple granola

Store-bought granola is the breakfast of choice for most of my friends who want to eat a little better. However, while cleverly branded as health foods, most granolas are full of sugar. This is why I make my own on Sunday night. Just 10 minutes' work yields a deeply satisfying and beautiful jar of breakfast for the rest of the week. I use a mixture of quinoa flakes and oats for balance, as I find oats a bit heavy for first thing in the morning, but this works just as well if you use 3 cups/300 g of one or the other (and using just quinoa will make it gluten free). Use whatever dried fruit you like here. I have kept it simple, but sometimes I like to add dried peaches, pears, or plums when I find them.

Quinoa flakes can be used anywhere you would use oats. I use them in my morning oatmeal. Quinoa is said to be one of the most complete foods in nature, as it contains a perfect balance of amino acids, enzymes, vitamins and minerals, fiber, and antioxidants. Most importantly, it is a complete source of protein, so it's perfect if you are cutting down or cutting out other proteins.

....

Preheat the oven to 375°F/190°C.

Mix the oats, quinoa flakes, seeds, chopped nuts, coconut, and lemon zest in a large bowl, then scatter over two large, lightly oiled baking trays.

Pour over the maple syrup or honey and mix well with your hands to coat everything. Bake for 20 minutes. Remember to give it a good stir every 5 minutes or so.

After 20 minutes, add all of the dried fruits and put back into the oven for another 10 minutes to get that slightly chewy, caramelized fruit texture. Then remove from the oven and allow to cool. Store in airtight jars or containers for up to 1 month.

**MAKES ABOUT
1½ POUNDS/700 G,
A NICE BIG JAR**

½ cup/170 g maple syrup or runny honey

2 large handfuls (1½ cups/150 g) rolled oats

2 large handfuls (1⅓ cups/150 g) quinoa flakes

2 handfuls (½ cup/80 g) seeds (I use sunflower and pumpkin)

2 handfuls (1 cup/150 g) nuts (I use skin-on almonds and pecans), chopped

a handful (¼ cup/30 g) unsweetened dried coconut

grated zest of 2 unwaxed lemons

a handful (¾ cup/100 g) raisins

2 handfuls (¾ cup/100 g) any other dried fruit, roughly chopped (I use dates and dried apricots)

SERVE WITH YOGURT AND FRUIT

Spring · vanilla-poached rhubarb and soy yogurt

Summer · roasted strawberries with coconut milk yogurt

Autumn · poached pears with maple syrup

Winter · dates poached in blood orange juice

Ten ways with avocado on toast

To me, avocado on toast is sunny food—it feels right on a summer's day and brightens up a dreary one. It is a go-to food when time is short and cupboards are bare. I often eat it as a hurried breakfast, very simply, with some lime, salt, and pepper. But these other ways have crept in too.

Since avocado is the star of the show, accept nothing less than soft, yielding, ripe, and perfect. Avocados are loaded with good fats and omega-3s (like the stuff you find in olive oil), and an artillery of vitamins and minerals. I would struggle to eat properly without them.

**EACH MAKES
2 PIECES OF TOAST**

- Mash an avocado with lemon juice, salt, and pepper. Pile onto toasted sourdough and top with tomatoes, a little balsamic vinegar, a bit of basil, and some olive oil.
- Mash an avocado with lemon juice and pile onto rye bread with a drizzle of honey.
- Mash an avocado with a little lemon juice. Pile onto hot buttered toast and top with a poached egg and some chile sauce.
- Mash an avocado with a little lemon juice. Spread a toasted bagel with a fine slick of cream cheese and top with the mashed avocado, generously grate over lemon zest, and sprinkle with lots of black pepper.
- Mash an avocado with a little lemon juice, pile onto toast, then top with a few thin slices of banana and a sprinkling of cinnamon.
- Mash an avocado with a little lemon juice, pile onto toast, and top with chopped pistachios, some toasted sesame seeds, and a little honey and cinnamon.
- Mash an avocado with a tiny bit of lemon juice. Top hot toast with a slick of coconut oil, the mashed avocado, and then some toasted almonds.
- Mash an avocado with some lime juice, salt, and pepper. Pile onto toasted bread and top with a good sprinkling of chopped, fresh red chile.
- Mash an avocado with a little lime juice, salt, and pepper and stir in a chopped scallion, a teaspoon of toasted mustard seeds, and some chopped cilantro. Pile onto hot toast.
- Blend some basil with a little olive oil. Mash an avocado with a little lemon juice and pile onto hot toast, crumble over some feta, and pour over the basil oil.

Herbed Parisian scrambled eggs

Sometimes I need a reminder that something simple and classic is really, really good. In my imaginary life where I spend my days roaming around Paris flea markets, this is what I would eat for breakfast. Classically, chervil is used with eggs, but it's not easy to find, so I've left it out; however, if you come across some, buy it—it's got such a piercingly delicate flavor and is great in green salads. Basil and mint can be thrown into the mix here too.

A note on how to keep soft herbs: I use herbs a lot—their flavors are like nothing else, and each is so completely different from the others, I couldn't cook without them. I appreciate that buying a lot of herbs for a little breakfast recipe feels extravagant. This is how I make herbs work harder for me. I buy a load once every week or so when they look good at the market, and I keep them like flowers, in glasses filled with a dash of cold water in the door of the fridge. This way they keep for a week or so. Every time I open the fridge, I am met with a heady smell and a grassy green wall of herbs, which means they are appreciated and make their way into much more of my cooking.

....

Everyone has their own way with eggs. This is how I scramble mine.

Heat a little oil or butter in a frying pan over medium-low heat. Crack the eggs into a bowl, mix with a fork, season well with salt and pepper, then pour into the hot pan and use a wooden spoon or a spatula to pull the eggs away from the sides of the pan, creating golden folds. Continue to do this until the eggs are how you like them. I like mine to just come together but keep a faint little bit of wobble.

Take the pan off the heat, taste, add more salt and pepper if necessary, and stir in the herbs. Pile on top of buttered toast.

SERVES 2

a little olive oil or butter

4 really good organic or free-range eggs

sea salt and freshly ground black pepper

a few sprigs each of fresh parsley, tarragon, and dill, leaves picked and roughly chopped

2 slices of good buttered toast (I like sourdough)

MY MORNING FRUIT

SPRING

APPLES · PEARS · RHUBARB ·
RASPBERRIES · EARLY STRAWBERRIES

·
·
·

QUICK RHUBARB COMPOTE

for 1 person

Take 4 stalks of rhubarb, chop small, and
put in a pan with 4 tablespoons of
good honey, a bit of vanilla, if you have it,
and the juice of ½ an orange.
Simmer for 15 minutes until soft through.

·
·
·

SPRING FRUIT BOWL

for 1 person

Cut up 1 apple and 1 pear, squeeze
over the juice of ½ a lime,
mash a handful of raspberries
with 1 teaspoon of honey,
and mix the two together.

SUMMER

STRAWBERRIES · CHERRIES · RASPBERRIES ·
PEACHES · APRICOTS ·
BLUEBERRIES · BLACKCURRANTS

·
·
·

RED FRUIT SALAD

for 2 people

Cut up 10 strawberries and 10 cherries.
Add a handful of raspberries and a
handful of halved red grapes. Squeeze over
the juice of ½ a lemon and, if you like,
add a little honey. Optional: Sprinkle with
crushed cilantro seeds.

·
·
·

QUICK APRICOT COMPOTE

makes a small jar

Put 9 ounces/250 g of apricots (pitted)
into a pan with 2 tablespoons of honey
and the juice of ½ an orange. Bring to a
slow simmer over medium heat and cook
for 10 minutes until softened.

To my mind there is no better way to start the day than with a bowl of in-season fruit. Here are the bowls I make as the seasons change. Some can be made in a batch for quick weekday breakfasts, and others can be put together in a few minutes—try with the granola on page 26.

AUTUMN

APPLES · PEARS · PEACHES · NECTARINES ·
PLUMS · BLACKBERRIES

·
·
·

ORCHARD FRUIT BOWL

for 2 people

Put 1 chopped apple, 1 chopped pear, and 2 chopped plums into a bowl with a handful of blackberries. Tear in some mint and mix well.

·
·
·

ROSEWATER PEACHES

for 1 person

Place 4 peach halves on a baking tray, drizzle with honey and vanilla, then sprinkle over some pistachios and a tablespoon of rosewater. Bake for 30 minutes until soft through. Serve with yogurt or goat cheese and some toast.

WINTER

APPLES · PEARS · WINTER CITRUS ·
CLEMENTINES · CRANBERRIES

·
·
·

POMEGRANATE-PEAR FRUIT BOWL

for 2 people

Chop up 3 ripe pears and add the seeds of ½ a pomegranate and 4 chopped-up dates. Squeeze over the juice of 1 lime and serve.

·
·
·

QUICK SPICED CLEMENTINES

for 2 people

Slice up 4 clementines and lay on a plate, sprinkle with ½ a teaspoon of ground cinnamon, and drizzle with honey.

A new eggs Benedict

I'm not sure I know anyone who doesn't like eggs Benedict in all its rich hollandaise glory. This is how I make mine. Roasted slices of sweet potato step in for English muffins, and avocado and cashews blend up creamily in seconds with a bit of tarragon to make a killer super-light hollandaise, creamy but not too rich. The caramelized onions and spinach sandwich it all together.

I like to make my hollandaise this way, as I find a butter-laden sauce too much of a treat with which to start the day (delicious though it is).

To get a creamy sauce I soak my cashew nuts in water overnight, but, if you forget, half an hour's soaking will do. See page 340 for more on soaking nuts.

For this recipe, you need to get your hands on large sweet potatoes so that they are wide enough to sit the poached egg on top.

....

SERVES 4

2 large sweet potatoes, scrubbed and sliced into ⅜-inch/1 cm rounds

sea salt and freshly ground black pepper

olive or rapeseed oil

2 medium red onions, peeled and finely sliced

6 handfuls of spinach, with any big stalks removed

4 organic or free-range eggs

FOR THE QUICK HOLLANDAISE

a small handful of cashew nuts, soaked in water (see above)

½ an avocado

a small bunch of fresh tarragon or dill, leaves picked

juice of ½ a lime

Preheat the oven to 425°F/220°C.

Lay the sweet potato slices on a couple of baking trays, season with salt and pepper, drizzle lightly with oil, and roast for 20 minutes until soft through and crisping at the edges.

Now on to the onions. Put a pan over medium heat, add a little oil, and then add the onions and a pinch of salt. Fry for 10 minutes, stirring from time to time, until the onions are soft and sweet and starting to brown. Scoop them into a bowl and set aside, keeping the pan to use later.

To make your hollandaise, grind the drained cashews in a food processor until you have a crumbly paste. Add the avocado and most of the tarragon or dill with the lime juice and a good pinch of salt and pepper and blend again. If you need to, thin the sauce with a little water until it is thick but pourable.

CONTINUED

Heat the pan you cooked the onions in over medium heat. Add the spinach and a drop of olive oil and cook for a couple of minutes until it starts to wilt but is still vivid green.

Next, poach the eggs. Heat a pan of water until boiling—I use a frying pan, but use whatever pan is most comfortable for you for poaching eggs. Turn the heat down until the water is barely bubbling, then crack in the eggs, and leave them to cook for 3 to 4 minutes. Scoop them out with a slotted spoon and drain on some paper towels.

To serve, lay some of the sweet potatoes in the middle of each plate. Top with the onions and wilted spinach, then add the egg and a spoonful of hollandaise. Scatter over the rest of the tarragon or dill, season with salt and pepper, and dig in.

Other ways to use your quick avocado hollandaise
- Spooned over grilled asparagus
- On top of a green spring risotto
- Next to a simple poached egg on toast
- In sandwiches in place of mayonnaise

Huevos rancheros

I make this dish a lot. It's the one thing I order without fail at breakfast tables in America. The holy trio of eggs, tomatoes, and avocado never fails me. It mostly crops up at my house mid-morning on a Saturday, after a walk to the store for the paper.

I have kept this version super simple, as it's a great thing to be able to throw together in a few minutes without having to run to the store. I use scallions, as they are quick to cook and have a milder note, more suited to the morning than onions, I think, but they can just as easily be swapped for thinly sliced red onion. I use fresh tomatoes in the summer, but good-quality canned ones work for the rest of the year.

The key here is cooking the eggs perfectly. I have tried a few different ways of getting just-set white and runny yolk perfection. The trick that works for me is using a frying pan with a lid and keeping the heat low so that the eggs poach and steam at the same time. I also make a version of this with roasted peppers or slices of smoked tofu instead of the eggs.

It's really worth investing as much as you can in the eggs you buy. I always buy organic free-range. Eggs are nutrient-loaded, perfectly packaged bundles of goodness. The yolks contain all the vitamins and minerals, and by keeping them runny, you actually preserve the nutrients that would be killed off by the heat if you were to cook them all the way through.

....

Heat a splash of olive oil in a medium frying pan (one with a lid that fits) over medium heat. Add the scallions and garlic and fry for 5 minutes, until soft and sweet. Add a good pinch of salt and pepper and the smoked paprika and cook for another couple of minutes.

SERVES 2
AS A HEARTY BRUNCH

olive oil

4 scallions, trimmed and finely chopped

1 clove garlic, peeled and finely sliced

sea salt and freshly ground black pepper

1 tablespoon sweet smoked paprika

1 (15-ounce/400 g) can of tomatoes, or 15 ounces/400 g cherry tomatoes, halved

1 ripe avocado

juice of 1 lime

a small bunch of fresh cilantro, leaves picked and finely chopped

4 organic or free-range eggs

2 whole wheat or corn tortillas

CONTINUED

Next, add the tomatoes and simmer for 5 minutes, until they have broken down and the sauce has thickened.

In the meantime, mash the avocado with the lime juice (I use a potato masher) and the chopped cilantro, season with salt and pepper, and set aside.

Once the tomatoes have broken down and thickened, turn the heat down to medium-low. Make 4 small holes in the sauce with the back of a wooden spoon by pushing the sauce out of the way. Crack an egg into each of the holes, season each egg with a little salt and pepper, then pop the lid on and leave to cook for exactly 5 minutes.

After 5 minutes the egg whites should be just set with a hint of a wobble, with the yolks runny in the middle. Remember, they will keep cooking as you take them to the table.

While the eggs are cooking, warm the tortillas—I do this by holding each one over a gas flame with a pair of tongs for a few seconds on each side to char, but 20 to 30 seconds on each side in a warm nonstick pan will work just as well.

Once the eggs are ready, pile them onto a plate with a decent helping of the spicy tomatoes and some mashed avocado, and scoop up with the charred tortillas.

Lemon ricotta cloud pancakes

Whenever I go out for breakfast, I order pancakes. This is my version of the pancakes I had at Gjelina in LA, which were quite simply the best pancakes I have ever eaten.

Chestnut flour makes an appearance here—you can get it in most natural food stores. It adds a depth and warmth to the flavor and is naturally gluten free; however, the pancakes would work with just plain flour. Any leftover chestnut flour can be used in cakes and baking (I use a 50/50 mix of chestnut and all-purpose flour) and works wonderfully in place of almond flour for a deeper, almost caramelly taste. Try it in the chocolate cake on page 284 and see page 290 for more information on it.

First put the ricotta into a sieve and leave it over a bowl for 10 minutes or so to allow the liquid to drain off.

Meanwhile, mix the flours, baking powder, and salt in a large bowl. In another bowl, whisk the egg whites until frothy, then add the sugar and whisk until you have stiff meringue-like peaks. In a bowl, whisk the egg yolks with the milk. Add to the flour mixture bit by bit and beat until smooth, then add the lemon and orange zest.

Using a spatula or metal spoon, gently fold half the egg whites into the flour and egg mixture. Now fold in the ricotta, then the rest of the egg whites— you should have a light and fluffy batter.

Heat a large nonstick frying pan over low heat and add a tiny bit of butter or oil. Working in batches, and using about half a ladleful for each pancake, cook until the bottom is golden and the edges are cooked. Once bubbles have risen to the top, flip and cook on the other side for a minute—then keep warm while you cook the rest. Stack the pancakes high on your plate with seasonal fruit spooned over and a squeeze of lemon juice.

SERVES 4
(MAKES 8 TO 10 PANCAKES)

1 (8-ounce/250 g) container ricotta cheese

½ cup/75 g plain white or light spelt flour

½ cup/50 g chestnut flour

1 tablespoon baking powder

a good pinch of salt

2 organic or free-range eggs, separated

2 tablespoons unrefined superfine sugar

⅞ cup/200 ml milk (I use almond milk, but regular milk works fine too)

grated zest of 2 unwaxed lemons

grated zest of ½ an unwaxed orange

butter or coconut oil, for frying

optional: lemon juice

SERVE WITH SEASONAL FRUIT

Spring · quick stewed rhubarb

Summer · raspberries mashed with lemon juice

Autumn · blueberries smashed up with a little maple syrup

Winter · quick sautéed apples and honey

Banana, blueberry, and pecan pancakes

The reason I became an expert on banana pancakes is a bleak but ultimately happy story. During an enthusiastic surfing lesson on the first day of a vacation in Bali, I got burned to a crisp, and, in order to stay out of the sun, I spent the rest of the vacation swathed in a sarong perfecting banana pancakes.

This is the result, though they are some way from the honey-drenched Indonesian ones that we ate on vacation. These have something of a banana bread feel to them and are vegan and gluten free, thanks to using pecans and oats instead of flour, and mashed bananas in place of butter.

A note on coconut milk: Most supermarkets sell a ready-to-drink coconut milk, which comes in a carton and lives next to the soy and rice milks. In the UK, I use the KoKo brand. It works in most recipes instead of milk and lies somewhere between thick canned coconut milk and cloudy coconut water. I have it on my morning cereal and in tea. This is the coconut milk I use in most of my cooking as it is lighter in fat and calories than the heavier canned version. If you can't get your hands on it, dilute canned coconut milk 50/50 with water or just use regular milk.

....

Preheat the oven to 250°F/120°C to keep everything warm.

Grind the oats in a food processor just slightly, until you have a rough oat flour. Add to a bowl with the pecans and throw in the baking powder and salt.

Mix the mashed banana with the milk (you can do this in the food processor, if you like). If the batter looks very thick, add a little extra milk. Beat the banana mixture into the flour and leave the batter to sit for a few minutes.

MAKES 8 LITTLE PANCAKES

FOR THE BATTER

1 cup/100 g oats

1 good handful of pecan nuts (about ½ cup/50 g), roughly chopped

1 teaspoon baking powder

pinch of sea salt

1 ripe banana, peeled and mashed

⅔ cup/150 ml coconut milk or almond milk (see note above)

2 bananas, peeled and cut into thin slices

a little coconut oil or butter

1⅓ cups/200 g blueberries

TO SERVE

a few pecan nuts, crumbled

lime wedges

honey, agave, or maple syrup

CONTINUED

Heat a nonstick pan over medium heat, then add the banana slices and fry on both sides in the dry pan until brown and caramelized. Keep warm in the oven.

Put the pan back over medium heat and add a little coconut oil or butter. Drop in a healthy tablespoonful of batter for each pancake. Once the sides are cooked and bubbles have risen to the top, scatter over a handful of blueberries and flip the pancake over. Cook for another couple of minutes on the other side. The pancakes will stay a little moist in the middle because of the banana, so don't worry. Keep them warm in the oven while you cook the rest.

Serve the pancakes piled with the banana slices. Add some crumbled pecans and a squeeze of lime, and, if you like, a little touch of honey, agave, or maple syrup.

A scoop of coconut and banana ice cream (see page 277) turns these into a homey dessert too.

Cherry poppy seed waffles

Like bottomless cups of coffee and inch-deep maple syrup and waitresses with name badges, waffles are very American territory to me. I started making them at home last year—I bought a $35 waffle iron—and I haven't looked back, as there is something so good about their crispy checkered exterior. They are quick and easy to make and more consistent than pancakes, and the waffle iron stays squeaky clean, so no dishes to wash. This is my poppy seed–flecked version. I make these waffles with a mixture of oats or quinoa, ground to a floury dust in the food processor, but whole wheat flour works well too.

Cherries are hands down my favorite fruit. When British cherries start filling my basket, they are all I eat for breakfast until they are gone again. They're high in iron, so they are useful for people cutting back on iron-rich meats. I keep pitted cherries in the freezer to use all year-round, and you can buy good frozen ones from most supermarkets too. These are equally good with raspberries mashed with a little rosewater in place of the cherries.

Instead of using eggs here, you can make these pancakes using the incredibly clever natural binding qualities of chia seeds. What I like best about chia seeds is how they work in baking and sweet things. You can use them in place of eggs in almost all baking: just mix 1 tablespoon of chia seeds with 3 tablespoons of water for each egg and leave to soak for a few minutes until you have a gloopy mix. I like the crunch of the chia seeds in my cake, but if you want to, you could grind them to a powder in your food processor before mixing with the water. This mixture works in all the baking in this book—just don't try scrambling them!

....

Put the cherries and honey into a saucepan and bring to a gentle simmer, then cook for 10 minutes, until just softened, slightly caramelized, and deep crimson.

MAKES 8 WAFFLES

FOR THE CHERRIES
1 pound/500 g pitted cherries, fresh or frozen
2 tablespoons honey

FOR THE BATTER
2 cups/200 g oats
4 tablespoons light brown sugar or coconut sugar (see page 275)
1 tablespoon baking powder
a pinch of sea salt
2 tablespoons poppy seeds, plus extra to serve
⅞ cup/200 ml all-natural yogurt or coconut milk yogurt
⅔ cup/150 ml milk of your choice
3 organic or free-range eggs (or see note on chia, above)
grated zest of 1 unwaxed lemon
butter or coconut oil, for cooking

TO SERVE
honey

 CONTINUED

Preheat your waffle iron over very low heat. I cook using a gas stove, which heats the waffle iron quite quickly, but you may need to wait a little longer if you have an electric stove. You could use an electric waffle maker (set to medium) too.

Grind the oats in a food processor until you have a fine powder, then put into a bowl with the sugar, baking powder, salt, and poppy seeds. In a bowl, whisk the yogurt, milk, eggs, and lemon zest. Pour the wet ingredients into the dry and beat until you have a smooth, thick batter, then pour into a pitcher to make it easier to fill your waffle iron.

Turn the heat up a little on your waffle iron. Drop a pat of butter or coconut oil on the base of it and use a brush to coat all the iron squares. Flip the iron and do the same for the other side.

Spoon one ladleful of mixture into one side of your hot iron and close the lid. Leave for 2 minutes to crisp up, then flip for another 3 minutes. The waffles are ready once they're an even golden brown and come away from the sides easily.

Serve with the warm cherries, a sprinkling of poppy seeds, a spoonful of yogurt, and a drizzle of honey.

Dosa-spiced potato cakes with quick cucumber pickle

The best breakfast I have ever eaten was a masala dosa in Fort Cochin, Kerala, India. This is how I like to work the deep, fragrant, southern Indian flavors into my day. It's an anytime dish with big flavor hitters in the shape of curry leaves and black mustard seeds, which give the potato the warm subtle punch that is the deeply clever balance of southern Indian food. It's also a great way to use up my leftover mashed potato. Any root vegetable mash works well here, but I find potato takes on the flavors best.

Mashing avocado with these spices is a revelation—I eat this on toast at least once a week.

If curry leaves aren't easy to get, you can just leave them out. However, curry leaves are wonderful, and if you haven't come across them before, try to get your hands on some. They have a curious but delicious flavor and add depth in a way that is difficult to explain, much like a truffle does. I buy a few packets whenever I see them—a lot of supermarkets stock them these days. Store them in a sandwich bag in the freezer and take a few out as you need them. They are addictive and also very good for you. They can be mixed with lime and a pinch of sugar in hot water to aid digestion.

Heat a splash of oil in a frying pan over medium heat and fry the onion for about 5 minutes, until soft and sweet. Add the mustard seeds and stand back while they pop. Scoop out a heaping tablespoon of the onion mixture and set aside to cool.

With the pan still on the heat, add the turmeric and curry leaves and fry for another minute or so, then scrape the contents of the pan into a bowl to cool slightly.

SERVES 4

FOR THE POTATO CAKES
olive or coconut oil
1 onion, peeled and finely chopped
1 tablespoon black mustard seeds
½ teaspoon ground turmeric
10 curry leaves
4 large potatoes, boiled, drained and coarsely mashed, or 4 big spoons of leftover mashed potatoes
sea salt and freshly ground black pepper

FOR THE AVOCADO
2 ripe avocados, pitted and halved
juice of ½ a lemon

FOR THE QUICK CUCUMBER PICKLE
½ a cucumber, halved and thinly sliced
1 teaspoon cilantro seeds, ground in a mortar and pestle
a pinch of sugar or a drizzle of agave syrup
grated zest and juice of ½ an unwaxed lemon
1 tablespoon white wine vinegar

CONTINUED

Add the mashed potato to the onion in the bowl, then season and mix well. Divide the mixture into 4 portions and shape them into 4 potato cakes. Put them into the fridge to chill while you prepare the avocado and pickles.

In another bowl, mash the avocados with the lemon juice (you can use a potato masher here), then stir in the reserved onion. Mix, then season well.

To make the pickles, put the sliced cucumber into a bowl and add all the other pickle ingredients. Using your hands, scrunch the cucumber slices to get the flavors going.

Now put your frying pan back on the heat. Take the potato cakes out of the fridge and fry them gently and carefully in a little oil for about 2 to 3 minutes on each side, until warmed through and crispy brown.

Serve each dosa cake piled with the mashed avocado and with a sprightly spoonful of pickle on the side.

Other ways to use your cucumber pickle
- Sandwiched inside a veggie burger
- Alongside a bowl of dal and rice
- In a bagel with some cream cheese and grated lemon zest
- In a cheese sandwich
- With any curry
- To make the best-ever cucumber sandwiches

Whole-grain Sunday brunch

Sometimes a fortifying breakfast or brunch is needed, but I have never been on board with heavy, greasy food to start off the day. For me breakfast sets the tone for how I want my day to be. I eat this breakfast after a night out or before a day of the same—I guess you could say this is my full English breakfast. In autumn and winter, when tomatoes are not at their best, use a few sun-dried tomatoes instead, added at the end.

You can make this in the time it takes someone else to go and buy the newspaper and to brew a decent cup of coffee. I encourage you to try grains rather than toast for breakfast. I find them so much more sustaining than bread, and they work perfectly here. If you like, though, a good slice of bread works wonderfully in place of the farro. Sometimes for a really filling brunch I sizzle up a couple of the chestnut sausages on page 201 too, or pan-fry a couple of slices of tofu, in place of the egg.

Sage is not perhaps the most obvious choice for a breakfast herb, but it works perfectly here. I love sage—the word, the taste, the bolstering flavor it brings—there is something ancient about it that I adore. In fact, it's a member of the mint family, and you can taste the relationship. I love to fry sage leaves in hot oil until perfectly crisp and sprinkle them on fried eggs or roasted squash.

....

Preheat your oven to 425°F/220°C.

Place the squash and mushrooms on a tray, season with salt and pepper, and drizzle with a little oil. Bake for 15 minutes.

Next, rinse the farro under cold water, then put it into a pan of boiling, salted water and cook for 20 to 25 minutes, until tender (or cook the quinoa for 10 minutes), making sure to add more water as needed.

SERVES 2, THOUGH THIS CAN EASILY BE SCALED UP FOR A BIG FRIENDLY BRUNCH

¼ of a butternut squash or similar, seeded and cut into ⅜-inch/ 1 cm slices

2 portobello mushrooms

sea salt and freshly ground black pepper

olive or rapeseed oil

½ cup/100 g farro or quinoa

handful of cherry tomatoes

a small handful (⅓ cup/50 g) of almonds

a few sprigs of fresh sage (about 20 leaves)

1 lemon

2 organic or free-range eggs, for poaching (more if you are hungry)

After the squash and mushrooms have baked for 20 minutes, take the tray out of the oven and add the tomatoes. Sprinkle with salt and pepper, drizzle with oil, and put back into the oven for another 20 minutes.

To make the sage and almond pesto, toast the almonds in a pan until fragrant and just browning, then remove from the heat. In a mortar and pestle, mash the sage leaves with a pinch of salt. Add the almonds and grind until you have a chunky paste, then pour in 4 tablespoons of oil, squeeze in the juice of a quarter of the lemon, and grind again until it's smoothish. (This can be done in a food processor too.) Season with salt and pepper, tasting and balancing to your liking.

Finally, bring a pan of water to a boil to poach your eggs (I use a frying pan). Turn the heat down until the water is barely bubbling, then crack in the eggs and leave to cook for 3 to 4 minutes. Scoop out with a slotted spoon onto paper towels.

Spoon the farro onto plates, pile on the roasted vegetables, top with an egg, then drizzle generously with the pesto and enjoy at a slow pace.

food for filling a gap

If you're going to snack, you might as well do it properly in every sense. Snacking between meals with something that is delicious, thought out, and healthy stops me from reaching for a chocolate cookie. Whether it's a simple slick of almond butter on a rice cake or a handful of kale chips or some homemade spicy caramel popcorn, a considered snack keeps me happy, fulfilled, and full of energy. All of these recipes are perfect for a crowd too—just double them as needed to fuel a party.

speedy sweet potato quesadillas · oven-baked kale chips · smokey walnut and cumin muhammara · maple peanut california wraps · hummus · homemade tortilla chips with charred-chile salsa · spiced salt caramel popcorn · caper, herb, and soft-boiled egg sandwich · killer smoked tofu club sandwich · quick sandwich ideas

Speedy sweet potato quesadillas

Quesadillas are an anytime meal. They take just 5 minutes to make, and everyone loves them. You can snack on them at a party, they make a late-home-from-work dinner, and they even work at breakfast with an egg inside.

These quesadillas are a bit different—the regular, white flour, cheese-loaded version doesn't do it for me. So instead, these are filled with a super-quick sweet potato and white bean mash. You will never look back.

Two types of chiles feature here, though don't worry—they are not super hot. I don't like that intense chile burn feeling. To me any food that sends your body into panic or out of balance can't be good. But I do crave heat, and this blend of the deep smokiness of the chipotle and the sweet raw heat of the fresh chile packs a well-rounded punch.

Many places have started to stock chipotle paste, which has made its sweet smokiness more easy to come by. If you can't get your hands on chipotle, ½ a teaspoon of hot smoked paprika will do.

It's worth making a mention of what chiles have hidden in their colorful little packages. They are super high in antioxidants and vitamins, and they boost the immune system and help speed your metabolism: chile magic.

....

Heat a small amount of olive oil in a pan, add the sweet potato and the maple syrup, and season with salt and pepper. Add the chipotle paste and the chopped chile and cook for a few minutes until the potato has softened and lost its rawness.

Transfer to a bowl and add the beans, then use a potato masher to mash everything a little—you will still have some flecks of unmashed sweet potato. Season if needed.

CONTINUED

SERVES 2 AS A DINNER OR 4 AS A SNACK

olive oil

1 sweet potato, peeled and grated

1 tablespoon maple syrup

sea salt and freshly ground black pepper

1 teaspoon chipotle paste

1 red chile, seeded and finely chopped

1 (15-ounce/400 g) can navy beans, rinsed and drained

1 avocado

½ a lime

a few sprigs of fresh mint or cilantro, leaves picked and chopped

4 corn tortillas (see note on page 13)

Mash the avocado with a little lime juice and stir in the herbs. I use the potato masher again here.

Now heat a frying pan big enough for your tortillas. Lay a tortilla flat in the pan, spoon a quarter of the mixture onto one half of it, then fold over the other half. Dry fry on one side until it's blistered and golden brown, then flip over and do the same on the other side. Keep the quesadilla warm in a low oven while you do this with the rest of the tortillas.

Serve straight from the pan with the mashed avocado.

As part of a bigger meal
- Serve with a couple of handfuls of lemon-dressed salad leaves.
- Serve with a crunchy salad of radishes, leaves, shaved fennel, and cilantro and a quick tomato salsa.

Oven-baked kale chips

Kale chips have found their way to the UK from health-conscious Americans. They are delicious—salty, sweet, crisp, and all-round good—a super-healthy alternative to a package of potato chips. The only downside is the price tag. I have seen them for as much as $14.50 for a little pot, which would last half an hour in my house.

I've got some friends who make them using their dehydrator, which slowly dries out and preserves food, but don't worry: I'm not about to tell you to go out and buy a $500 piece of equipment either.

The answer is a $2 bunch of kale and the trusty oven. Cooking the chips in the oven means they don't have quite the same "raw" credentials as their dehydrated brothers, but I like compromise and this is a good one— oven-baked kale for deep-fried potato.

I couldn't decide which flavor was best, so here are both. The miso and sesame seed version has all the sweet savoriness of a killer sushi roll. The tarragon mustard chips are sweet and fragrant. Give both a try and then experiment with your own—stick to a combination of salt, acid, and sweet, and you can't go wrong.

These are a great way to get greens haters onto the good stuff. Disguised as little flavor pop chips, these could persuade anyone to like kale.

....

Preheat the oven to 250°F/120°C. Line two baking trays with parchment paper.

Tear the kale off its stalks into chip-size pieces (remember, they will shrink a bit). Little stalks are fine, you just don't want any of the big ones. Lay them well spaced out on the baking trays.

MAKES ENOUGH FOR A FEW FRIENDS TO NIBBLE, OR A FEW DAYS' SNACKING FOR 1

7 ounces/200 g curly kale, washed and spun dry (I use a mix of white, green, and purple)

FOR THE TARRAGON
AND MUSTARD DRESSING

1 tablespoon whole grain mustard

1 tablespoon olive oil

1 tablespoon honey or agave syrup

½ a bunch of fresh tarragon, leaves picked and chopped

juice of 1 lemon

a good pinch of sea salt

FOR THE SESAME
MISO DRESSING

1 teaspoon red miso paste

1 tablespoon soy sauce or tamari

1 tablespoon olive oil

1 tablespoon maple syrup

juice of 1 lime

3 tablespoons sesame seeds

CONTINUED

Make whichever dressing you choose, mixing the ingredients in a bowl. Drizzle the dressing evenly over the trays of kale. Now get your hands in and toss and turn the kale in the dressing until everything feels coated.

Put your kale into the oven for 30 minutes. Then take both trays out and loosen the kale from the parchment paper with a spatula. Pop the trays back in, turn the oven off, and leave them until they have crisped right up, which will take about another 30 minutes.

Lift the kale chips from the tray and store them in a jar or an airtight container. They will keep for up to a week, but they will be gone long before that.

Smoky walnut and cumin muhammara

If there is someone in your life who thinks vegetarian food is bland, hand them a bowl of this and some charred flatbreads and give them 5 minutes. It's a riot of flavors: musky sweetness from the peppers, earthy spice from the cumin, and buttery depth from the walnuts. And it's so versatile. I keep a jar of it in the fridge for spicing up pretty much any meal.

Pomegranate molasses is traditionally used to add a sweet piquant roundness. Most larger supermarkets and Middle Eastern stores stock it, but if you can't get your hands on it, you can substitute a tablespoon of balsamic vinegar and a tablespoon of maple syrup, dark honey, or agave syrup.

....

Preheat your oven to 425°F/ 220°C

Put the nuts and cumin seeds on a baking tray and roast for 6 minutes until the nuts are just starting to turn golden and the cumin smells wonderful and has released its oils. Transfer to a food processor and add the red peppers. Blend to a paste, then add the breadcrumbs, tomato purée, pomegranate molasses, chile flakes, lemon juice, and a good pinch of salt and pepper. Blend again until smooth.

With the food processor on, slowly pour in the oil and blend until really smooth. Taste, season if needed, and blend again. Keep tasting and balancing the flavors—you may need a bit more lemon juice or more molasses and seasoning. Get it how you like it. This will keep well in the fridge for at least a week.

Ways to use your muhammara
· For breakfast, spread on toast and topped with a poached egg
· As a marinade for barbecued tofu or vegetables
· Thinned with a little oil as a dressing for roasted root vegetables, beets, and squash
· Piled on the side of a plate of lentils or beans with a little yogurt and some herbs

MAKES A GOOD JARFUL, ENOUGH FOR A CROWD TO DIP INTO

½ cup/75 g shelled walnuts

1 teaspoon cumin seeds

1 (8-ounce/200 g) jar of roasted red peppers, or 3 freshly roasted red peppers, peeled, seeded, and chopped

2 slices of good brown bread, ground to breadcrumbs

2 tablespoons good-quality tomato purée

2 tablespoons pomegranate molasses (for alternative, see note above)

1 teaspoon Turkish chile flakes (see page 22) or a pinch of red pepper flakes

juice of ½ a lemon

sea salt and freshly ground black pepper

4 tablespoons extra virgin olive oil

Maple peanut California wraps

This wrap sustained me through a week in the desert, listening to music, a few years ago. It's just the right combination of refreshing greens, vitamin-loaded carrot, and good protein energy from tempeh and seeds.

But the crowning glory here is the sauce—it's one of those sauces that hits every flavor note and leaves you wanting more. It's good on a salad too. I have been known to eat two of these in one sitting. They are that good. Super quick to put together, these are a weekday lunch for me at least once a week and often make an appearance in summer for supper, with some roasted sweet potato wedges.

Tempeh is a cake of pressed soybeans. It is a great source of protein and works well in most recipes where you might use tofu. I buy my tempeh from my local health food store. Tempeh is a fermented food, which actually makes it much easier to digest than other types of soy. Tempeh does need a bit of special treatment, such as this marinade, as its flavor is quite neutral. Firm tofu would work here too.

MAKES 4 WRAPS

FOR THE TEMPEH

1 tablespoon maple syrup

1 tablespoon soy sauce

1 tablespoon olive oil

1 tablespoon balsamic vinegar

8 ounces/200 g tempeh, cut into ⅜-inch/1 cm slices

FOR THE PEANUT DRESSING

2 tablespoons all-natural peanut butter

2 teaspoons miso paste

2 teaspoons soy sauce

2 tablespoons maple syrup

2 tablespoons tahini

juice of 1 lemon

FOR THE WRAP

4 whole wheat tortillas

2 carrots, grated

4 tablespoons mixed toasted seeds

4 handfuls of salad greens

Mix the maple syrup, soy sauce, olive oil, and vinegar in a bowl. Add the tempeh and turn to coat in the marinade. Set aside.

Next, make the dressing. Whisk all of the ingredients together, with a tablespoon of water if it's too thick, taste, and check for balance, then set aside.

Heat a dry pan and fry the tempeh for a couple of minutes on each side until browned and starting to caramelize.

Warm the tortillas—I do this by holding them with tongs over a gas flame for a few seconds, but the oven or a dry nonstick pan will work too. To assemble each wrap, place some tempeh on each tortilla; top with a quarter of the grated carrot, seeds, and greens; then add a quarter of the dressing. Repeat with the rest of the wraps.

HUMMUS

DATE AND BLACK SESAME

●

1 (15-ounce/400 g) can cannellini beans, rinsed and drained

1 tablespoon olive oil

4 medjool dates, roughly chopped

juice of ½ a lemon

½ tablespoon miso paste

sea salt

2 tablespoons date syrup

2 tablespoons toasted black sesame seeds

If you don't have date syrup handy, a drizzle of dark honey or dark agave syrup would work really well. Well-toasted white sesame seeds will work here if you can't get black ones.

....

Put your beans into a food processor with the olive oil, dates, lemon juice, miso, and a pinch of salt and blend to your desired consistency. Taste, add more salt if necessary, and thin with a bit of water or more olive oil if it looks too thick. I like to blend throughly for a light and fluffy result, but some like more texture—you decide.

Once the texture is how you like it, scoop it into a bowl, drizzle over the date syrup and sprinkle with the black sesame seeds.

BLACK BEAN AND PUMPKIN SEED

●

1 (15-ounce/400 g) can black beans, rinsed and drained

1 green chile, stemmed and roughly chopped, plus more chopped chile for garnish

a small bunch of fresh cilantro, roughly chopped, plus more chopped cilantro for garnish

grated zest and juice of 1 unwaxed lime

1 tablespoon maple syrup

a good handful of pumpkin seeds

sea salt and freshly ground black pepper

a good drizzle of olive oil

A classic Mexican combination for a reason—this is especially addictive with the homemade tortilla chips.

....

Put everything except the extra chile and cilantro garnishes into a food processor and blend until it's the texture you like. Taste and add more salt and pepper if needed, and thin with more oil or water if it's too thick.

Scoop into a bowl. Mix the remaining chile and cilantro with a little olive oil and drizzle on top.

If your house is anything like mine, or those of most of my friends for that matter, then a lot of containers of hummus find their way into fridges and onto tables. I usually make my own, as I like being able to adapt the flavors to what's going on at the time, seasons, moods, and what else is in the fridge. The chickpea/tahini format can get a bit boring, so here are some offbeat versions you won't find in stores. The principle can be followed with pretty much anything, as long as you keep to roughly the same quantities of beans/citrus/seasonings below.

These recipes are a great way to use up leftover beans.

All these keep in the fridge for 5 days. Each recipe makes a good jarful.

LIMA BEAN, ALMOND, AND ROSEMARY

•

1 (15-ounce/400 g) can lima beans, drained
grated zest and juice of 1 unwaxed lemon
a handful of whole almonds
2 sprigs of fresh rosemary, leaves picked
2 to 3 teaspoons almond milk or water
sea salt and freshly ground black pepper
a good drizzle of olive oil
a few whole almonds, toasted and chopped, for garnish

Here the rosemary and almonds come together in an Italian way. This is a good start to a meal, with some grilled olive-oil-drizzled toast. I make mine with untoasted nuts, but toasted nuts add smokiness, so try both.

....

Put all the ingredients except the toasted almonds into a food processor and blend until it's as smooth as you like. Add a little extra water if needed until it's a good consistency.

Top with the chopped almonds and another drizzle of olive oil.

PEA AND GREEN HERB

•

10½ ounces/300 g frozen peas
a small bunch of fresh mint
a small bunch of fresh basil
2 tablespoons good extra virgin olive oil
grated zest and juice of 1 unwaxed lemon
sea salt and freshly ground black pepper

Who says you can't make hummus with peas? Not me. Slather this on bruschetta or spoon it on top of a simple risotto; leftovers can even be stirred into pasta. Kids love this one. Sometimes I add an avocado for a bit of extra creaminess. Fava beans work just as well here. I use fresh peas in springtime—the rest of the year, frozen peas are your friend.

....

Place the peas in a bowl and cover them with hot water. Let sit for a minute, then drain. Put them into a food processor with everything else and blend until you have a bright green paste (a hand blender works well too), then taste and season with more salt and pepper or lemon if needed.

Homemade tortilla chips with charred-chile salsa

These tortilla chips are a massive hit every time I make them, so much so that I have taken to making them every time anyone comes over. Even the sniff of a visitor and these are in the oven and I'm blending up some salsa. I love the compliments. I sort of feel a bit guilty about how much people like them, as they are so easy a five-year-old could make them, which makes people love them even more.

These can be made easily with tortillas, wraps, pitas, leftover chapatis, or whatever you have on hand. Corn tortillas are my choice. Below is my favorite way to flavor them, but most spices work really well: cumin and cilantro are favorites, and a bit of lemon zest and some chopped thyme or rosemary also goes down well.

Eat these with anything you can dip them into. In my house it's most often this smoky salsa, but mashed avocado, hummus, and spice-spiked yogurt are also really good. Try the Indian mashed avocado on page 45 with chips made from chapatis and spiced with cilantro and some lemon zest, for another winning combination.

MAKES A BIG BOWLFUL

FOR THE SALSA
4 scallions
1 red chile, pricked with a knife
20 cherry tomatoes or
8 big tomatoes
a small bunch of fresh cilantro
olive oil
juice of 1 lime
sea salt and freshly ground
black pepper

FOR THE TORTILLAS
8 tortillas, wraps, flatbreads,
or chapatis
olive oil
1 teaspoon smoked paprika
sea salt

Preheat the oven to 400°F/200°C.

Place a griddle pan over very hot heat. Once it's smoking hot, put the scallions, chile, and tomatoes on the griddle and let char on each side. Remove the scallions once they are black, then the chile, and finally the tomatoes. This will take 5 minutes or so. Transfer to a bowl to cool.

Once cool enough to handle, transfer to a cutting board. Use a big knife to chop everything together until you have a chunky salsa consistency, discarding the green top of the chile as you go. When the salsa is nearly there, add the cilantro and chop it into the mixture.

Put the mixture into a bowl with a good glug of olive oil, the lime juice, and a good pinch of salt and pepper. Taste, balancing the flavors with more lime, salt, or oil if needed.

Cut each tortilla, wrap, flatbread, or chapati into 8 triangles and spread out on a couple of baking trays. You don't want them to be too crowded or they won't crisp up.

Drizzle them with oil and sprinkle over the smoked paprika and a good pinch of sea salt.

Bake for 10 minutes, until crisped and delicious. Serve piled high in bowls with the salsa.

Other ways to use your salsa
- To top quesadillas (see page 52)
- In a toasted cheese sandwich
- To top a baked sweet potato
- To dip potato wedges into
- Alongside a poached or fried egg for breakfast
- To top some avocado on toast

Spiced salt caramel popcorn

Salty-sweet caramel-coated popcorn—serve it in big bowls or in cinema-style paper containers for a special movie night. And make lots—it goes quickly.

I love cinnamon—it's such a comforting spice. Half a teaspoon of ground cinnamon a day mixed into tea or hot water can help with digestion problems. Be careful to buy real or Ceylon cinnamon and not cassia. Cassia is the outer bark of the cinnamon tree—it's darker and comes in a stick-like curl of bark. It has a punchy medicinal aroma and is used widely in the United States. Real cinnamon is sweeter and more calming. The sticks are lighter in color and crumble very easily. If you buy from a good natural foods store or spice shop, you should know what you are getting.

First get your popcorn popping. Heat a very large pan (make sure it's one with a lid) over medium heat and add a splash of oil. If you don't have a very large pan, two smaller ones will do. Once it's hot, add the popcorn kernels, put on the lid, and turn the heat down to low. Give it a good shake every 30 seconds or so to move the kernels around and keep them from burning. It will be a while before the popping starts. But when it does, it will come thick and fast, so don't be tempted to lift the lid.

While your corn is popping, make the caramel. Put the sugar into a pan with scant ½ cup/100 ml water, place over medium heat, and bring to a simmer, being careful not to touch it. Keep it bubbling until the water has reduced and you have a deep caramel color. Don't be tempted to stir or you will end up with crystallized caramel.

Once your popcorn has finished popping, remove it from the heat and pour it into a deep baking tray. Very carefully pour over your caramel, using a metal spoon to mix it throughout the popcorn—do not touch the popcorn with your hands, as the caramel will be very hot. Sprinkle over the cinnamon and salt, grate over the nutmeg and orange zest, and mix again with a spoon. Allow the caramel to cool completely before eating.

SERVES 10

a splash of vegetable oil

2¼ cups/400 g popping corn

scant 1 cup/200 g packed unrefined light brown sugar

1 tablespoon ground cinnamon

a pinch of sea salt

½ a nutmeg, freshly grated

grated zest of 1 unwaxed orange

Caper, herb, and soft-boiled egg sandwich

I never used to like egg sandwiches—I always steered clear of them. My boyfriend John loves them, so one day I set out to make the best one he'd ever eaten. The kickback was, I liked it too: soft, just-set yolks, plenty of character from an almost tartare-style dressing, and a bit of zip from some snipped green herbs. This is quick fresh food at its best: freshly made straight onto the plate. It's the only way to eat egg sandwiches to my mind.

I find yogurt really useful in the kitchen—it makes its way into cakes, batters, and breads. I use good organic Greek yogurt in place of mayonnaise and in more indulgent desserts, and a natural one for breakfasts and toppings. For me it's important to vary my diet so as not to become reliant on one thing too much, so I also keep coconut milk yogurt on hand for days when I'm feeling like changing things up a little.

MAKES 4 SANDWICHES

6 organic or free-range eggs

6 cornichons or 2 large pickles, chopped up small

2 tablespoons little capers in brine, or big ones chopped up

2 tablespoons Greek yogurt

1 teaspoon good Dijon mustard

grated zest and juice of ½ an unwaxed lemon

a few sprigs of fresh dill, chopped

a few sprigs of fresh parsley, chopped

optional: 1 stick of celery, chopped up small

sea salt and freshly ground black pepper

8 slices of good bread (I like seeded bread)

First put the eggs into a pan, cover with cold water, and bring to a boil. Once the water is boiling, set the timer for 6 minutes (you may need a touch longer for large eggs).

Once the eggs have had 6 minutes, drain them and put them under running cold water until they have cooled a little. Then leave them in a bowl of cold water until they are cool enough to peel.

Put the rest of the ingredients except the bread into a bowl and mix together. Once the eggs are cool, peel and roughly chop them and add them to the bowl. Taste and adjust the seasoning, adding more salt, pepper, or lemon as needed. If your bread is super-fresh, there's no need to toast it, but if it's a little firm, pop it into the toaster. Pile the eggs on to 4 of the pieces of toast and top with the other 4 pieces.

I sometimes add a handful of seasonal salad leaves too—pea shoots, watercress, and arugula all work well.

Killer smoked tofu club sandwich

John thinks this might be the best thing I have ever made. It's basically an assembly job, putting a few good things between two slices of bread, as a sandwich should be.

....

Heat a nonstick frying pan over medium heat, then add the tofu slices and warm them on both sides.

Put the chipotle paste, mayonnaise, and lime juice into a bowl, season with a little salt and pepper if needed, and mix well.

Toast your bread and get everything ready to assemble your sandwich.

Spread 2 slices of the toast with the chipotle sauce and the other 2 slices with the mashed avocado. Top the avocado with the tofu, lettuce, and tomatoes. Place the chipotle-coated slices on top, cut in half, and eat immediately.

MAKES 2 HEALTHY SANDWICHES

3½ ounces/100 g smoked tofu, cut into 6 slices

1 tablespoon chipotle paste

1 tablespoon mayonnaise or vegan mayonnaise

juice of ½ a lime

sea salt and freshly ground black pepper

4 slices of good bread (I use sourdough or a seeded bread)

½ an avocado, roughly mashed

1 Little Gem lettuce, shredded

8 sun-blushed tomatoes

QUICK SANDWICH IDEAS

Sandwiches are one of my favorite things. Something great happens when the right combination of fillings is sandwiched between two slices of bread. These are modern, vegetable-packed sandwiches. I use good bread—sourdough, rye, seeded, or even millet.

HUMMUS

SLICED TOMATO

SUN-DRIED TOMATOES

HUMMUS

BLACK OLIVES

HARISSA

TOASTED SEEDS

FALAFEL

FALAFEL

CAPER BERRIES

TOMATOES

HUMMUS

PICKLED BEETS

SPINACH

LEMON JUICE

VEGETABLE

SPROUTS

GRATED CARROT

SPINACH

MASHED AVOCADO

CHERRY TOMATOES

PESTO

CLUB

SMOKED TOFU

SLICED CHEDDAR

PICKLES

LETTUCE

CHERRY TOMATOES

MUSTARD

MAYONNAISE

SAN FRAN

PESTO

ALMONDS

PECORINO

ARUGULA

HONEY

LEMON JUICE

AVOCADO

MASHED AVOCADO

FETA

CILANTRO

LIME

CHERRY TOMATOES

LETTUCE

CHILE/CHIPOTLE

ASPARAGUS

BLANCHED ASPARAGUS

PARMESAN

AVOCADO

PUMPKIN SEEDS

ARUGULA

LEMON JUICE

BEET

COOKED BEETS

GOAT CHEESE

PUMPKIN SEEDS

ARUGULA

LEMON ZEST

a bowl of broth, soup, or stew

There is something about one-pot cooking that feels very nourishing. All the goodness of every ingredient is released into the soupy mix. Most of these soups and stews come together in under 30 minutes and require only a little bit of up-front chopping. In the colder months, I tend to make a pot of soup on a Monday night, usually a double recipe in my biggest cast-iron pot. We then dip into it for lunches and dinners for the rest of the week, varying the toppings so that boredom doesn't creep in. We start with a chunky soup and after a couple of bowls, I blend it up and it feels brand new.

chickpea and preserved lemon stew · seeded bread and roast tomato soup · one soup: one thousand variations · walnut miso broth with udon noodles · restorative coconut broth · sweet tomato and black bean tortilla bowls · charred pepper and halloumi stew · celeriac soup with hazelnuts and crispy sage · lemony lentil and crispy kale soup · white beans, greens, olive oil—my ribollita · cardamom and star anise winter squash soup

Chickpea and preserved lemon stew

This was a quick evening creation, one of those moments when the stars align. Even though you haven't been to the store, a few ingredients jump out of the fridge, and they effortlessly come together in the pan to make something special.

I make this when I want the warmth of a soup but need something a little heartier. The depth of flavor from the cinnamon, preserved lemon, and tomato tastes like something cooked slowly for hours, but in fact this is a really quick recipe to make, and the warming flavors of Arabic spices are all the more heartening on a cold evening.

I use Israeli couscous here, as it's bigger, heartier, and more substantial than the finer couscous and I think stands up very well to being cooked in a stew. It is available in most supermarkets, though you could swap it for bulgur wheat if you like, or quinoa if you are avoiding gluten.

A note on preserving lemons: the unique salty-but-scented zippiness of preserved lemons introduces a punchy note to this stew. Use them too in salads, to add to a rice pilaf, in spiced soups, and to liven up grains and beans. They are best added toward the end of cooking. I use a super-simple variation of the classic Claudia Roden recipe to make them. Cut 4 lemons into quarters, without going all the way through to the bottom, then pack the cuts generously with sea salt. Squash them into a canning jar, seal, and leave for a couple of days so that the salt draws out the juice. Top the jar up with the juice from 4 more lemons, to cover everything completely. Leave in a cool place for a month, then they are ready to use.

Heat a little olive oil in a pan over medium heat, then add the onion, carrot, garlic, and a good pinch of sea salt. Cook for 10 minutes, until the onion is soft and sweet.

CONTINUED

SERVES 4

olive oil

1 red onion, peeled and finely sliced

2 carrots, peeled and finely chopped

1 clove of garlic, peeled and sliced

sea salt and freshly ground black pepper

1 (15-ounce/400 g) can chopped tomatoes

1 (15-ounce/400 g) can chickpeas, rinsed and drained

½ vegetable stock cube, or 1 teaspoon vegetable stock powder

1 stick of cinnamon

1 preserved lemon, halved, seeds removed

a handful of raisins

½ cup/100 g Israeli couscous

a small bunch of fresh parsley, leaves picked and chopped

TO SERVE

a good pinch of saffron strands

4 tablespoons yogurt of your choice

½ a clove of garlic, peeled and chopped super fine

4 handfuls arugula

a small handful of toasted pine nuts

Next, add the tomatoes and chickpeas. Fill both cans with water and add to the pan too. Add the stock cube, cinnamon stick, preserved lemon halves, and raisins. Season with salt and pepper and simmer over medium heat for 15 to 20 minutes until the tomato broth has thickened slightly and tastes wonderfully full and fragrant.

Add the couscous and cook for another 10 minutes, making sure you add a little extra water here if necessary. I like more of a soup than a stew, so I usually add another can of water.

Meanwhile, put the saffron into a bowl with a small splash of boiling water and allow it to sit for 5 minutes. Then add the yogurt, garlic, and a pinch of salt and mix well.

After 10 minutes the couscous should be cooked while still keeping a little chewy bite. Check the seasoning and add more salt and pepper if needed, stir in the parsley, and then scoop out the preserved lemon halves. Ladle your stew into bowls. Top with a crown of arugula, a good spoonful of saffron yogurt, and a pile of toasted pine nuts.

Seeded bread and roast tomato soup

A few years ago I spent a glorious six months living and working among the Chianti vines in the deep green heart of Tuscany. I was an hour's walk from the nearest bus and cooking was all there was to do. We worked hand in hand with what was going on around us, and it was glorious. We made this traditional Tuscan favorite, pappa pomodoro, for our staff lunch at least twice a week—comfort eating at its best.

The flame-red tomatoes turn scarlet pink when slowly roasted, and the bread softens and soaks up the tomato juices to become almost milky. The seeded bread is my way of doing things—I love the pops of texture it adds. I still make this in deepest winter with four cans of really good cherry tomatoes and rosemary or thyme—it's a different soup but still killer.

Preheat the oven to 425°F/220°C.

Place the fresh tomatoes in a large deep ovenproof casserole dish with the garlic, half the basil, and a good pinch of salt and pepper, and drizzle with olive oil. Place in the oven for 20 minutes to roast and intensify. Once your tomatoes are roasted, take the pan out of the oven and place it on the stove top, remembering to be careful, as your pan will be very hot.

Add the canned tomatoes and a can of water and break up the tomatoes a little with the back of a wooden spoon. Bring to a simmer, and then cook for 20 minutes.

Once the soup is thick and sweet, tear the slices of bread and most of the rest of the basil over the top, cover with a lid, and let sit for 10 minutes. Then give it a stir so it all comes together. Ladle into bowls, drizzle generously with very good olive oil, scatter with the remaining basil, and eat with enthusiasm and a fine Chianti.

SERVES 4

1 pound/500 g vine-ripened tomatoes, halved

2 cloves of garlic, peeled and finely chopped

a large bunch of fresh basil, leaves picked

sea salt and freshly ground black pepper

olive oil

2 (15-ounce/400 g) cans of good-quality plum tomatoes

4 slices of good-quality seeded bread

ONE SOUP: ONE THOUSAND VARIATION

1	2	3
CREATE THE BASE LAYER	**CHOOSE AN HERB**	**CHOOSE A SPICE**
↓	↓	↓
1 ONION OR LEEK, FINELY CHOPPED	A FEW SPRIGS THYME	CUMIN SEEDS
+	/	/
2 STALKS OF CELERY, TRIMMED AND FINELY CHOPPED	A COUPLE OF SPRIGS ROSEMARY	CILANTRO SEEDS
+	/	/
2 CARROTS, ROUGHLY CHOPPED	10 LEAVES SAGE	3 PODS CARDAMOM
	/	/
Chop up all 3 and sweat over medium heat with a little olive oil until soft and sweet.	3 BAY LEAVES	½ STICK CINNAMON
	/	/
→	A FEW SPRIGS OREGANO	MUSTARD SEEDS
	/	/
	BASIL STEMS	SMOKED PAPRIKA
	/	/
	CILANTRO STEMS	BLACK PEPPER
		/
	Add the herb and sizzle for a couple of minutes to release its flavor.	CRUSHED RED PEPPER FLAKES
	→	Add 1 tablespoon or the quantity suggested and sizzle for a minute or two.
		→

4	**5**	**6**	**7**
CHOOSE THE MAIN BODY OF YOUR SOUP	**CHOOSE A BACK-UP FLAVOR**	**HOW TO MAKE IT MORE SUBSTANTIAL**	**HOW WILL YOU FINISH YOUR SOUP?**
↓	↓	↓	↓

BUTTERNUT SQUASH	SPINACH (ADD AT THE END)	QUINOA (COOKED)	ROASTED SEEDS
/	/	/	/
SWEET POTATO	BROCCOLI	DRAINED BEANS (COOKED)	YOGURT
/	/	/	/
PEAS	PEAS	AMARANTH (COOKED)	TAHINI
/	/	/	/
CELERIAC	FAVA BEANS	TORN-UP BREAD	TOASTED NUTS
/	/	/	/
PARSNIPS	ARTICHOKES	SMALL OR CUT-UP PASTA (COOKED)	QUICK CROUTONS
/	/	/	/
TOMATOES	ASPARAGUS	BROWN RICE (COOKED)	CHOPPED SOFT HERBS
/		/	/
CARROTS		BROKEN-UP NOODLES (COOKED)	HERB OIL
/			
BROCCOLI			
/			
CAULIFLOWER			

CHOOSE THE MAIN BODY:
Add a handful per person of your main vegetable, peeled and chopped if needed, and enough hot stock to cover. Simmer for 40 minutes.

→

CHOOSE A BACK-UP FLAVOR:
Add a couple of handfuls of chopped vegetable and simmer for 5 more minutes.

→

HOW TO MAKE IT MORE SUBSTANTIAL:
This is optional. If using, add a couple of handfuls just before your soup is ready, warm through, and blend if you like.

→

HOW WILL YOU FINISH YOUR SOUP?
Top with 1 or 2 of these options and a drizzle of olive oil.

Walnut miso broth with udon noodles

One of my favorite meals to go out and eat is this one, sitting on my own at the noodle bar in Koya in Soho. Their udon noodles are from the gods, just the right side of chewy. But it's the walnut miso paste that comes next to them in a little bowl that really crowns it. I am sure they make it in a far more sophisticated way—I've never asked but this is my version.

This is a soup that has everything. Deep umami flavor, cleansing sharpness, and a delicious bundle of vegetables. Both udon and soba noodles work here. The broth is a very simple and clean one, and you'll need to stir in the walnut and miso for the flavors to really work. At Koya they add one of those amazing Japanese eggs, poached in its shell. I sometimes add a poached egg too, but it divides opinion, so I have left it out here.

Walnuts and I have a curious relationship. After a year working at a high-end restaurant in Knightsbridge where I had to individually peel the bitter skins from each walnut, weaving delicately in and out of those dainty, frilly edges without breaking it, I fell out of love with them. But I have ditched the peeling and have since fallen back into their arms. They are a delicious vegetarian source of omega-3s, which is key for brain health—a handful will provide you with almost all you need in a day, so get snacking on some walnuts.

Most vegetables would work well in this broth—chard, asparagus, sugar snap peas, spinach. Don't be tied to what I have suggested here.

....

Preheat your oven to 425°F/220°C.

Put the walnuts on a baking tray and toast them in the oven for 5 to 10 minutes, until just browned and smelling fragrant. Set aside to cool.

SERVES 2

FOR THE WALNUT MISO PASTE

¾ cup/100 g walnuts, lightly toasted

2 tablespoons dark miso paste (I use brown rice miso)

2 tablespoons honey or agave syrup

1 tablespoon sweet soy sauce or tamari

a splash of white wine vinegar

FOR THE BROTH

2 scallions, trimmed and finely sliced

a thumb-size piece of fresh ginger, peeled and chopped into matchsticks

1 vegetable stock cube, or 1 tablespoon vegetable stock powder

1 head of kale, collard greens, or other leafy green, stemmed and shredded

a handful of shimeji mushrooms (about 6 ounces/150 g)

a handful of enoki mushrooms (about 6 ounces/150 g)

9 ounces/250 g dried udon noodles

Now get the broth going. Put the scallions, ginger, and vegetable stock cube or powder into a pan with 8½ cups/2 L of water, over medium-high heat, and bring to a boil. Reduce the heat and simmer for 10 minutes, then add the greens and mushrooms and turn off the heat.

Meanwhile, bring another pan of water to a boil. Add the noodles and cook for 6 to 8 minutes (or follow the instructions on the packet).

Pulse the toasted walnuts in a food processor until they resemble very coarse breadcrumbs. Mix with the other walnut miso paste ingredients.

Once the noodles are cooked, drain and divide them between two bowls. Ladle over the hot broth (about two ladles' worth for each bowl), top with a generous spoonful of walnut miso in the middle of each, and stir in.

Restorative coconut broth

There are some evenings when I feel like I've absorbed the day, when all the frenetic activity around me has somehow seeped in. Whenever I am feeling off center and need some calming, this is what I have for dinner. The clean white of this broth is like a blanket on a cold night and whispers away the hustle and bustle. The coconut milk calms and soothes, the chile boosts and wakens, the lime leaves and lemongrass cleanse, and the vegetables add fuel and freshness.

I pick up bundles of lemongrass and kaffir lime leaves whenever I see them. If you haven't used them before, you will be amazed at the powerful citrus depth they impart in minutes. If you use them frequently, you can keep them in the fridge, where they will last about a month. If you are less likely to use them up that fast, pop them into the freezer—they keep well and can be used frozen.

SERVES 4

2 (15-ounce/400 g) cans
coconut milk

1 vegetable stock cube, or
1 tablespoon vegetable stock powder

4 stalks lemongrass

optional: 4 kaffir lime leaves

1 shallot, peeled and finely sliced

2 cloves garlic, peeled and halved

1 red chile, roughly chopped

2 tablespoons coconut sugar
(see page 275) or unrefined
superfine sugar

a bunch of fresh cilantro

4 generous handfuls (about
9 ounces/250 g) of green leaves,
shredded (collard greens,
bok choi, or kale)

2 handfuls (about 4 ounces/120 g)
of sliced mushrooms (enoki, shitake,
oyster, or cremini would do well)

2 tablespoons soy sauce or tamari

juice of 2 limes

Pour the coconut milk into a large pan and add a canful of water and the stock cube or powder. Smash the lemongrass with a rolling pin to help release the flavors more quickly. Add to the pan with the lime leaves, shallot, garlic, chile, and sugar. Cut the roots off the cilantro and add these too.

Push all the aromatics into the liquid so they are covered and turn the heat on under the pan. Bring to a gentle simmer, then allow to bubble for 15 minutes until you have an intensely flavored coconut broth.

Take the pan off the heat and strain the broth through a fine-mesh sieve into a bowl, discarding all the aromatics (they have done their work now). Then pour the broth back into the pan. Add the shredded greens and mushrooms, and warm through for 2 to 3 minutes. Then take off the heat and add the soy sauce and lime juice.

Ladle the soup into bowls and top with the roughly chopped cilantro leaves. I like the neatness of this simple, soothing soup on its own, but if you are hungry, try adding some cooked soba noodles.

Sweet tomato and black bean tortilla bowls

I love Mexican food for its attention to different textures and its layers of flavor, crunch, softness, creaminess, citrus punch, and chile heat, and that's what I like about this bowl.

The soupy-stew is great on its own, but when you top it with popping roasted tomatoes, buttery avocado, and even a perfectly poached egg, it becomes a serious team of flavors in a bowl. Don't be fooled by the title—this is not one of those greasy bowls made from a baked tortilla that you see in Americanized Mexican restaurants.

Smoked paprika is a good friend—if I can find any excuse to shake some of the sweet smoky stuff on to my food, I will. Last year I visited my holy grail: the chile fields of La Vera in Spain. Over the years I have been lucky enough to tour a bunch of different artisans and producers, but this was my favorite one of all—fields and fields of brave red chiles, picked by hand and carted to huge kilns in a beautiful old smokery in the middle of the fields where fires were lit below ceilings made of wire racks holding thousands of chiles, to smoke them and get that wonderful taste.

....

Preheat your oven to 400°F/200°C.

Place the sweet potatoes on one side of a baking tray and the halved cherry tomatoes on the other. Then sprinkle everything with a good amount of salt and pepper, drizzle with a little oil, and roast for 20 to 25 minutes.

Heat a little oil in a large pan over medium heat. Add the scallions and garlic and sizzle for a few minutes until the garlic has just started to brown, then add all the spices and stir a couple of times. Add the canned tomatoes and simmer for 5 minutes, until all the flavors have come together.

SERVES 4

1 medium sweet potato, washed and chopped into little pieces

20 cherry tomatoes, halved

sea salt and freshly ground black pepper

olive or rapeseed oil

a bunch of scallions, trimmed and finely sliced

2 cloves garlic, peeled and finely sliced

1 teaspoon sweet smoked paprika

1 teaspoon ground cilantro

1 teaspoon ground cumin

1 teaspoon ground cinnamon

1 (15-ounce/400 g) can chopped tomatoes

3¼ cups/750 ml hot vegetable stock

1 (15-ounce/400 g) can of black beans, drained

6 corn tortillas (see page 13)

optional: a few organic or free-range eggs, for poaching

optional: 1 avocado, peeled and cut into chunks

a small bunch of fresh cilantro, leaves picked

CONTINUED

Add the stock and bring to a boil, then simmer for another 5 minutes. I like to blend the broth with an immersion blender now, but feel free to skip this if you like it with more texture. After simmering, add the beans.

By now the tomatoes and sweet potatoes should be roasted. Take the tray out of the oven and add the sweet potatoes to the broth, then keep it simmering over low heat. Set the roasted tomatoes aside—they will go in later.

Cut the tortillas into ¼-inch/½ cm wide strips and put them on another baking tray. Season with a little salt, drizzle over some oil, toss to coat, and bake in the oven for 4 to 5 minutes until crisp and lightly golden.

I like to serve poached eggs on top of my soup, so if you like the idea, poach 1 egg per person (see page 34 for my method).

Once the tortilla strips are golden, take them out of the oven. Ladle the soup into bowls, top with the roasted tomatoes and crunchy tortilla strips, a poached egg, some chopped avocado, and a scattering of cilantro.

Charred pepper and halloumi stew

There seems to be a huge fascination with halloumi, especially among vegetarians. Every barbecue in the summer seems to include a couple of blocks. While I like the squeaky cheese, I think it needs a bit of help in the flavor department. Here it sits in a warm blanket of blackened peppers and a flash-cooked tomato stew that coats the just-crisped halloumi in its balmy juices—somewhere between a warm salad and a fresh herby stew.

....

If you have a gas stove, turn on the flame and use tongs to balance all 3 peppers around the burner, turning them every few minutes until they are charred all over. This will take 10 minutes or so. They are done when they are almost completely black and they have softened and lost their rawness. If you don't have a gas stove, use a really hot griddle pan to char them in the same way instead, or put them under a very hot broiler. Once black and charred all over, put the peppers into a bowl and cover with plastic wrap. Let sit for 5 minutes.

Put the tomatoes into a bowl with the pitted olives, capers, lemon zest, and 1 tablespoon of olive oil. Season well with salt and pepper and let the flavors meld while you peel the peppers. Take the peppers out of the bowl and use your fingers to peel the blackened skin into the bowl, cleaning off as much of the skin as you can. Don't be tempted to rinse them under the faucet, as this will wash away all the flavor. Seed the peppers, cut them into ⅜-inch/1 cm strips, and add them to the bowl of tomatoes.

Now heat a frying pan over medium heat. Add the rest of the olive oil and allow to heat up, then add the slices of halloumi and fry for 30 seconds or so on each side until they have just turned golden. Place the halloumi on a plate, then add the tomato mixture to the hot pan, and return to the heat for a couple of minutes to warm through and release some juices.

Finally, add the chopped herbs and halloumi to the pan and serve immediately, warm, with some good bread and spritely greens.

SERVES 4

3 red peppers

1 pound/500 g mixed cherry and vine-ripened tomatoes, halved

2 handfuls (about 20) kalamata olives, pitted

2 tablespoons little capers

grated zest of 1 unwaxed lemon

3 tablespoons good olive oil

sea salt and freshly ground black pepper

1 (8-ounce/250 g) package of halloumi cheese, cut into 12 slices

½ bunch of fresh mint, leaves picked and chopped

½ bunch of fresh parsley, leaves picked and chopped

½ bunch of fresh basil, leaves picked and chopped

Celeriac soup with hazelnuts and crispy sage

Celeriac is an underused star. I love it and champion it in my kitchen. Sometimes it's simply roasted with salt and pepper; other times it's smashed with lemon and thyme or just eaten raw, finely sliced in a remoulade.

Here it's the centerpiece of a comforting soup. Apples are the perfect foil for adding sweetness, while the lima beans bring creaminess, so no need for cream or crème fraîche here. The soup can be eaten simply as it is, but try it with the brown butter—it amps it up and makes this soup a real winner. If you haven't made brown butter before, it's got a deep nutty flavor that melds with the crispy sage and toasted hazelnuts to send this soup to a different dimension.

Celeriac is a bit of a beast to look at. But looks are not everything—beneath the gnarled, knobby exterior lies a creamy white flesh with a sweet, nutty, super-savory flavor. It packs some serious health benefits. It's high in fiber, potassium, magnesium, and vitamin B6. Peel your celeriac thickly to get rid of any green tinges around the edge.

SERVES 6

olive oil

1 leek, washed, trimmed, and finely sliced

1 celeriac, washed, peeled, and roughly chopped

4 apples, cored and roughly chopped

a few sprigs of fresh thyme, leaves picked

6⅓ cups/1½ L vegetable stock

1 (15-ounce/400 g) can lima beans, drained

sea salt and freshly ground black pepper

TO SERVE

a handful of hazelnuts

4 tablespoons butter

a few sprigs of fresh sage, leaves picked

Heat a splash of oil in a large pan, then add the leek and cook over medium heat for 10 minutes until soft and sweet. Add the celeriac, apples, and thyme and cook for 2 to 3 minutes, then add the stock and lima beans and season well. Simmer over low heat for 20 to 30 minutes, until the celeriac is tender, then remove from the heat and blend with an immersion blender until smooth.

Toast the hazelnuts in a frying pan until golden brown, remove them from the pan, and put to one side. Add the butter to the pan and, once it is hot, add the sage and fry until it is crispy and the butter is light brown. Keep the heat low for this last bit and take the pan off as soon as you see the butter turn brown, as it can burn really quickly.

Ladle into bowls and top with the sage and hazelnut brown butter.

Lemony lentil and crispy kale soup

I love this simple soup, which is somewhere between a dal and a soup—it reminds me of the curry that is served in southern India with dosas. This soup is cleansing and clean, thanks to being spiked with turmeric and a lot of lemon. It's what I crave if I've overindulged or been around food too long (an occupational hazard—a very nice one). I serve this with a kitchari (page 163).

Turmeric is a favorite spice of mine. If I am feeling out of sorts, I stir a teaspoon into hot water and sip it as a reviving tonic. I love the vibrant, deep saffron-gold color; the clean, sharp, savory acid note; and the hard-to-put-your-finger-on flavor. It's a real star on the health front, as it is an anti-inflammatory and has anticarcinogenic properties—what a spice.

Place a large pan over medium heat. Add a little oil. Add the leek and fry for a few minutes until it has softened and smells sweet. Then add the spices and fry for another couple of minutes. Squeeze in the juice of 1 lemon and stir to scrape up all the spices from the bottom of the pan.

Next, add the lentils, 6⅓ cups/1½ L of water, and the stock cube or powder and allow to bubble away for 20 to 35 minutes, until the lentils are cooked and the soup has thickened.

Turn off the heat and, if you like, you can blend with an immersion blender to a thin dal consistency, then squeeze in the juice of the remaining 2 lemons, tasting as you go to make sure it doesn't get too lemony. It may seem like a lot, but you really want the lemony tang to come through.

Just before you're ready to serve, sauté the kale in a little olive oil until it slightly softens but begins to crisp at the edges.

Ladle into bowls and top with the salted yogurt and the crispy kale.

SERVES 4 TO 6

a splash of olive or rapeseed oil

1 leek, washed, trimmed, and finely sliced

1 teaspoon ground turmeric

2 teaspoons ground cumin

2 teaspoons black mustard seeds

juice of 2 to 3 lemons

1¼ cup/250 g split red lentils

1 vegetable stock cube, or 1 tablespoon vegetable stock powder

4 handfuls of kale (or other greens), washed, trimmed, and shredded

TO SERVE (OPTIONAL)

yogurt, mixed with a little sea salt

White beans, greens, olive oil—my ribollita

SERVES 6

olive oil

2 red onions, peeled and chopped

3 cloves of garlic, peeled and chopped

1 carrot, peeled and chopped

6 stalks celery, trimmed and chopped, yellow leaves reserved

a small bunch of fresh parsley, roughly chopped

1 (15-ounce/400 g) can of plum tomatoes

1 medium potato, peeled and chopped

1 (15-ounce/400 g) can of white beans (liquid reserved)

3 big handfuls of dinosaur kale or curly kale (about 14-ounces/ 400 g), stalks removed, leaves roughly chopped

8½ cups/2 L vegetable stock

4 slices of good-quality bread (best if it's a little stale)

very good extra virgin olive oil, for drizzling

I spent a good few years of my life cooking Italian food, and I am still in the midst of what I know will be a lifelong love. This is one of the dishes that made me love it so. It is a diva of a dish and it demands you use the very best of everything for it to perform. A ribollita made from the best oil, tomatoes, dinosaur kale, and bread is hard to beat.

I remember every note of my first taste of this in the kitchen of Fifteen London, at the hands of a wonderful chef, Ben Arthur, a Londoner who cooks like an Italian. Dishes like this changed how I looked at food, how I understood it—why the oil needed to be the very best, why there needed to be a lot of it, why traditions were followed and techniques respected. It was a life-changing bowl of soup, you could say.

This is an autumn version. In summer I use chard or spinach in place of the dinosaur kale and squashed fresh tomatoes instead of canned ones. I use canned beans here for ease, but you could cook your own too.

A good vegetable stock is useful here, as it adds depth of flavor and backbone that is hard to get with stock cubes. (See pages 344 and 345 for my vegetable stock recipes.) Good textured bread is a must too—I use a good sourdough or country-style loaf from my local bakery. Spongy white bread won't work in the same way.

Dinosaur kale is a deep black green and shows up in late summer and hangs around for a couple of months. I love its deep mineral flavor and its robust nature—the leaves lend themselves very well to cooking in stews. It seems to team with olive oil in some kind of divine partnership. If you can't get dinosaur kale, then curly kale will stand in just as well.

CONTINUED

Heat a little oil in a large saucepan and fry the onions, garlic, carrot, and celery over medium heat for about 30 minutes until they are soft and slightly caramelized. Add most of the parsley and cook for another few minutes.

Next, add the tomatoes and the potato. Squash the tomatoes with a wooden spoon and cook over a low heat for 15 minutes longer, stirring from time to time. The tomato liquid should be almost completely absorbed by now, and the vegetable should be looking quite dry.

Add the beans and their liquid along with the kale and the stock. Bring to a gentle simmer, and then cook for 30 minutes.

Turn the heat off and lay the slices of bread on top of the soup like a lid. Generously drizzle with extra virgin olive oil and let sit for 10 minutes or so.

Then stir to combine everything—the ribollita should be thick, almost stewy, and deeply delicious. Season with salt and pepper and more parsley, the yellow celery leaves, and more good olive oil, and ladle into big bowls.

If you have leftovers, reheat in a pan with more hot stock or water, as the soup will thicken once cool.

Cardamom and star anise winter squash soup

A bowl of good stuff for a cold winter's day: this is a meal of a soup with two of my favorite spices shining through, the most fragrant of all, cardamom, and the super-pretty star anise. They come together with the vivid orange sweetness of the squash and the sweet potato to make something wonderful—a soup with depth and character.

I like to serve this with a few spoonfuls of brown rice in the bottom of the bowl, a dollop of yogurt, and some nigella seeds. If you don't have nigella (black onion) seeds, toasted sesame seeds work too. The soup and brown rice take about the same time, so put the rice on as you start the soup.

Heat a large heavy pan over medium heat. Add a little oil and sauté the leek, ginger, garlic, and chile for 10 minutes until soft and sweet.

Crush the cardamoms in a mortar and pestle and discard the pods, leaving the seeds behind in the mortar. Add the cilantro seeds and grind as fine as you can. Add these, with the tumeric, to the pan of leeks, and stir for another couple of minutes to release their fragrance.

Add the squash, sweet potatoes, and star anise and cover with the stock. Bring to a boil, then turn the heat down and simmer for 20 minutes until the squash is tender when pierced with a fork. Add more water as you go, if needed.

Season with salt and pepper, and then blend with an immersion blender. Stir in the spinach and allow it to wilt.

Spoon into bowls, topped with a few spoonfuls of brown rice, some chopped cilantro, nigella seeds, more chile, and some lime wedges.

SERVES 4

olive or rapeseed oil

1 leek, washed and chopped

1 thumb-size piece of fresh ginger, peeled and finely chopped

1 clove garlic, peeled and finely chopped

1 green chile, seeded and finely chopped

6 cardamom pods

1 tablespoon cilantro seeds

1 tablespoon ground turmeric

½ a butternut squash, or a 1-pound/500 g piece of pumpkin

3 sweet potatoes, peeled and roughly chopped

2 star anise

8½ cups/2 L vegetable stock

sea salt and freshly ground black pepper

3 handfuls of spinach

TO SERVE (OPTIONAL)

cooked brown rice

a small bunch of fresh cilantro

nigella (black onion) seeds or sesame seeds

green chile, chopped

lime wedges, for squeezing

satisfying salads

Salads are more than lettuce leaves. To me, salads are a modern way of eating. Brightly colored piles of well-thought-out leaves and carefully roasted or thinly sliced raw vegetables, good bread, grassy olive oil, and toasted seeds or nuts are the lunch (and dinner) of kings. Add some interesting grains or roasted root vegetables for a heartier meal, or pare everything right back with spritely green salad leaves and a killer dressing. Whether simple or complex, light and airy, or hearty and filling, make sure to embrace your salad days.

laura's herbed green quinoa · california miso, avocado, and lima bean salad · warm salad of roasted kale, coconut, and tomatoes · caramelized leek and new potato salad · cilantro and orange-scented buckwheat · how to make a great salad · sunchoke salad · cucumber satay crunch salad · autumn roasted root panzanella · figs with sticky date dressing · charred spring vegetables with watercress vinaigrette · spiced carrot and cashew salad with fresh coconut and cilantro · lemon-roasted feta with traffic-light tomatoes · raw thai citrus crunch salad · charred corn, scrunched kale, and sweet potato salad · seeded squash, pomegranate, and za'atar

Laura's herbed green quinoa

2 unwaxed lemons

1½ cups/250 g quinoa

½ vegetable stock cube, or
1 teaspoon vegetable stock powder

a bunch (about 9 ounces/250 g)
of purple sprouting broccoli, stalks
chopped, florets left whole

a good handful of frozen peas

extra virgin olive oil

1 leek, washed, trimmed,
and finely sliced

a small bunch of fresh basil,
leaves picked and chopped

a small bunch of fresh mint,
leaves picked and chopped

3 big handfuls of spinach,
washed and shredded

2 tablespoons toasted
pumpkin seeds

2 tablespoons toasted
sesame seeds

optional: 9 ounces/200 g feta cheese

sea salt and freshly ground
black pepper

My beautiful sister, Laura, is the queen of feel-good food. She often cooks for our family and always manages to put on an incredible spread where every mouthful is as insanely tasty as it is healthy. Laura makes this all the time. It is in my opinion the best quinoa I have ever eaten, full of grassy green freshness and deeply toasted flavors. So I've hijacked it.

Purple sprouting broccoli is my broccoli of choice for most dishes. I love its violet plumes, the fact that it's grown right here in the UK for most of the year, and that when the long winters draw in, the flowers of this hardy little brassica are the only green thing above the ground. With heaps of vitamin C and fiber, among many other vitamins and minerals, these are amazing little stems. If you can't get purple sprouting broccoli, or it's not in season, a small head of regular broccoli, or, to use its proper name, calabrese broccoli, will do. Be sure to use the stalk too—it can be finely sliced and blanched along with the florets. Be careful not to overcook broccoli—for me, a minute or two in boiling water or a steamer is more than enough to take the raw edge off while retaining its minerally character and vivid deep green color.

Quinoa is often grouped with whole grains, but it is actually the seed of a plant that is a relative of leafy green vegetables like spinach and Swiss chard. It is an energy-rich food that delivers heaps of fibre and protein but very little fat and no gluten. The amino acids in quinoa make it a complete protein, so it's a really good choice for vegetarians and vegans. And it tastes so good too—fluffy and creamy, yet slightly crunchy. I love the stuff. Try the black and the red quinoa too; they cook in just the same way.

This quinoa salad works with pretty much all green vegetable—spinach, fava beans, edamame beans, kale, asparagus . . . the list goes on. Just pick what's good and in season and swap as you like.

CONTINUED

Cut 1 of the lemons in half and place both halves in a pan with the quinoa. Cover with 2½ cups/600 ml of water and crumble in the stock cube, bring to a boil, then reduce the heat and simmer for about 15 minutes until most of the water has been absorbed. Add more boiling water, if needed, as you go.

Just before the quinoa has fully absorbed all the water and your 15 minutes are nearly up, lay the broccoli and peas directly on top of the quinoa, put a lid on, and allow to steam for a couple of minutes.

Meanwhile, place a frying pan over medium heat, add a splash of olive oil and the sliced leek and cook slowly for 10 minutes or so, until soft and sweet.

You'll know when the quinoa is ready—it will still have a little bite, it will have turned lightly opaque, and its curly grain will have been released from the seed. Drain off any excess water, remove the lemon halves, and use tongs to squeeze the lemon juice into the quinoa.

Put the quinoa, broccoli, and peas into a bowl and add the chopped herbs, shredded spinach, toasted seeds, and cooked leek. Squeeze over the juice of half of the second lemon, add a couple of tablespoons of olive oil, and mix well.

Crumble over the feta cheese. Taste and season with salt and pepper and add a little more lemon juice if needed.

This is a meal in its own right, but sometimes a little salted yogurt and a whole wheat flatbread work well with it, as do a few slices of avocado.

California miso, avocado, and lima bean salad

This is a great quick-as-a-flash meal to throw together. It echoes the fantastic way Californians work Asian flavors into their sunshine food. Any seasonal green leaves work well here—my favorites are mustard greens, arugula, and oakleaf lettuce.

Ponzu is a sweet-sour-salty mixture of soy sauce and a Japanese citrus called yuzu lime—the zippiest citrus flavor I know. It's available in most Japanese shops. If you don't have ponzu, a little soy mixed with lime juice will work.

Miso paste is one of my favorite ingredients. It's a paste made from fermented rice, barley, or soy beans and adds an incredible umami depth—a deep savoriness—to just about anything. I use it to roast vegetables (carrots are especially good), and in dressings, broths, and dips. Miso comes dark, white, and in a number of shades in between. Here I use a dark, sweet, almost mushroomy brown rice miso. The white stuff would work too, though, and is a good choice if you are steering clear of gluten. Miso is great to eat if you are vegan or cutting back on dairy—it contains vitamin B12, which helps keep our nervous system and blood healthy and is usually found only in animal products.

....

First make the dressing. Mix all your dressing ingredients together in a bowl, adding a little salt, depending on how salty your miso is.

Next, blanch the broccoli in boiling water for a minute or so, until it has lost its rawness and is a lovely bright green. Drain and let cool.

Toast the pumpkin and sesame seeds in a pan until lightly golden, then spread on a plate to cool.

Pile the leaves into a serving bowl, then chop the avocado into chunks and add them to the bowl along with the lima beans. Once the broccoli and seeds are cool, add them too. Pour over the dressing and toss well. Serve with steamed brown rice or soba noodles for a more substantial dinner.

SERVES 2 OR 4 AS PART OF A MEAL

FOR THE DRESSING
1 tablespoon brown rice miso paste
1 tablespoon brown rice vinegar
1 tablespoon ponzu or soy sauce
juice of ½ a lime
4 tablespoons cow's milk or soy yogurt
sea salt

5 ounces/150 g broccoli, stems chopped, florets broken into little heads
2 tablespoons pumpkin seeds
2 tablespoons sesame seeds
2 handfuls of baby salad leaves, washed and dried
1 ripe avocado, pitted and halved
1 (15-ounce/400 g) can lima beans, drained

Warm salad of roasted kale, coconut, and tomatoes

Roasted kale is a revelation. Here I've paired it with sweet roasted tomatoes, coconut, and a quick miso dressing. Roasting this wonderful brassica gives a deep savory flavor and an amazing crunchy texture, not too far away from the Chinese restaurant crispy seaweed of my childhood.

During the winter months, I eat kale most days. I love its minerally sweetness. It's good roasted, sautéed, steamed, blanched, slow-baked to a crisp, and even eaten raw (see page 124). It's a super-hardy plant with bubbly looking fronds that provide us with some green freshness when all the other greens are taking the winter off. The most common kale is curly kale, and it's the one found in most grocers and supermarkets, but deep green dinosaur kale and the majestic purple kale work too.

To make this a more substantial meal you could add a handful or two of cooked quinoa or pearl barley too.

SERVES 4

14 ounces/400 g cherry tomatoes

sea salt and freshly ground black pepper

olive oil

2 unwaxed limes

1 head of green or purple kale (about 7 ounces/200 g), stalks removed, leaves roughly torn into bite-size pieces

a handful of unsweetened shaved or dried coconut

1 tablespoon soy sauce or tamari

FOR THE DRESSING

a thumb-size piece of fresh ginger, peeled and finely chopped

1 tablespoon white miso paste (see page 101)

1 tablespoon tahini

1 tablespoon honey or agave syrup

1 tablespoon coconut or olive oil

1 red chile, finely chopped

Preheat your oven to 425°F/220°C.

Halve the tomatoes and place them on a baking tray with some salt and pepper, a good drizzle of olive oil, the zest of both limes, and the juice of one. Roast for 20 minutes until blistered and golden.

Next, pile the kale on to a baking tray with the coconut. Pour over the soy sauce and toss well until everything is coated. Roast in the oven with the tomatoes for the last 5 to 10 minutes of their cooking time, until crisp.

Meanwhile, mix all the dressing ingredients together in a bowl with the juice of the second lime. Taste and add a little more seasoning or lime juice if needed, letting your taste buds guide you—remember the dressing will be less punchy once it hits the salad. Pull the kale and tomatoes out of the oven and transfer to a big bowl. Toss with the miso dressing, adding a little at a time and tasting as you go, and serve still warm.

Caramelized leek and new potato salad

I love potato salad and I make it a bunch of different ways, depending on the season and on what is being served. Sometimes it's capers and cornichons with dill-spiked yogurt. Other times the potatoes are roasted with charred broccoli, lemon, and chile.

Of all the variations, this is my new favorite, as it hits all the flavor and texture notes. Caramelized leeks, punchy mustard in two guises, and a contrasting crunch from the celery and radishes. I often make this for a crowd, as the recipe doubles nicely and forms the center of most gatherings at my house.

....

Put the potatoes into a pan with a good pinch of salt, cover with boiling water, then return to a boil, and allow to simmer for 20 to 25 minutes until they are tender all the way through.

Next, place a pan over medium heat and add a splash of oil and the leeks. Throw in a pinch of salt, turn down the heat to low, and cook for 20 to 25 minutes until the leeks are soft, sweet, and starting to turn a caramel brown in places.

Meanwhile, make your dressing by mixing all the ingredients together in a bowl with a good pinch of salt and some pepper.

Once the potatoes are ready, drain them and return them to the pan. Now, using a little knife, roughly swipe across the potatoes, roughing them up a little. Add the leeks.

Allow the potatoes to cool a little, then transfer to a serving bowl; stir in the radishes, celery, and dill, and mix gently with a spoon. Pour over the dressing and serve immediately, still warm. If you are making this ahead of time, make a double batch of dressing, as you may need to add a bit more just before serving.

SERVES 4

FOR THE SALAD

1¾ pounds/750 g small new potatoes, scrubbed clean

sea salt and freshly ground black pepper

olive or rapeseed oil

2 good-size leeks, washed, trimmed, halved, and thickly sliced

a handful of radishes, trimmed and cut into little chunks

2 stalks celery, trimmed and roughly chopped

a good bunch of fresh dill

FOR THE DRESSING

1 teaspoon honey

1 tablespoon cider vinegar

4 tablespoons olive oil

1 tablespoon whole grain Dijon mustard

1 tablespoon Dijon mustard

juice of ½ a lemon

Cilantro and orange-scented buckwheat

I love the East Side of London, and for the last twelve years or so, I have lived near Broadway Market in Hackney, a busy strip of shops with a Saturday market. Over the years I've watched it become a wonderful buzzing mix of food, music, and beers in the sunshine. On Saturdays my sister and I roam the market, checking on each and every food stall before deciding what to eat. More often than not, we end up at the stall that makes a killer vegetable salad and a really good buckwheat. Inspired by this delicious stall and the desire to get some more buckwheat in my kitchen, I made this salad.

There is a brave use of cilantro seeds here, which sits well with the chewiness of the buckwheat and the rounded sweetness of the roasted squash and onions. For more on buckwheat, see page 185.

SERVES 4

1 butternut squash, peeled, seeded, and cut into rough chunks

2 red onions, peeled and cut into thin wedges

1 heaped tablespoon cilantro seeds, roughly ground in a mortar and pestle

sea salt and freshly ground black pepper

olive oil

1 unwaxed orange

½ cup/100 g toasted buckwheat or kasha

a small bunch of fresh mint, leaves picked and roughly chopped

a small bunch of fresh cilantro, roughly chopped

extra virgin olive oil

optional: a squeeze of honey

TO SERVE

a little Greek yogurt

Preheat your oven to 425°F/220°C.

Put the squash on a baking tray with the onions and cilantro seeds. Sprinkle with salt and pepper and drizzle with olive oil. Cut the orange in half and squeeze the juice over the squash and onions, then put the orange halves on the tray. Toss to coat everything and put into the oven to roast for 30 minutes.

Next, cook the buckwheat. Put the wheat into a pan and add twice its volume of hot water. Bring to a boil, then reduce the heat and simmer for 20 minutes, until all the water has been absorbed and the grains are tender but not mushy. Drain off any excess water if needed, then cover to keep warm and set aside.

Once the squash is roasted, transfer to a serving bowl. Add the buckwheat and chopped herbs along with the extra virgin olive oil and honey. Mix well, taste, and season again if needed. Serve this simply with a little Greek yogurt and some lemon-dressed salad leaves—I sometimes add a charred flatbread if I'm really hungry.

HOW TO MAKE A GREAT SALAD

1	**2**	**3**
START WITH SOME SALAD LEAVES	**ADD SOME INTEREST**	**ADD SOME TEXTURE**
2 handfuls per person	½ a handful per person	a small handful per person
↓	↓	↓
SPINACH	ROASTED SQUASH	CROUTONS
/	/	/
ARUGULA	SEASONED TOMATOES	TOASTED SEEDS
/	/	/
LITTLE GEM	BLANCHED PEAS	TOASTED NUTS
/	/	/
CHICORY (RED OR WHITE)	CORN ON THE COB	TOASTED TORTILLA STRIPS (SEE PAGE 85)
/	/	/
OAKLEAF LETTUCE	ROASTED LEEKS	QUICK MAPLE SEEDS (SEE PAGE 246)
/	/	/
BIBB OR BUTTERHEAD LETTUCE	AVOCADO	SPROUTS
/	/	/
SHREDDED KALE	SUGAR SNAPS	POMEGRANATE SEEDS
/	/	/
WATERCRESS	RADISHES	FLASH-FRIED BREADCRUMBS
/	/	
COLLARD GREENS	RIBBONED ZUCCHINI	
	/	
	FETA	

A great salad is a combination of flavors, textures, and colors, all topped off with a balanced dressing. Salads are so much more than a bowl of leaves—whether they sit beside another dish or are a meal in themselves, they are a great way to be creative. Follow the basic flow of the recipe below, but feel free to experiment.

4

ADD SOME FRESHNESS

a small handful per person

↓

BASIL

/

MINT

/

CHERVIL

/

TARRAGON

/

PARSLEY

/

CILANTRO

/

FRIED CRISPY SAGE

/

DILL

/

FENNEL TOPS

/

CELERY LEAVES

5

MAKE IT HEARTY (IF YOU LIKE)

a couple of tablespoons per person

↓

QUINOA

/

DRAINED BEANS

/

LENTILS

/

COUSCOUS

/

PEARL BARLEY

/

TORN-UP BREAD

/

AMARANTH

/

BULGUR WHEAT

/

A POACHED EGG

/

CHEESE

6

MAKE A GREAT DRESSING

Follow 2:1 ratio and then add your flavors and seasoning.

↓

OIL: 2 PARTS

OLIVE OIL · HAZELNUT OIL · RAPESEED OIL · MASHED AVOCADO · COCONUT MILK · PUMPKIN SEED OIL

ACID: 1 PART

CITRUS: LEMON · LIME · ORANGE · GRAPEFRUIT

VINEGARS: RICE · WHITE WINE · RED WINE · HERB · BALSAMIC

FLAVORS AND SEASONINGS

MISO · CHIPOTLE · TOASTED SPICES · RED OR GREEN CHILE · MUSTARD · CAPERS · PARMESAN · PECORINO · SALT AND PEPPER

Mix with a fork in a bowl, or put into a jam jar and shake.

Sunchoke salad

In America, Jerusalem artichokes go by the far more charming name of Jerusalem artichokes. Along with artichokes, chamomile, and marigolds, they are actually part of the sunflower family, hence their cheerful name.

I adore these nutrient-packed knobby little vegetables and I love eating them raw as they have a refreshing juiciness to them and their flavor is much more sweet and subtle before they are cooked. If you want to slice them ahead of time, keep them in a bowl of water with the juice of half a lemon squeezed in to keep them from turning brown.

This is also my go-to salad recipe. The dressing is a winner, sweet with a perky lemon zing; I tend to make a big batch and keep it on hand in a jar in the fridge. Use any seasonal salad leaves you like—a mixture of frisée and arugula works for me, or, if it's in season, escarole, radicchio, or the pink-flecked Castelfranco.

I use smoked almonds here—I like how they sit alongside these flavors—but toasted almonds will work too. This salad works as a side, but if you want to make it part of a meal, it goes well with roasted feta (see page 119) and some warmed flatbreads.

....

First make your dressing by putting all the ingredients into a food processor and blending until smooth and emulsified. If you don't have a food processor, finely chop the preserved lemon into very small bits and mix with all the other dressing ingredients in a jug.

Next, slice the artichokes paper thin—I use a mandoline, but a sharp knife and a bit of care will do the trick.

Put the salad leaves into a bowl with the sliced artichokes and roughly chopped almonds. Pour over the dressing, toss to coat, taste, and season with salt and pepper if needed.

SERVES 4 AS A SIDE

FOR THE DRESSING

½ a preserved lemon, seeds removed

3 tablespoons olive oil

1 tablespoon white wine vinegar

1 teaspoon honey or agave syrup

a good pinch of sea salt

FOR THE SALAD

2 small Jerusalem artichokes

4 good handfuls of perky bitter lettuce leaves

a handful of smoked almonds, roughly chopped

sea salt and freshly ground black pepper

Cucumber satay crunch salad

Refreshing, crunchy, and zippy all at the same time, this fresh salad is great to serve alongside Indian and Thai curries or as part of an easy summer dinner. It is, of course, also good to eat on its own for lunch or a light dinner with a flatbread or two.

Don't be put off by the amount of fresh cilantro here—it makes the salad. I use a big bunch from my farmers' market, but if you are buying little ones from the supermarket, you may want to buy two.

This recipe allows the cucumber to shine. A very British vegetable and a member of the squash family, it's packed full of vitamin C.

See page 39 for a note on the coconut milk. Here you use the ready-to-drink variety.

....

Peel and halve your cucumber and then use a teaspoon to scrape out the seeds. Cut into half-moons about ¼ inch/½ cm thick and put into a big serving bowl.

Smash the peanuts in a mortar and pestle until they are crumbled and add to the bowl with the chopped cilantro leaves and stalks and the shredded spinach.

Squeeze the juice of the lemon into a little jar. Add the honey, soy sauce, coconut milk, and ginger and mix well.

Pour the dressing over the salad, mix well, and top with the toasted coconut flakes.

SERVES 4

1 cucumber

2 handfuls of unsalted peanuts

a large bunch of fresh cilantro, roughly chopped, roots and all

3 good handfuls of spinach, washed and shredded

1 lemon

1 tablespoon honey

1 teaspoon soy sauce

2 tablespoons light coconut milk or olive oil

½ a small thumb-size piece of fresh ginger, peeled and finely chopped

a handful of coconut flakes, toasted

Autumn roasted root panzanella

SERVES 4

FOR THE SALAD

6 medium beets, peeled and quartered

2 tablespoons sherry or red wine vinegar

sea salt and freshly ground black pepper

olive oil

2 red onions, peeled and cut into eighths

6 smallish carrots, peeled and halved lengthways

½ a butternut squash, seeded and cut into ⅜-inch/1 cm slices (see note on squash above)

a few sprigs of fresh sage or thyme, leaves picked

5 slices of good seeded bread

a handful of roasted pumpkin or roasted squash seeds

1 unwaxed lemon

FOR THE DRESSING

2 tablespoons good extra virgin olive oil

a small bunch of fresh mint, leaves picked and roughly chopped

1 tablespoon whole grain mustard

Panzanella by its tomatoey nature is something I only really enjoy in late summer, when the tomatoes are at their ripest and best, with good bread soaking up all the precious juices of the best tomatoes.

But I love the idea of panzanella, so I made a version for autumn too. Here, gently roasted squash hugs the seeded bread, onions add background sweetness, and the beets are roasted with a brave amount of vinegar, which becomes a deep amethyst liquor that is the base of the killer dressing. In this recipe, the oven does all the work for you (you'll need a few roasting trays).

More often than not, I suggest using butternut squash as it is easily and readily available. But I encourage you to try other squash too when they fill the market through the autumn and into winter. Deep green acorn squashes work well or golden-fleshed kabocha. My favorite, though, is the dusty pale-green-skinned Crown Prince squash. They are huge, so just a quarter will do here. They will all cook in a similar time, provided you cut them into ⅜-inch/1 cm slices.

I love to make use of the squash seeds and roast them for using in salads and cereals. It is a bit of work but worth the effort as they taste much better than any store-bought ones. Just rinse the seeds under cold water and soak them in salted water for a couple of hours—the orange fibers of the squash that cling to them will then peel away easily. Roast them at 400°F/200°C for 15 minutes with a little salt and oil—adding soy sauce and spices works too. Bear in mind, they crisp up as they cool.

Preheat your oven to 400°F/200°C.

⋮⋮ CONTINUED

Put the beets into a deep roasting tray with the vinegar, some salt and pepper, and a good splash of olive oil. Turn them to coat everything, then cover the tray with foil and put into the oven to roast for 15 minutes.

Next, lay the onions and carrots on a second tray and the squash on a third. Sprinkle with salt and pepper and drizzle with a little olive oil, then scatter the sage or thyme over both. Once the beets have had 15 minutes in the oven, put in the other two trays and roast everything for a further 40 minutes.

Once the vegetables are roasted, tender, and golden, take everything out of the oven and scrape the onions and carrots onto the tray with the squash. Tear the bread into little chunks and spread them onto the now-empty tray and then scatter over the seeds. Season with salt and pepper and grate over the lemon zest. Drizzle with olive oil and bake for 5 to 10 minutes, until just starting to crisp.

While the bread is toasting, make your dressing. Carefully pour the juices from the roasted beets into a bowl; add the olive oil, mint, and mustard; season with salt and pepper; and mix well.

Transfer all the vegetables into a big bowl and top with the crisp bread and seeds. Stir in the dressing, turning everything so that it's coated with the deep violet color.

This is wonderful with a little goat cheese or even a spoonful of lemony yogurt, and some green leaves, if you like.

Figs with sticky date dressing

This recipe is for when you see great figs, dusty white and deeply purple. The little boxes turn up a few times a year in the market near me, and when they do, I make this.

This is a killer dressing for any robust salad. If figs aren't in season, peaches, thinly sliced apples, or clementines are all good too.

I use date syrup here—I always have a bottle in the cupboard for sweetening oatmeal, dressings, marinades, smoothies, and for drizzling on pancakes. It's a great, completely natural sugar with a wonderful deep malty backnote. If you can't get date syrup, a couple of dates blended with a little oil will work, as will some good thick balsamic.

Goat cheese works wonderfully with fruit and is actually much easier for us to digest than cow's milk products due to its smaller protein molecules. It contains more calcium and minerals than cow's milk and has an alkalinizing effect on the system. I love it.

....

Put the chopped shallot, mustard, date syrup, and the juice of the lemon into a bowl, season with salt and pepper, and drizzle in the oil, whisking as you go. Chop the mint, add to the bowl, and set aside.

Put the salad leaves into a bowl and scatter the figs over. Give the dressing a good mix, then drizzle it over the salad. Pick the basil leaves off the stems and scatter over the salad; then toss everything together.

Dot the goat cheese over the top, and it's ready to serve.

SERVES 4

FOR THE DRESSING

1 shallot, peeled and very finely chopped

½ teaspoon Dijon mustard

2 tablespoons date syrup or 2 dates blended with a little oil

1 lemon

sea salt and freshly ground black pepper

2 tablespoons good extra virgin olive oil

a small bunch of fresh mint

FOR THE SALAD

8 big handfuls of mixed salad leaves (I use arugula, radicchio, baby chard, and mustard greens)

6 fresh figs, quartered

a small bunch of fresh basil

3½ ounces/100 g soft goat cheese

Charred spring vegetables with watercress vinaigrette

This is one of those delicious stand-alone salads. I roast the potatoes and asparagus here as I like the nutty character that's brought out in the asparagus. In winter I use purple sprouting broccoli and chunks of potato, which cook in the same time and work just as well.

One of the reasons I love to cook is the connection to what's going on in the fields and gardens up and down the country. Asparagus to me marks a change in the year, heralding warmer times ahead. Keep the woody ends of the asparagus you have snapped off here to flavor a stock for a soup or risotto. Although too tough to eat, they still have a lot of flavor.

....

Preheat your oven to 425°F/220°C.

Put the new potatoes on a baking tray with a good pinch of salt and pepper and drizzle with olive oil. Once the oven is hot, put the potatoes in to roast for 30 minutes.

SERVES 4

1⅔ pounds/750 g small new potatoes, scrubbed clean

sea salt and freshly ground black pepper

extra virgin olive oil

4 organic or free-range eggs

a bunch of asparagus, woody ends snapped off

a few sprigs each of fresh parsley, mint, and tarragon, leaves picked

a good bunch of watercress, roughly chopped

8 cornichons, roughly chopped

2 tablespoons little capers

1 tablespoon red wine vinegar

1 teaspoon Dijon mustard

Next, put the eggs into a pan, cover with cold water, bring to a boil, and then turn the heat off and leave for 7 minutes. Take them out of the pan and run them under cold water. Then, once they are cool, peel and set aside.

When the potatoes have had 30 minutes in the oven, throw in all but 2 stems of the asparagus, toss to coat in the oil, and roast for 15 minutes longer.

Chop the herbs and watercress with the cornichons and capers and put them into a bowl or jar. Add 3 tablespoons of olive oil, the red wine vinegar, and the Dijon mustard, and shake or whisk to mix. Peel the remaining spears of asparagus into long thin strips with a vegetable peeler.

Once the potatoes and asparagus are ready, transfer them to a bowl. Roughly chop the eggs and add them to the bowl, then pour over the dressing, scatter with the asparagus strips, and toss gently while everything is still hot.

Spiced carrot and cashew salad with fresh coconut and cilantro

Indian flavors creep into this fresh and upbeat salad, taught to me by my friend Emily. Roasting the carrots adds depth, while the clean cucumber and ripe red tomatoes keep things fresh. I use my beloved curry leaves here, but if you can't get them, don't worry—it will be really good without.

I love making spiced nuts, and these are a good stand-alone snack for any day, but scattering them over the carefully thought-out salad amplifies this dish to something majorly delicious.

....

Preheat the oven to 400°F/200°C.

Put the carrots into a roasting tray and add a good drizzle of oil and the honey. Scatter over the mustard seeds and nigella seeds and roast in the oven for 30 minutes.

Put the cucumber, tomatoes, red onion, and chile into a bowl. Toss with a little oil and a good pinch of salt and squeeze over the lime.

Heat a little olive oil in a frying pan, add the curry leaves, and turmeric and stir for a minute or so until the curry leaves start to crisp. Add the onion and fry for another couple of minutes, then add the cashew nuts and continue to fry until the nuts are golden and toasted. Season with salt and transfer to a bowl to cool.

Remove the carrots from the oven and add to the bowl of cucumber and tomatoes.

To serve, lay the carrot salad on a big platter. Scatter over the cilantro and then the spiced cashew nuts. Sprinkle with the chopped chile and coconut and squeeze over the juice of the remaining lime. Serve with warm chapati and mango chutney (or the nectarine chutney on page 339).

SERVES 4

FOR THE SALAD

1 pound/500 g carrots, peeled and cut in half lengthwise and into 1¼-inch/3 cm lengths

olive or coconut oil

1 tablespoon honey or agave syrup

2 teaspoons mustard seeds

1 teaspoon nigella (black onion) seeds

½ cucumber, peeled into ribbons

4 ripe tomatoes, roughly chopped

1 small red onion, peeled and very finely sliced

1 large red chile, seeded and finely chopped

sea salt

1 lime

FOR THE SPICED CASHEWS

optional: 20 curry leaves

1 teaspoon ground turmeric

1 onion, peeled and finely sliced

⅔ cup/100 g cashew nuts

TO SERVE

a large bunch of fresh cilantro, roughly chopped

1 large red chile, seeded and finely chopped

3½ ounces/100 g fresh coconut, or coconut cream

1 lime

Lemon-roasted feta with traffic-light tomatoes

Where I live in Hackney, East London, every corner store sells feta and tomatoes, so I make this in summer when I don't have the time (or the inclination) to wander very far.

Here I roast the feta with lemon and cilantro as both add such heady citrus tones to the salty cheese. Roasting feta gives it an unexpectedly wonderful milky wobbly curd interior and a crisped golden exterior. I like to serve it just out of the oven so it's milky soft.

Basil is the predictable partner of tomato, but mint comes from the same herb family and in my mind goes just as well. I sometimes stir in some half-moons of peeled, seeded cucumber, a handful of shredded spinach, and even a few toasted pumpkin seeds.

I like to make the most of the variety of different colored and shaped tomatoes to which we now have access. I can't think of a more beautiful plate than a mixture of bright yellow, vibrant orange, and flaming red tomatoes, carefully sliced, with a drizzle of decent olive oil and a scattering of sea salt.

Tomatoes contain a powerful antioxidant called lycopene, which is better absorbed by the body if the tomatoes are cooked. And, even better, olive oil actually allows us to absorb lycopene more easily, which goes to show that nature always knows best.

....

Preheat the oven to 425°F/220°C.

Place the feta on a baking tray lined with parchment paper. Grate over the zest of half the lemon, sprinkle over the smashed cilantro seeds, season with some black pepper (no salt needed here), and drizzle with a touch

SERVES 2 OR 4 AS PART OF A MEAL

8 ounces/200 g of feta cheese

1 unwaxed lemon

1 teaspoon cilantro seeds, bashed in a mortar and pestle

sea salt and freshly ground black pepper

olive oil

1¾ pounds/800 g tomatoes, different colors, sizes, and shapes

a small bunch of fresh mint, leaves picked and finely chopped

CONTINUED

of oil. Roast in the oven for 25 minutes, until the feta is starting to turn nicely golden.

While your feta is roasting, chop the tomatoes into interesting different chunks and slices and place them in a bowl. Season well with salt and pepper, grate over the zest of the rest of the lemon and drizzle with a couple of tablespoons of olive oil. Add half the lemon juice, then taste and add more if needed. Mix well with your hands and set aside so the flavors can meld.

Once the feta is roasted, lay the tomatoes on a serving platter and scatter over the mint. Use a spoon to dot chunks of the feta over the tomatoes and serve right away, with plenty of warmed pitas or olive-oil–drizzled toast and, if you like, some green leaves.

Roasted feta also works really well

· with finely sliced zucchini dressed with lemon and chile.
· on top of a quinoa or couscous salad.
· crumbled over roasted squash.
· crumbled on top of soups and stews.
· piled on top of hunks of good bread drizzled with olive oil.
· in a Greek salad.

Raw Thai citrus crunch salad

This salad borrows its flavors from one of my all-time favorite comfort dishes, pad Thai. Unlike pad Thai, though, you'll notice there aren't any noodles here—instead, ribbons of zucchini and carrot take their place. I make this salad all year round: in autumn and winter I swap the basil for more cilantro and the zucchini for celeriac or parsnip.

Everything used in this salad is completely raw. It's good to have some raw food in your diet—it helps us appreciate food in its cleanest, purest form. This salad is a good stepping-stone for people who think raw food is all beansprouts and hemp seeds.

SERVES 4

FOR THE SALAD

1 zucchini

3 medium carrots, peeled

½ head white or napa cabbage

1 red pepper, seeded

2 scallions

1 pink grapefruit

1 lime

a small bunch of fresh basil

a large bunch of fresh cilantro

2 good handfuls of beansprouts

FOR THE DRESSING

2 medjool dates

a handful (about 3½ ounces/100 g) cashew nuts, soaked overnight in water if you have time

1 (¾-inch/2 cm) piece of fresh ginger, peeled and roughly chopped

½ clove garlic, peeled, green center removed, roughly chopped

1 red chile, seeded and finely chopped

juice of 2 limes

2 tablespoons soy sauce or tamari

TO SERVE

a handful of cashews, crushed

Use a vegetable peeler to peel the zucchini and carrots into ribbons and place them in a big bowl—it's okay to leave a little bit of the middle behind for the sake of your fingers. Shred the cabbage finely, slice the red pepper and scallions as finely as you can, and add to the bowl.

Now use a knife to peel the grapefruit and lime. Then with the knife, roughly cut out all the segments from both, leaving the pith and membrane behind. Put the segments into a bowl, then mash them up so you are left with little juicy jewels of lime and grapefruit. Add these to the big bowl too.

Roughly chop the basil and cilantro, then add all the basil, half the cilantro, and all the beansprouts to the bowl. This will all keep well in the fridge until you are ready to eat.

When ready to serve, make your dressing by putting all the ingredients into a blender with ⅔ cup/150 ml of water and blending until you have a dressing just thick enough to coat and hold on to the vegetables. Thin with a little more water if you need to. If you don't have a blender, mash the dates in a bowl until you have a paste, then finely chop the nuts, ginger, garlic, and chile and stir in the lime juice and soy sauce. Pour the dressing over the salad, mix well, and top with the crushed cashews and the rest of the cilantro.

Charred corn, scrunched kale, and sweet potato salad

This is a mix of popping Mexican spices and fresh Californian flavors. It's a riot of color in a bowl and often takes center stage when I have people over for dinner. This is a wonderful midweek supper too, as it comes together in no time, with some black or brown rice alongside.

Here I keep the kale raw, which might seem a bit unusual. I love to eat kale raw—but I always scrunch it with lemon or lime juice and a pinch of salt first. This does something amazingly fresh and different to it—the cellulose breaks down, so it softens and sweetens into buttery little ribbons. It is super quick, and because you aren't cooking it, all the nutrients stay intact. I scrunch any greens before using in a salad—spinach, dinosaur kale, and collards all work.

SERVES 4

4 sweet potatoes, peeled and roughly chopped

1 teaspoon smoked paprika

½ teaspoon cumin seeds

1 teaspoon runny honey

extra virgin olive oil

sea salt and freshly ground black pepper

½ pound/250 g head of curly kale

juice of ½ a lime

2 corn on the cob

1 ripe avocado, peeled, pitted, and sliced

FOR THE DRESSING

juice of ½ a lime

a handful of cashews (soaked overnight if you have time—see note on page 340)

½ a bunch of fresh cilantro

2 tablespoons coconut milk (see note on page 39)

Preheat your oven to 400°F/200°C.

Place the sweet potatoes on a roasting tray with the paprika, cumin, honey, a good splash of olive oil, and some salt and pepper. Toss together, and then roast for 40 minutes until soft on the inside and charred and caramelized outside.

Strip the kale from its stems and rip or chop it into little bite-size pieces. Put into a large bowl, squeeze over the lime juice, and add a pinch of salt. Use your hands to scrunch the kale for a minute or so, then set aside.

Next, heat a griddle pan until screaming hot. Add the corn and char it on each side, turning it from time to time. Once charred all over, let it cool, then cut the kernels from the corn cobs and add them to the bowl of kale.

Put all the dressing ingredients into a blender with 2 tablespoons of water and a good pinch of salt. Blend until almost smooth and grassy green. Taste; add more lime juice or salt if you think it needs it.

Add the sweet potatoes to the kale and corn and then add the avocado to the bowl too. Pour over the dressing and toss everything together.

Seeded squash, pomegranate, and za'atar spices

This is a warming salad that will brighten up the grayest day. A riot of vivid orange and ruby, this squash salad plays around with the flavors of the Middle Eastern spice blend za'atar. Za'atar is a blend of thyme, sumac, and sesame seeds that's sprinkled on everything from flatbreads to soups and is a quick fix to amp up any dinner.

I could eat squash for every meal. Its bright orange color means it's packed with beta-carotene and vitamins, and it will keep all year round. Bitter leaves like chicory and radicchio are a foil for the sweetness of this salad.

....

SERVES 4

1 medium butternut squash or 2 smaller squash such as acorn, seeded and cut into chunks (you can leave the skin on)

a little olive oil

1 heaping tablespoon poppy seeds

1 heaping tablespoon sesame seeds

1 teaspoon fennel seeds, crushed up a bit in a mortar and pestle

1 teaspoon red pepper flakes

1 teaspoon ground cinnamon

sea salt and freshly ground black pepper

2 red chicory or 1 head of raddichio

½ a pomegranate

a few sprigs of fresh mint

FOR THE DRESSING

2 medjool dates, pitted

2 tablespoons good balsamic vinegar

2 tablespoons olive oil

juice of ½ a lemon

Preheat your oven to 425°F/220°C.

Spread the squash on to a baking tray, add a splash of oil, and scatter over the seeds (poppy, sesame, and fennel seeds), red pepper flakes, and cinnamon. Season with salt and pepper and toss together to coat in the seedy spices. Cover with foil and roast for 40 minutes.

Meanwhile, shred the chicory or radicchio and pop the pomegranate jewels from the fruit. Put them into a big bowl and then roughly chop the mint and add that too. Mash up the dates in a bowl with a fork, add the rest of the dressing ingredients, and mix well. You can use a food processor here if your dates are not soft enough to mash.

After 40 minutes, remove the foil from the baking tray, check that the squash is yielding and tender, and then return it to the oven without the foil for 10 minutes to crisp up a bit.

Take the squash out of the oven and add it to the bowl. Drizzle over the dressing and toss everything together. For a really hearty meal, serve this with flatbread and some more green leaves. Sometimes a bit of feta finds its way on to the top of this salad too.

easy lunches and laid-back suppers

Food for easy days and laid-back nights: I love to eat light and clean, as it makes heading out for an after-dinner stroll or curling up to watch a film far more enjoyable and comfortable. These recipes are as perfect for a weeknight dinner as they are for a weekend lunch and come together in less than 30 minutes, leaving you feeling satisfied but light as a feather.

dal with crispy sweet potato and quick coconut chutney · popcorn tacos · walnut and marjoram pesto with radicchio · three go-to pasta recipes · avocado and lemon zest spaghetti · kale and black sesame sushi bowl · lentils and beets with salsa verde · sweet red onion and hazelnut pizzette · asparagus and toasted cashew stir-fry · farro with roasted leeks and smoky-sweet romesco · full-of-greens fritters · beet curry with spiced cottage cheese · pan-dressed noodles with crunchy cabbage and crispy tofu · gentle brown rice pilaf with toasted nuts and seeds · lemon chard aloo · kitchari · in season · ezekiel's charred eggplant with baba ghanoush · golden roasted roots with leeks, tarragon, and quinoa · lime and chipotle black bean tacos · gado gado · pestos · sweet potato tortilla with almond salsa

Dal with crispy sweet potato and quick coconut chutney

SERVES 4

FOR THE SWEET POTATOES

2 sweet potatoes, skins on, washed and roughly chopped into ½-inch/1½ cm cubes

sea salt and freshly ground black pepper

1 teaspoon cumin seeds

½ teaspoon fennel seeds

olive oil

FOR THE DAL

2 cloves garlic, peeled and chopped

a thumb-size piece of fresh ginger, peeled and roughly chopped

1 green chile, finely chopped

1 red onion, peeled and roughly chopped

1 teaspoon cumin seeds

1 teaspoon cilantro seeds

1 teaspoon ground turmeric

1 teaspoon ground cinnamon

1 cup/200 g red lentils

1 (15-ounce/400 g) can coconut milk

1⅔ cups/400 ml vegetable stock

2 large handfuls of spinach

a bunch of fresh cilantro, roughly chopped, stems and all

juice of 1 lemon

FOR THE COCONUT CHUTNEY

½ cup/50 g unsweetened dried coconut

1 teaspoon black mustard seeds

10 curry leaves

a small amount of vegetable or coconut oil

1-ounce/20 g piece of fresh ginger, grated

1 red chile, finely chopped

This dal is one of my favorite recipes. It is a killer dal, and the roasted sweet potatoes and rose-colored coconut chutney lift it to something stellar. Everyone I have given the recipe to tells me that this has become their "compliment" dish—everyone loves it. And it all comes from the humble little lentil.

For the chutney, fresh grated coconut is the best, but I don't often have time to crack coconuts for my dinner, so this version uses unsweetened dried coconut. If you have the time to grate a fresh coconut, the chutney will be out of this world. If you are short of time, this chutney can be swapped for a good spoonful of mango chutney.

I keep a bag of curry leaves in the freezer. They bring back brightly colored memories of southern India, and their deep yet delicate flavor can't be mimicked. If you can't find fresh curry leaves, dried ones will do.

....

Preheat your oven to 425°F/220°C.

Pour ⅔ cup/150 ml of boiling water over the coconut and leave to soak.

Put your sweet potatoes on a roasting tray and add a good pinch of salt and pepper, the cumin and fennel seeds, and a drizzle of olive oil. Roast in the oven for 20 to 25 minutes until soft and sweet in the middle and crispy brown on the outside.

In a large saucepan, sauté the garlic, ginger, chile, and red onion in a little oil for about 10 minutes, until soft and sweet.

CONTINUED

Grind the cumin and cilantro seeds in a mortar and pestle, then add to the pan with the other spices, and cook for a couple of minutes to toast and release the oils. Add the lentils, coconut milk, and stock to the pan and bring to a simmer; then turn the heat down and simmer for 25–30 minutes.

While that is cooking, make your chutney. Drain the coconut and put it into a bowl. Fry the mustard seeds and curry leaves in a little oil until they begin to crackle and then pour the mixture over the coconut. Season with salt and pepper, then stir in the ginger and chile, and give it a good mix.

To finish your dal, take it off the heat, then stir in the spinach and allow it to wilt a little, stirring in half the chopped cilantro and the lemon juice too. Pile into bowls and top with the crispy sweet potatoes, spoonfuls of the coconut chutney, and the remaining cilantro. I serve this with charred chapatis or roti, and if you are really hungry, you can have some fluffed brown basmati rice too.

Popcorn tacos

Elote is a Mexican street snack sold on every corner in Mexico. It's a pretty offbeat combination of corn, chile powder, butter, and lime (and sometimes even mayonnaise), served in a polystyrene cup and normally topped with crema (sour cream). Sounds weird but it tastes delicious.

I like making my version of *elote* by caramelizing corn and adding lime and chile, popping it into a taco, and topping it with agave-spiced popcorn. It's got a bit of Jeff Koons kitsch and tastes ridiculously good.

I love that corn is used in three ways here: the charred corn kernels, the popped corn, and the corn tortillas. Corn is such a clever and versatile food. I spent some time on an Indian reservation a few years back and I was blown away by the ingenuity of the cooks with corn: breads, cakes, stews—it seems to be part of everything. Eating corn in three different ways here means you maximize its vitamins and minerals, and different ways of preparing it bring different benefits for your body.

These are a perfect supper or lunch. I eat two mini ones and feel satisfied, so that's what I have accounted for here, but someone really hungry (my John) could eat three or four.

I use cayenne pepper, as it packs a good heat punch that is backed up with a deep roasted red pepper and almost sun-dried tomato flavor. It has recently been in the limelight, mixed with maple syrup as the "master cleanse" detox choice of many celebrities. Reap the benefits in this delicious recipe rather than sipping miserably from a bottle of watery spicy syrup.

First get the popcorn going. Place a large pan over low heat and add a splash of oil. Add the popcorn kernels and put the lid on. Shake the pan vigorously every minute or so to keep the kernels from burning. The corn will start to

⁘ CONTINUED

SERVES 4

FOR THE POPCORN
olive oil
3 tablespoons popcorn kernels
½ teaspoon sea salt
½ teaspoon cumin seeds
½ teaspoon cayenne pepper
1 tablespoon honey or agave syrup

FOR THE CARAMELIZED CORN
4 corn on the cob
sea salt and freshly ground black pepper
grated zest and juice of 1 unwaxed lime
½ teaspoon cayenne pepper
1 red or green chile, finely chopped
scant ½ cup/100 ml all-natural yogurt or crème fraîche

TO SERVE
2 avocados
juice of ½ a lime
8 mini corn or wheat tortillas, or 4 big ones
3½ ounces/100 g feta cheese, drained and crumbled
a bunch of cilantro, roughly chopped

pop after a couple of minutes. Once the popping has stopped, remove the pan from the heat and allow to cool a little.

Next, mix together the popcorn spice. Mix the salt, spices, and honey or agave syrup in a little pan; warm and mix. Next, toss with the popcorn until everything is coated.

Using a sharp knife, cut the kernels from the corn cobs. Heat a little olive oil in a pan and fry the kernels for 5 to 10 minutes, until charred and caramelized. Add salt and pepper, the lime zest and juice, and the cayenne and chile; then take off the heat, stir in a tablespoon of yogurt, and cover the pan with foil to keep the corn warm.

Peel the avocados, remove the pits, and then chop the flesh into little pieces. Put them into a bowl and squeeze over a little lime juice.

Warm your tortillas—I do this by holding them in a gas flame with a pair of tongs, but warming them in the oven or frying them in a dry nonstick pan will work just as well.

Divide the corn kernels between the tortillas and top with a spoonful of yogurt or crème fraîche, some avocado, some crumbled feta, and a pinch of chopped cilantro. Top with a scattering of popcorn and then fold up in your hands and eat.

Walnut and marjoram pesto with radicchio

I may get into some trouble with the pasta purists here, but these flavors are worth it for me. Strozzapreti is my favorite pasta—I love its chewy plumpness. You can find it in Italian delis and some good supermarkets, but fusilli would do nicely too.

This is a great weeknight supper, since the sauce takes as long to throw together as the pasta takes to cook.

Radicchio is a vibrant magenta lettuce with a slightly bitter taste. It's a member of the chicory family, hence red chicory will work well here too. Bitter leaves need to be treated with some forethought. Here the radicchio is finely shredded so that in each bite the bitterness is balanced by the sweetness of the roasted walnuts. These leaves can also help with digestion, much like the bitter after-meal digestifs you find in France and Italy.

SERVES 4

1 pound/400 g strozzapreti or fusilli pasta

1 head of radicchio (about 7 ounces/200 g), shredded

FOR THE PESTO

⅓ cup/50 g shelled walnuts

1 small clove garlic, peeled

sea salt and freshly ground black pepper

a bunch fresh marjoram or oregano, leaves picked

a bunch fresh flat-leaf parsley, leaves picked

3 tablespoons extra virgin olive oil

2 ounces/50 g pecorino cheese, freshly grated (see note on page 136)

juice of 1 lemon

Toast the walnuts in a pan for a few minutes until golden. Then grind them in a mortar and pestle with the garlic and some sea salt until you have a thick paste. You can do this in a food processor if you like—just take care not to overmix it, as a little texture is good.

Add the herbs, grind again, then add the oil; mix everything together into a slick deep-green paste. Add the pecorino and some lemon juice to taste and season with a bit more salt and pepper if needed. Set aside.

Next, bring a pan of salted water to a boil and add the pasta. Simmer for however long it says on the package—it will usually be around 8 minutes. Just before you drain the pasta, scoop out a cup of the pasta water for later.

Put the pasta back into the pan, add some of the pesto, and mix well, adding enough of the cooking water to thin and make a creamy sauce. Finally, stir in the shredded radicchio and serve with more pecorino.

THREE
GO-TO PASTA
RECIPES

QUICK GREENS SPAGHETTI

1 pound/400 g spaghetti (I like brown rice, whole wheat, or spelt—see pasta cooking instructions at left)

extra virgin olive oil

2 cloves garlic, peeled and finely sliced

1 to 2 red chiles, seeded and finely chopped, depending on how hot you like it

1 sprig fresh rosemary, leaves picked

1 large head of leafy greens (about 1 pound/400 g), rinsed and finely sliced, with any big stems removed

grated zest and juice of 1 large unwaxed lemon (plus an extra lemon for juice if needed)

sea salt and freshly ground black pepper

a good handful of finely grated Parmesan or pecorino cheese

To cook your pasta: Put a large pan of boiling water on to boil and add a couple of generous pinches of salt. Once the water is at a rolling boil, add your pasta and cook according to the package directions or until just al dente. Meanwhile get on with your chosen sauce. Each recipe serves 4.

Heat a good drizzle of olive oil in a large frying pan and add the garlic, chile, and rosemary. Fry for a minute or so, until the garlic is starting to color, then add the greens and sauté, stirring occasionally, for 3 to 4 minutes, or until the greens have wilted a little.

Transfer to a blender and blend with the lemon zest and juice, another 2 tablespoons of olive oil and a good pinch of salt and pepper. Thin with a little of the pasta water if you need to—you want a thin pesto-like consistency. Return the greens mix to the pan.

Drain the pasta, reserving a cupful of water. Add to the greens with a splash of the pasta water and mix well. Squeeze over a little more lemon juice if needed, and serve topped with a drizzle of olive oil and a wispy pile of grated Parmesan or pecorino.

MY GOLDEN RULES WHEN COOKING PASTA

· Use your biggest pan so the pasta has space to move around.
· Be brave with the salt you add to the water; remember, only a little bit of the salt you add will be absorbed into the pasta.
· Only add your pasta once the water is at a rolling boil.
· Always cook it to just al dente—it will cook a little more as it cools.
· Always dip a heatproof cup into the pan and fill it with pasta water just before draining the pasta. You can add this water to your drained pasta and sauce to help it come together.

A NOTE ON PARMESAN AND PECORINO

I often like to use pecorino with pasta as I like the flavor and it is easier in my experience to find vegetarian pecorino than Parmesan. Parmesan and some pecorinos are not vegetarian as they are made with animal rennet. You can buy special vegetarian Parmesan-style cheese that is pretty good, so you may want to search this out or use another cheese instead.

SPEEDY SUMMER ZUCCHINI SPAGHETTINI

1 pound/400 g spaghettini or spaghetti of your choice (I like buckwheat or whole wheat—see pasta cooking instructions at left)

4 zucchini

1 red chile, seeded and finely chopped

a bunch of fresh mint, leaves picked and chopped

a bunch of fresh parsley, leaves picked and chopped

grated zest and juice of 1 unwaxed lemon

7 ounces/200 g feta cheese

good extra virgin olive oil

sea salt and freshly ground black pepper

Grate the zucchini into a big bowl. Add the chopped chile, mint, and parsley and the zest and juice of the lemon, then crumble in the feta. Add a couple of tablespoons of good olive oil and mix well.

Before you drain the pasta, carefully scoop out half a cupful of the pasta water—you'll need this later. Drain the pasta and put it back into the empty pan, then add the zucchini mixture and a good pinch of salt and pepper. Stir in a little splash of pasta water to make a bit more of a sauce. Serve immediately in the middle of the table for everyone to help themselves.

SUMMER SPAGHETTI POMODORO

1 pound/400 g spaghetti (I like to use buckwheat spaghetti—see pasta cooking instructions at left)

olive oil

2 cloves garlic, peeled and finely sliced

a bunch of fresh basil

1 pound/500 g cherry or vine-ripened tomatoes, cherries halved, vine ones chopped

sea salt

good olive oil, for drizzling

optional: Parmesan or pecorino cheese

Heat a good-sized frying pan and add a glug of olive oil. Once the oil is warm but not too hot, add the garlic and cook over medium heat until the edges are just beginning to brown. Add the basil stems and swish around the pan. Next, add the tomatoes and a good pinch of salt and cook over medium heat for 10 minutes, until they have broken down and the sauce has thickened and sweetened.

Once the pasta is cooked, carefully scoop out a cupful of pasta water, then drain the pasta and add it to the tomato sauce. Toss everything together, adding a little of the pasta water as needed. Tear over the basil leaves.

Serve immediately, topped with good olive oil and grated Parmesan or pecorino, if you like.

↓

THINGS TO ADD

· 1 tablespoon harissa and some pitted black olives
· 1 tablespoon toasted fennel seeds and some shredded kale
· 1 tablespoon cilantro seeds and some crumbled feta
· 1 tablespoon capers, a handful of pitted green olives and some oregano
· A couple handfuls of frozen peas and some fresh mint
· 1 tablespoon za'atar (see page 125) and some roasted squash
· 7 ounces/200 g chopped green beans and some crushed red pepper flakes
· Some ribbons of zucchini and a crumbling of goat cheese

Avocado and lemon zest spaghetti

At my house supper is almost always quick, but it has to be flavor- and nutrition-packed, and this hits all the right notes.

I tend to use whole wheat spaghetti as it works really well with the avocado. Whole wheat spaghetti will soak up more oil than the other kinds, though, so you may need to add a trickle more at the end.

I prefer to use the capers that come sitting in little jars of brine. I find the salt-crusted ones just too salty, even if they are washed. Use whichever you prefer but remember all capers are salty, so be sparing about adding more salt.

I often top this pasta with a poached egg, partly because it makes a more filling dinner but also because of the sunshine yellow sauce it makes for the pasta. Definitely try it.

....

Fill a big pan with water and add a good pinch of salt. Bring to a rolling boil, add the pasta, and cook for 8 to 10 minutes, or according to the package instructions, until perfectly al dente.

Heat some olive oil in a large frying pan over low heat, then add the capers and garlic, and sauté gently until the edges of the garlic start to very slightly brown. Remove from the heat and add the lemon zest.

Chop the herbs and add them to the pan. Halve and pit the avocados, then use a knife to make criss-cross cuts through the flesh, chopping it inside the skin. Use a spoon to scoop out each half into the pan, and stir to mix all the flavors together.

Before you drain the pasta, carefully scoop out half a cupful of the pasta water. Drain the pasta and add it to the frying pan with a little of the cooking water and a good drizzle of olive oil. Taste and add salt, pepper, and lemon juice as needed. Scoop the pasta into bowls and eat on your lap.

SERVES 4

sea salt and freshly ground black pepper

1 pound/400 g dried spaghetti of your choice (I use whole wheat, but rice, quinoa, or regular spaghetti will work too)

olive oil

4 tablespoons capers in brine, roughly chopped

1 clove garlic, peeled and very finely sliced

grated zest of 2 unwaxed lemons, and juice of ½ a lemon

a bunch of fresh basil, leaves picked

a bunch of fresh parsley, leaves picked

2 ripe avocados

Kale and black sesame sushi bowl

SERVES 2

1 cup/200 g brown sushi rice
(or regular brown rice)

sea salt

2 handfuls of frozen edamame
beans (without the pods, about
4 ounces/120 g)

1 good-sized pomegranate

a dash of sesame oil

2 big handfuls of kale or other leafy
greens, stalks removed, leaves
finely shredded

4 sheets of nori seaweed,
torn into bits

2 tablespoons black sesame seeds

a small bunch of fresh cilantro,
leaves picked and chopped

1 avocado, halved and sliced

FOR THE DRESSING

grated zest and juice of
1 unwaxed lemon

grated zest and juice of ½ an
unwaxed orange

1 tablespoon honey or agave syrup

2 tablespoons soy sauce or tamari

1 tablespoon Japanese rice vinegar

This is clean food. Nutty brown sushi rice provides the comforting base for a colorful, satisfying bowl of crisp, zingy, taste-popping flavors. It's the kind of food I crave for a weekday lunch when I need sustenance for running around. There are a couple of Japanese places in London where they do a bento box full of rice, avocado, and seaweed, which I often pick up on the fly.

If I'm at home, though, or if I have time the night before, I make this; it's as good cold as it is warm. I have written the recipe to serve two but you can double it for a dinner for four—it's a perfectly complete one-bowl light dinner on a sunny day.

Black sesame seeds are pretty dark blue-black seeds and have a distinct, deeper sesame taste than their white counterparts. Black sesame seeds are high in both vitamin E and antioxidants. I buy black sesame seeds from Chinese or Japanese food stores or spice shops. If you can't find them, just use some well-toasted white ones instead.

Rinse the rice in a sieve under cold running water to get rid of some of the starch, then place it in a pan with a pinch of salt and cover with twice the volume of water (about ⅔ cups/400 ml). Bring to a boil, then reduce the heat and simmer, covered, for 45 minutes, until all the water has been absorbed and the rice is fully cooked. Add more hot water from time to time, if needed, to keep the rice from drying out. If you are using regular brown rice, follow the instructions on the package.

Meanwhile, defrost the edamame beans by putting them into a bowl and covering them with boiling water. Leave for 10 minutes.

CONTINUED

Cut the pomegranate in half. Lay a sieve over a bowl, put one half of the pomegranate in your hand, seed side down, then squeeze it over the bowl, allowing the juice to pour through your fingers. Set aside.

Take the other half of the pomegranate and hold it above a clean bowl, cut-side down. Tap the back of the pomegranate with a wooden spoon so that the jewels fall through your fingers into the bowl, tapping a little harder if the seeds resist falling out. Once all the jewels are in the bowl, discard the shell and pick out any little pithy white bits that may have fallen into the bowl.

Heat a frying pan over medium heat. Add a splash of sesame oil and sauté the kale or greens for a couple of minutes, then add the nori and cook for a minute longer, to toast. Remove from the heat, cover, and keep warm.

Add the dressing ingredients to the bowl of pomegranate juice and mix well.

Once the rice is cooked, drain it and pour over most of the dressing. Add half the black sesame seeds and stir so that the dressing coats the grains.

Pile the rice into two bowls, top with little piles of edamame beans, pomegranate seeds, warm kale, chopped cilantro, sliced avocado, and more black sesame seeds, and pour over the rest of the dressing.

Eat and feel clean and calm.

Lentils and beets with salsa verde

This is a simple dinner with a lot going on. Here, beets and lentils are cooked simply but carefully in my favorite way. Topped with a salsa verde, this dish might just make it into my top five dinners.

Cooking lentils this way is a wonder—the tomatoes, garlic, and bay leaves come together to make a really full-flavored bowl. If you haven't tried it before, give it a try—they will be the best lentils you have ever eaten. Be sure to buy Puy lentils, as they are much richer in flavor and hold their shape when cooked.

If beets aren't in season, top the lentils with steamed broccoli, roasted squash, or celeriac. Sometimes I top this with a little goat cheese, or even good thick Greek yogurt.

SERVES 4

FOR THE BEETS
8 medium firm beets (red, candy cane, or yellow), peeled and quartered
4 tablespoons red wine vinegar
extra virgin olive oil
sea salt and freshly ground black pepper

FOR THE LENTILS
2 cups/400 g Puy lentils, rinsed
4 cloves garlic
1 small tomato
1 bay leaf
a few sprigs of fresh thyme
4¼ cups/1 L vegetable stock

FOR THE SALSA VERDE
2 tablespoons capers
2 tablespoons cornichons
a bunch of fresh mint
a bunch of fresh parsley
a bunch of fresh basil
extra virgin olive oil
juice of ½ a lemon

Preheat your oven to 350°F/ 180°C.

Put the quartered beets on a tray with the vinegar, a good glug of olive oil, and a splash of water. Then season with salt and pepper and toss everything to coat. Cover with foil and roast in the oven for 1 hour until the beets are cooked through and the juices are neon pink.

While the beets are roasting, make the lentils. Put them into a pan with the unpeeled garlic, whole tomato, and herbs. Add vegetable stock to just cover, place over medium heat, bring to a simmer, and simmer for 20 to 25 minutes, until they are cooked and the water has evaporated. If they are looking too dry, add a little boiling water as needed.

Next, make your salsa verde. On a big cutting board, chop the capers and cornichons until they are pretty fine, and then add the herbs and chop everything together until you have a fine mass of green. Scoop

CONTINUED

everything into a bowl and add 3 tablespoons of olive oil and the lemon juice. Season with salt and pepper, tasting and balancing to your liking: more oil? more salt? more lemon?

Once the lentils are cooked and all the water has evaporated, scoop out the tomato and the garlic cloves and put them into a bowl to cool. Once cool enough to handle, pop the garlic out of its skins, put back into the bowl with the tomato, and use a fork to mash everything together. Stir this garlic and tomato paste into the lentils. Taste, season with salt and pepper, then dress with a generous glug of olive oil and a splash of red wine vinegar.

Once the beets are cooked, pile the lentils onto plates, top with the roasted beets, and drizzle their dark pink roasting juices over the top. Spoon on the salsa verde to finish. If you have some leftover salsa verde, it will keep in a jar in the fridge for 2 to 3 days.

Ways with salsa verde
- As a marinade for vegetables or tofu
- Smothered over mozzarella or roasted feta
- As a dressing for grains or beans
- In place of pesto stirred into pasta
- Spooned on top of a simple soup
- As a dip for chunks of good toasted bread

Sweet red onion and hazelnut pizzette

These little pizzettes are somewhere in the territory of a pizza but they are made with spelt flour, which gives them a deeper, nuttier tone. Hazelnuts are folded into the dough too and toast as they bake to add an amazingly sweet, nutty backnote.

The depth of the spelt and hazelnut crust stands up to the clean fresh goat cheese, caramelized onion topping, and the nourishing green from the wilted spinach. I serve these for a crowd or with a simple salad for an offbeat supper.

MAKES 8 PIZZETTE

FOR THE DOUGH

3½ cups/550 g light spelt flour (regular bread flour would work too)

1 teaspoon sea salt

1 teaspoon dry yeast or a ½-ounce/15 g package

a good handful of toasted and crushed hazelnuts

1 cup and 1 tablespoon/260 ml warm water

scant ¼ cup/50 ml rapeseed or olive oil, plus more as needed

FOR THE TOPPING

3 red onions, peeled and sliced

olive oil

14 ounces/400 g spinach

a good grating of nutmeg

1 clove garlic, peeled

a bunch of fresh marjoram or oregano, leaves picked

6 tablespoons rapeseed or olive oil

8 ounces/250 g soft goat cheese or ricotta cheese

a good pinch of salt

Weigh all the dry dough ingredients into a mixing bowl. Add the warm water bit by bit, mixing as you go. Then add the oil in the same way. Mix until everything comes together into a dough. This can be done in a stand mixer (like a KitchenAid—using the dough hook) or a food processor.

Knead the dough until it's elastic and superstretchy. This will take 15 minutes by hand or 10 minutes if done in a mixer. Don't skip the kneading, as this is what will make a great dough.

Once it is a smooth, even, springy ball, put the dough back into the mixing bowl, cover, and leave in a warm place to rise for 1 hour or so—it should double in size.

Once it has risen, turn out the dough on to a clean work surface and divide it into 8 equal pieces. Shape each piece of dough into a tight round roll.

Slosh a good glug of rapeseed oil into a big roasting pan and roll the dough balls around, coating each one with oil. This'll stop them from sticking to

CONTINUED

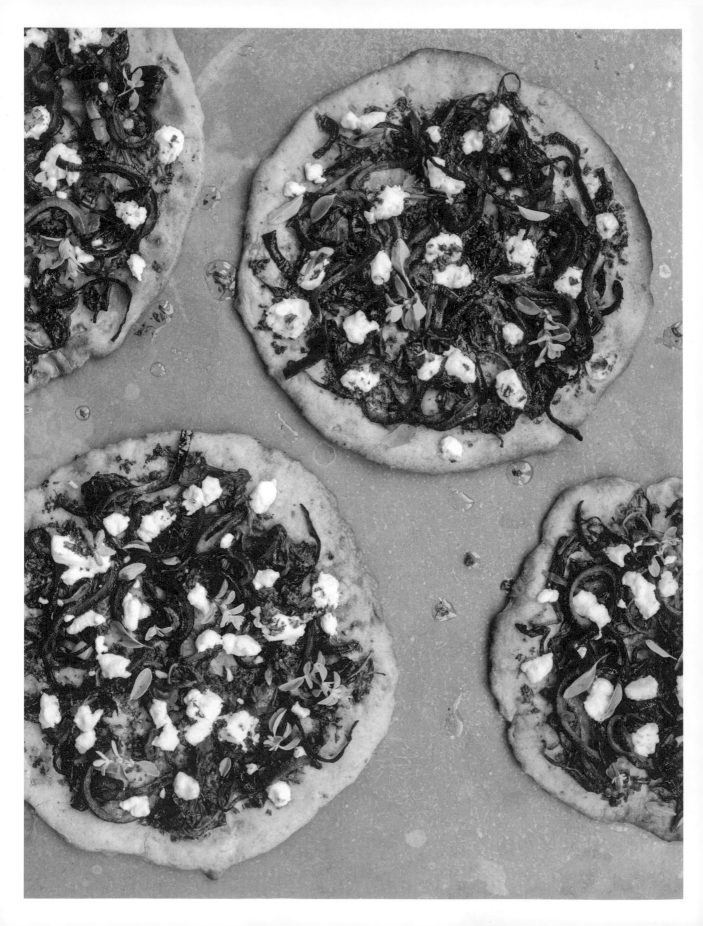

each other and give the pizza base a lush crust. Leave the pan of pizza bases covered in a warm place to rise for another 30 minutes.

Meanwhile, preheat your oven as hot as it'll go—anything above 475°F/ 240°C is good. Place a pizza stone or a heavy baking sheet in the middle of the oven to heat up.

Now on to the toppings: fry the onions slow and low for about 15 minutes in a little olive oil until soft and sweet—then add the spinach and nutmeg. Set aside. Chop the garlic with the marjoram until fine and mix with the oil.

Once the dough balls have had their final 30 minutes' rise, carefully roll each one into a rough circle, patching up little holes that the crushed hazelnuts might make. Top with the marjoram oil, spoon on the spinach mixture, and dot with the goat cheese or ricotta. Bake on a pizza stone or baking sheet in the super-hot oven for 8 to 10 minutes. Eat the pizzettes as soon as they are cool enough.

Asparagus and toasted cashew stir-fry

I crave this stir-fry and eat it for dinner often. It's fresh, green, and delivers on flavor in a big way. This is a super-quick supper that comes together in 10 minutes. Serve with brown rice or some noodles—I like soba noodles, but rice or egg noodles would work too.

The key with a stir-fry is to make sure everything is prepped and close at hand before you start to cook. This recipe is just for two, as it's best not to overcrowd the pan when stir-frying—if you want to serve more, I suggest you cook it in a couple of batches. I make this in autumn and winter with purple sprouting broccoli and kale or winter greens, and sometimes I throw in a few sesame seeds too.

....

Heat your biggest frying pan or wok and add a splash of sesame oil. Add the scallions and ginger and fry for a minute or two; then add the asparagus and sugar snap peas and stir for a couple of minutes until they have just lost their rawness. Add the spinach or greens and stir until wilted.

Next, add the red pepper flakes, maple syrup, soy sauce, and lime juice and zest and cook for another minute or two.

Remove from the heat, stir in the herbs, and scatter over the cashews. Serve immediately with rice or noodles.

SERVES 2

sesame oil

6 scallions, sliced

a thumb-size piece of fresh ginger, peeled and finely chopped

1 bunch of asparagus, ends snapped off, spears cut into ¾-inch/2 cm pieces

7 ounces/200 g sugar snap peas or halved green beans

2 good handfuls of spinach or shredded leafy greens

a pinch of crushed red pepper flakes

1 tablespoon maple syrup

1 tablespoon soy sauce

grated zest and juice of 1 unwaxed lime

a small bunch of fresh mint or cilantro, or both, roughly chopped

a big handful of toasted cashew nuts

Farro with roasted leeks and smoky-sweet romesco

SERVES 4 TO 6, WITH SOME ROMESCO LEFT OVER

1 butternut squash, seeded and cut into rough chunks

12 whole baby leeks, washed

1 unwaxed lemon

1 cup/200 g farro

a few sprigs of fresh parsley, leaves picked

FOR THE ROMESCO

⅔ cup/100 g blanched almonds

⅓ cup/50 g hazelnuts

olive oil

2 slices of good stale white bread (about 1½ ounces/40 g), torn into chunks

2 cloves garlic, peeled and finely chopped

1 teaspoon sweet smoked paprika

1 (8-ounce/220 g) jar of roasted red peppers, drained (see page 87 for how to roast them yourself)

6 tablespoons extra virgin olive oil

2 tablespoons sherry vinegar

1 small dried chile, crumbled, or a pinch of crushed red pepper flakes

a generous pinch of saffron strands

1 tablespoon tomato purée

sea salt and freshly ground black pepper

If I had my way, this smoky tangy-sweet Catalan sauce would find its way into a meal a day. The recipe will make enough for this dinner plus an extra jam jar full to keep in the fridge for a week or so.

Farro is one of my favorite grains—it has a chewy, almost gummy texture that is so pleasing. Farro is much lower in gluten than most grains, so if you have a mild sensitivity to gluten, it might be okay for you. It's available in most natural food stores and good supermarkets. If you can't get your hands on farro, then pearl barley or bulgur wheat would also work, as would quinoa if you prefer it. Just adjust the cooking times accordingly (see pages 184–5).

Use the best jarred Spanish peppers you can find—piquillo are the ones to look for. If you can't find baby leeks, regular leeks are fine too. Just wash, trim, halve them lengthways, and cut them into 1¼-inch/3 cm lengths.

....

Preheat the oven to 400°F/200°C.

First make your romesco sauce. Scatter the nuts on a baking tray and roast in the hot oven for 10 to 15 minutes, until golden. While they are roasting, heat a little olive oil in a pan and fry the bread until golden brown all over. Add the garlic and smoked paprika and cook for a minute longer and then remove from the heat.

Leaving the oven on, transfer the nuts and toasted bread to a food processor. Add the peppers and blend until you have a coarse paste—you still want a nice bit of texture.

Transfer to a mixing bowl and stir in the extra virgin olive oil, sherry vinegar, dried chile, saffron, and tomato purée. Season to taste and mix well, adjusting the flavors if need be. Romesco is about a balance of punchy flavors. Too

CONTINUED

thick? Add a little water. Too sweet? Add a little vinegar. Too sharp? Add a little oil to soften. Set aside to mellow.

Next, put the squash on a large roasting tray with the leeks. Drizzle over some olive oil, grate over the zest of the lemon, and season with salt and pepper. Roast in the oven for 40 minutes until the squash is golden and the leeks are sweet. Meanwhile, cook the farro in salted boiling water for 35 to 40 minutes, until it is soft but still has a good gummy bite.

Drain the farro, toss with the roasted squash and leeks and a good few tablespoons of the romesco, and finish off with a good sprinkling of parsley.

Ways to use romesco
- Spread on toast and topped with a smear of goat cheese for a quick snack
- As a dip for baby carrots and spring vegetables
- As a marinade for barbecued vegetables
- Piled onto roasted vegetables for extra flavor
- Tossed with cooked noodles with pan-fried greens
- Stirred into a bowl of brown rice and topped with a poached egg
- Alongside your morning eggs
- With flatbread and feta for a quick simple lunch
- Spooned on top of a bowl of soup

Full-of-greens fritters

These were made for me on a trip to Piedmont. A pile of them was laid in the middle of the table just after a breakfast of local cheese, bread, and dark melata honey, and still we polished off the whole thing.

These make their way from the chopping board to the table in 10 minutes, so are often a late-home dinner with a shock of mustardy green salad. Also a great start to a meal if you have a tableful—the fritters will keep well in a low oven, so you can make them early on.

I change the greens depending on what is around, but my two favorite combinations are zucchini with spinach and basil and sprouting broccoli with greens and dill. Any quick-cooking green will do. I use whatever soft cheese I can easily come by here, which more often than not is feta, but look out for robiola, a Piedmontese sheep's milk cheese, which takes these fritters to a different level.

**SERVES 4
(MAKES 12 FRITTERS)**

9 ounces/250 g zucchinis, grated, or purple sprouting broccoli, finely chopped

2 handfuls (about 3½ ounces/ 100 g) of spinach or collard greens, shredded

4 tablespoons soft crumbly cheese (such as feta, robiola, or goat cheese)

3 tablespoons freshly grated Parmesan or pecorino cheese (see note on page 136)

½ clove garlic, peeled and finely chopped

a few sprigs of fresh dill or basil, roughly chopped

grated zest of 1 unwaxed lemon

sea salt and freshly ground black pepper

5 organic or free-range eggs

olive oil

Put all the grated, chopped, and shredded vegetables into a bowl. Crumble in all the cheeses, add the garlic, herbs, and lemon zest and a good pinch of salt and pepper, and mix. Now crack in the eggs and mix well.

Place a large frying pan over medium heat and add a good glug of olive oil— you want to be generous with the oil here.

Once the oil is hot, carefully lower in tablespoons of the mixture and flatten them out to form little patties. Fry for 2 to 3 minutes, then carefully flip and fry on the other side for a final 2 minutes, until the egg is completely cooked.

Place on a plate in a low oven to keep warm until you are ready to eat.

Serve a few fritters on a plate next to some bright salad dressed with lemon, oil, and a little mustard.

Beet curry with spiced cottage cheese

SERVES 4 TO 6

2 tablespoons coconut or sunflower oil

a good handful (about 20) curry leaves

2 tablespoons mustard seeds

2 teaspoons cumin seeds

1 teaspoon ground turmeric

1 tablespoon curry powder

8 small shallots, peeled and finely sliced

1 to 2 green chiles, finely chopped

2 cloves garlic, peeled and crushed

a thumb-size piece of fresh ginger, peeled and finely chopped

10 tablespoons unsweetened dried coconut

1 teaspoon sea salt

juice of 2 lemons

2¼ pounds/1 kg beets, with stalks and leaves, beets peeled and coarsely grated, stalks and leaves washed and finely chopped

⅞ cup/200 ml coconut milk

1 (8-ounce/260 g) bag of washed young leaf spinach

freshly ground black pepper

7 ounces/200 g cottage cheese

a small bunch of fresh cilantro, leaves roughly chopped

My local Indian restaurant is incredible. It does out-of-this-world Keralan vegetarian food, which I adore, with big chile flavors swathed in calming coconut milk. The brash pink decor and knockout food can make the rainiest London day feel a bit sunnier.

The beet part of this dish comes from a trip to Kerala, where I was lucky enough to cook with a lovely lady named Leelu. This is my version of the beet thoran we made: a coconut-heavy beet curry with curry leaves, lemon, and spinach. It may seem like you are adding a lot of dried coconut, but please trust me—you need a lot to allow the sweetness to come through the earthy beets.

I added my own little riff by spooning some spice-spiked cottage cheese on top—beets and cottage cheese are a killer combination. You can use coconut or soy yogurt instead of cottage cheese.

Heat the oil in a large saucepan over medium heat, then add the curry leaves, mustard seeds, and cumin seeds and sauté until fragrant. Watch out—the mustard seeds will pop a little.

Add the turmeric, curry powder, shallots, chiles, garlic, and ginger and cook until the shallots are translucent. Stir in the dried coconut and salt and cook for a couple more minutes, stirring the whole time. Next, squeeze in the juice of 1 of the lemons and give everything a good mix. Take out 1 tablespoon of the spice mix and pop it into a bowl for later.

Add the grated beets and the stalks and leaves to the pan. Pour in the coconut milk, turn the heat up, and stir until everything is vivid

CONTINUED

magenta. Bring to a boil, then lower the heat, cover with a lid, and simmer for 35 to 45 minutes.

When the beets are soft, turn off the heat and add the spinach. Stir it through the curry to wilt it, adding the juice of half the second lemon. Taste and add a little more salt and pepper if needed, then put the lid back on.

In another bowl, mix the cottage cheese with the reserved tablespoon of coconut spice mix and the cilantro. Add the juice of the last lemon half and season to taste.

Serve your beet curry with a spoonful of spiced cottage cheese and warm chapatis. Add some steamed brown rice if you are really hungry.

Pan-dressed noodles with crunchy cabbage and crispy tofu

SERVES 2

1 bunch of purple sprouting broccoli (about 7 ounces/200 g), spears trimmed, or other green vegetable

7 ounces/200 g soba noodles

¼ of a small red cabbage, finely shredded

sea salt

2 tablespoons brown rice vinegar

3 tablespoons maple syrup or agave syrup

olive or rapeseed oil

1 (8-ounce/200 g) block of smoked tofu (I use the almond and sesame one), cut into ⅜-inch/1 cm pieces

1 tablespoon sesame seeds

6 scallions, finely chopped

1 teaspoon sesame oil

1 tablespoon soy sauce or tamari

juice of 1 lemon

a small handful of toasted sesame seeds

a small bunch of fresh cilantro, roughly chopped

To me this supper hits the right note— a clean-eating, tasty but hearty bowl of colors and flavors and just what the people I know want to eat. This is another really quick supper that goes from cutting board to table in 15 minutes if you move quickly, 20 if you take it easy.

I use smoked tofu in this noodle bowl. I also use it in sandwiches and to add to brown rice and stews. The smoky sesame flavor will get the tofu-haters on your side. But what I like most about it is that it is reliable and easy to cook. This tofu is firm, easy to slice, and fries to a satisfying crisp in a nonstick pan in a minute or two.

I favor 100 percent buckwheat soba noodles here. They can be pretty pricey though, so I often use regular soba noodles, which are a blend of buckwheat and wheat flour. Buckwheat is not a grain at all, but the seed of a plant and a cousin of rhubarb. You can buy it whole to make hot cereal for breakfast or use it as a grain in soups and salads, and of course you can use the flour in pancakes, baking, and most famously, blinis. It has a wholesome nutty flavor, slightly malty and altogether delicious. Buckwheat, like quinoa, is high in protein.

....

Bring a pan of water to a boil, then drop in the broccoli and allow to simmer for a couple of minutes, just until it has lost its rawness. Don't cook for any longer, as it's good with a bit of a bite.

Remove your broccoli with a slotted spoon, keeping the pan of water on the heat. Drop in your noodles and cook for 6 to 8 minutes, until they are soft, with a tiny bit of bite. Drain, then run cold water over them to cool them and keep them from sticking.

CONTINUED

Put the shredded cabbage into a bowl and add a big pinch of salt, 1 tablespoon of rice vinegar, and 1 tablespoon of maple syrup. Scrunch it all together with your hands for a minute, then set aside. Wash your hands, as they will be purple from the cabbage.

Heat a nonstick frying pan and add a splash of olive oil. Once it's hot, add the tofu and sauté, turning it until every side is crisp. Toss in the sesame seeds and stir to coat, then remove the tofu from the pan, set aside, and put the pan back on the heat.

Add a little splash of sesame oil and the scallions and cook for a few minutes until softened. Add the remaining tablespoon of vinegar and 2 tablespoons of maple syrup along with the sesame oil, soy sauce, and lemon juice. Cook for 30 seconds or so, until it thickens to a sweet, warm dressing.

Add the drained noodles to the pan and stir to coat them in the dressing. Divide between two bowls and top each one with a handful of pickled cabbage, half the tofu and broccoli, a sprinkling of sesame seeds, and some chopped cilantro.

Gentle brown rice pilaf with toasted nuts and seeds

This is a fantastic dish to have under your belt, as it's a pantry dinner made from next to nothing. I vary the spices by sometimes throwing in a pinch of saffron or some cardamom pods, but the allspice and cinnamon never budge.

I go heavy on the nuts here, as it changes a bowl of rice to a real dinner. Occasionally I swap the nuts, though, for jarred artichokes or sautéed wild mushrooms or chopped dried apricots. Brown basmati releases its energy into your body more slowly than white rice, so it's a better option for feeling full and satisfied.

My favorite herbs to use here are the aniseed-flavored tarragon, dill, chervil, or even mint for its freshness and lightening flavor, which sits well against the warming spices and nuts.

SERVES 4 TO 6

1⅔ cup/300 g brown basmati rice
⅓ cup/50 g pine nuts
⅓ cup/50 g cashew nuts
⅓ cup/50 g pumpkin seeds
a good pat of butter or olive oil
2 red onions, peeled and sliced
1 teaspoon ground allspice
1 teaspoon ground cinnamon
1 teaspoon cumin seeds
sea salt
1 unwaxed lemon, halved

TO SERVE

all-natural yogurt
a small bunch of mixed fresh soft herbs (usually mint and dill, but parsley, chervil, and tarragon work well too)

Soak your rice in cold water for about 15 minutes. Meanwhile, put a large pan (one that has a lid) over medium heat and toast the nuts and seeds without any oil until golden brown. Remove them from the pan and set aside.

Next, add a good pat of butter or olive oil to the pan and fry the onions over medium heat for 10 minutes, until soft and sweet. Add the spices and cook for 5 minutes to allow them to release their fragrant oils and warming smell.

Drain the rice and then wash it under cold running water until the water runs clear. Add it to the pan and cook for a couple of minutes, stirring as you go.

Add a really good pinch of salt (there is a lot of rice here, so be brave with the salt) and the lemon halves, then add enough cold water to cover the rice (2 cups/450-500 ml is about right). Put the lid on the pan, then follow this method: high cook, low cook, no cook. Turn the heat to high for 5 minutes, then turn it down to low and cook for 15 minutes. Now turn the heat off and leave without touching for 10 minutes—don't even peek or lift the lid.

Take off the lid, take out the lemon halves, and squeeze the juice over the rice. Stir in the toasted nuts and seeds. Check for seasoning—add a little more salt and lemon juice if needed.

Spoon into bowls and top with the yogurt and chopped herbs.

To make this a hearty meal
· Add a fried egg to each plate and sprinkle with minced chile
· Add some dried apricots and raisins to the rice before cooking
· Add some finely sliced fennel
· Serve the rice pilaf on top of some blanched greens
· Stir in some peas and extra mint
· Top with sautéed kale and a poached egg

Lemon chard aloo

Saag aloo is a staple in Indian restaurants up and down the UK and seems always to be a side dish, but here it shines in all its worthy glory as the main event. I use chard instead of spinach here as I like its more robust character. (Spinach would work though; just cook it for half the time.)

I follow the rule of eating the rainbow, so it's pretty obvious that chard must be really good for us. With its candy neon stems of ruby reds, saffron yellows, pinks, and deep sea greens, no other vegetable can boast such variety and vivid color. These colors mean that a bounty of vitamins and minerals and antioxidants lie in the leafy greens and stalks.

Chard is tricky to cook if you haven't come across it before, as the delicate leaves and the stalks need to be treated differently. The leaves can be stripped from the stalks and braised for a few minutes or quickly blanched. The stalks need a little more cooking, but not much—if you cut them into ⅜-inch/1 cm slices, they'll take no time to cook. I also like to chop the stalks really finely and throw them into salads.

Heat a splash of oil in a big heavy-bottomed pan and once it's nice and hot, add the mustard seeds. Step back and let them crackle and pop, then add the onions, ginger, garlic, chile, cumin seeds, and turmeric and cook for 5 minutes over medium heat, until the onions are just soft.

Now add the potatoes, the chard stalks, and a good pinch of salt. Pour in ⅞ cup/200 ml of water and cook over medium heat with the lid on for 30 to 35 minutes, until the potatoes are cooked. Add the chard leaves and cook for few minutes, until they have wilted and lost their rawness. Season with plenty of sea salt and add more water if it starts to look dry.

Remove from the heat, grate over the zest of half the lemon, and squeeze over the juice. Pile the chard aloo into bowls and top with fresh cilantro, spoonfuls of chutney, and yogurt. Serve with warm breads for dipping.

SERVES 4

olive or peanut oil

2 teaspoon black mustard seeds

2 red onions, peeled and finely sliced

a thumb-size piece of fresh ginger, peeled and finely chopped

2 cloves garlic, peeled and sliced

1 red chile, roughly chopped

1 teaspoon cumin seeds

1 teaspoon ground turmeric

1½ pounds/700 g waxy potatoes, washed and cut into little rough ⅜-inch/1 cm cubes

1 head of chard (about 11 ounces/ 300 g), leaves roughly chopped, stalks cut into ⅜-inch/1 cm slices

sea salt

1 unwaxed lemon

TO SERVE

a small bunch of fresh cilantro, chopped

mango chutney

all-natural yogurt

warmed Indian breads (chapatis or roti)

Kitchari

Kitchari is an Ayurvedic Indian dish made up of rice and lentils and is thought to cleanse and detoxify the body. It has a simple nurturing quality, with warming spices and soft textures. This is how I like to eat it, with more spices than perhaps is traditional and a spike of ginger, coconut, and cilantro.

I eat this with yogurt, into which I stir a little salt, some chopped cilantro, and some lemon juice. It is equally good alongside any curry in place of rice or bread.

....

Pick through your lentils to make sure no stones have made their way into the package. Then soak the lentils and rice in cold water; try to soak them for at least an hour—though if you have longer, that's great.

Put the fresh cilantro, ginger, and coconut into a food processor with a generous 1 cup/250 ml of water, and blend. If you don't have a food processor, chop everything up very small and stir into the water.

Once the lentils and rice have soaked, heat the ghee or oil in a heavy-based pan over medium heat and add all your spices. Stir and fry for a minute or so, until they have released their wonderful aroma.

Drain the lentils and add them to the pan, then add the cilantro mixture and 3 cups/700 ml of water. Now drain the rice and add that too. Bring to a boil and simmer for 30 to 35 minutes, until the liquid is completely absorbed and the rice and lentils are cooked—you are looking for a soft, almost oatmeal-like texture here. Add a little more water if you need to, as you go.

Serve with cilantro-spiked yogurt and, if you are hungry, next to a bowl of curry.

SERVES 4 TO 6

1 cup/200 g split yellow lentils

1 cup/200 g brown basmati rice

a small bunch of fresh cilantro

a thumb-size piece of fresh ginger, peeled and roughly chopped

4 tablespoons unsweetened dried coconut

1 good tablespoon ghee or rapeseed oil

1 tablespoon black mustard seeds

1 teaspoon each of ground cilantro, cumin, and cardamom (I grind these freshly from seeds)

1 teaspoon each of ground turmeric, cloves, black pepper, and cinnamon

IN SEASON

SPRING

VEGETABLES

artichokes

arugula

asparagus

cauliflower

celery

chicory

dandelion greens

fava beans

leeks

morels

new potatoes

parsnips

peas

purple sprouting broccoli

radishes

salad leaves

scallions

spinach

watercress

wild garlic

young cabbage

FRUIT

apricot

blood oranges

grapefruit

mandarins

mango

pomelo

rhubarb

HERBS

basil

bay leaf

chervil

chives

cilantro

dill

elderflowers

marjoram

oregano

parsley

rosemary

tarragon

thyme

SUMMER

FRUIT

apricots

blackberries

blueberries

cherries

figs

grapes

melon

nectarines

peaches

pears

plums

pluots

strawberries

raspberries

rhubarb

VEGETABLES

arugula

beets

chard

corn

cucumber

eggplant

fava beans

fennel

green beans

peas

peppers

potatoes

radishes

runner beans

tomatoes

zucchini

HERBS

basil

bay leaf

chervil

chives

cilantro

dill

marjoram

mint

oregano

parsley

rosemary

sage

tarragon

thyme

Eating with the seasons is now part of how we eat. I am usually led by what is at the farmers' market. If I am writing recipes, planning a dinner, or shopping at a supermarket or online, I find it's really useful to remind myself what is good now. I get good value and much tastier produce.

AUTUMN

FRUIT
apples
blackberries
clementines
figs
grapes
kiwi
nectarines
pears
persimmons
plums
pomegranates
quince
raspberries

VEGETABLES
arugula
beets
cabbages
celeriac
celery
chestnuts
eggplants
fennel
hazelnuts
Jerusalem artichokes
kale
late tomatoes
leeks
mushrooms
onions
parsnips
peppers
potatoes
pumpkin
rutabaga
squash
zucchini

HERBS
basil
bay leaf
chives
marjoram
mint
oregano
parsley
rosemary
sage
thyme

WINTER

FRUIT
blood oranges
clementines
cranberries
grapefruit
kiwi
kumquats
mandarins
pomegranate
pomelo
quince

VEGETABLES
broccoli
Brussels sprouts
butternut squash
cauliflower
celeriac
celery
chestnuts
chicory
Jerusalem artichokes
kale
leeks
onions
parsnips
potatoes
red cabbage
rutabaga
turnips

HERBS
bay leaf
rosemary
sage

Ezekiel's charred eggplant with baba ghanoush

SERVES 4 TO 6

FOR THE BABA GHANOUSH DRESSING

2 eggplants

1 preserved lemon, seeded and very finely chopped

1 teaspoon smoked paprika

¼ cup/60 ml all-natural yogurt or unsweetened soy yogurt

1 tablespoon tahini

juice of ½ a lemon

sea salt and freshly ground black pepper

FOR THE SALAD

5 sweet potatoes, each cut into 8 long wedges

olive oil

juice of ½ a lemon

1 teaspoon cumin seeds, crushed in a mortar and pestle

1 teaspoon cilantro seeds, crushed in a mortar and pestle

2 eggplants, ends cut off and cut into ⅜-inch/1 cm discs

extra virgin olive oil

4 Baby Gem lettuces, quartered

⅔ cup/100 g sliced almonds, toasted

seeds from 1 pomegranate

a bunch of fresh mint, leaves picked and roughly chopped

a large bunch of fresh parsley, leaves picked and roughly chopped

1 red chile, finely chopped

Emily Ezekiel is my culinary sidekick, and over the years, we have picked perfect strawberries, baked giant pies, and made cakes in sandcastle buckets. Our culinary travels have taken us from Cotswold farms to Caribbean spice plantations and everywhere in between. Emily is a complete babe and a seriously good cook, and this recipe is one of her best.

Here eggplants get used in two ways, some to make a quick smoky baba ghanoush, others charred and tossed with sweet potatoes.

You must be brave with your grill heat here, as to cook eggplants properly you need some serious heat. Make sure they are charred on the outside but cooked through and soft in the middle—there is nothing worse than an uncooked eggplant.

Preheat the oven to 400°F/200°C.

While it is heating up, make your baba ghanoush. I use my biggest gas burner, but if you don't have a gas stove you can use a smoking hot griddle pan.

Prick the skin of the eggplants and place them directly on the flame. Use tongs to turn them every minute or so, making sure the skin is getting charred and turning matte black on all sides. Once both eggplants are charred and feel soft right through (after about 10 minutes), take them off the heat and set aside to cool.

Put the sweet potatoes into a large roasting tray. Drizzle with olive oil and the lemon juice and scatter over the cumin and cilantro seeds. Season with salt and pepper, then toss well so everything is evenly coated, and roast in the oven for 15 minutes.

 CONTINUED

Once the eggplants for the baba ghanoush are cool enough to handle, cut them in half lengthwise and scoop out the flesh, leaving the skin behind. Put the flesh into a bowl with the rest of the baba ghanoush ingredients, season with salt and pepper, and mix well with a fork, mashing any big bits of eggplant as you go.

Next, put a griddle pan over high heat until smoking hot and grill the sliced eggplants until charred on both sides and cooked through. You will have to do this in a few batches. Once all your eggplants are charred, put them into a roasting tray and toss them with a little extra virgin olive oil. Leave the griddle on.

Once the sweet potatoes have had 15 minutes in the oven, put the eggplant tray into the oven too and roast both together for a final 15 minutes.

Put the lettuce quarters on the griddle and char them on each side until they are nicely marked. Lay them on a big cutting board or platter.

Remove the sweet potatoes and eggplants from the oven. They should both be crisp on the outside and soft and cooked through on the inside. If not, give them a few more minutes.

To serve, lay the sweet potatoes and eggplants over the charred lettuce. Scatter over the toasted almonds, pomegranate seeds, chopped herbs and chile, and finish with a good drizzle of extra virgin olive oil and a squeeze of lemon juice. Serve with a big bowl of the baba ghanoush and warm flatbreads.

A few of the million ways baba ghanoush can be used
- To top a roasted sweet potato
- Spooned on the side of a grain salad
- As a dip for raw vegetables
- Spread on top of garlic-and-oil-rubbed toast

Golden roasted roots with leeks, tarragon, and quinoa

This is what my sister, Laura, often makes on a Sunday when it's hot outside or just when we feel like something lighter. It's packed with good English Sunday roast flavors—caramelized roasted parsnips, sweet roasted beets, bright squash, and peppery watercress. We eat it around the table with our family, spooned into big bowls and accompanied with glasses of red wine. It's just as good on the sofa with the newspaper, though.

Tarragon splits opinion—I love its liquorice basil notes and its lemony backup, but if you're not a lover, swap the tarragon for parsley or mint, both delicious.

....

Preheat your oven to 425°F/220°C. Get 2 baking trays and spread the parsnips, beets, and squash over them. Drizzle with olive oil, season well with salt and pepper, and roast in the oven for 40 to 45 minutes until golden, sweet, and burnished. Check them every 15 minutes or so to turn them.

SERVES 4

2 medium parsnips, peeled and cut into little sticks

2 medium beets, washed, peeled and cut into half-moons

½ a butternut squash, peeled, seeded, and cut into thin chunks

olive or rapeseed oil

sea salt and freshly ground black pepper

2 large leeks, washed, trimmed, and finely sliced

¾ cup/150 g quinoa

a small bunch of fresh tarragon, leaves picked

grated zest and juice of ½ an unwaxed lemon

2 tablespoons olive oil

2 big handfuls of watercress

Meanwhile, fry the leeks over low heat in a little oil until soft and sweet. This should take about 20 minutes.

Next, cook your quinoa. First rinse the quinoa under cold water, as you would rice. Place it in a pan with double the volume of water and a good pinch of salt. Bring to a boil, then turn the heat down to medium and simmer for 10 to 12 minutes until the grains are just tender.

Place the tarragon in a food processor with the lemon juice and zest, the olive oil, and a pinch of salt and pepper. Blend to a grassy pulp, adding a little more oil if it's too thick (if you don't have a food processor, you can do this in a mortar and pestle).

To serve, pile the leeks and roasted vegetables into a bowl, add the quinoa and watercress, and mix well. Then drizzle with the grassy green tarragon oil and serve in the middle of the table for everyone to help themselves.

Lime and chipotle black bean tacos

SERVES 4

FOR THE BEANS

2 cloves garlic, peeled and finely chopped

olive oil

1 teaspoon ground cinnamon

1 teaspoon ground cumin

1 teaspoon chipotle paste or 1 red chile, finely chopped

2 (15-ounce/400 g) cans of black beans

sea salt and freshly ground black pepper

FOR THE SALSA

20 cherry tomatoes

½ a red chile, seeded and finely chopped

a few sprigs of fresh cilantro, leaves picked

juice of ½ a lime

extra virgin olive oil

FOR THE GUACAMOLE

1 avocado

juice of ½ a lime

FOR THE CRUNCH SALAD

1 small apple

juice of ½ a lime

a few leaves of white cabbage or a Baby Gem lettuce

4 radishes, sliced

a few sprigs of fresh cilantro

olive oil

INGREDIENTS CONTINUE →

I have yet to find anyone who doesn't love these tacos, and I think that's because they hit all the spots on flavor, texture, and feel-good food. This is probably the supper I make the most—it's quick and flavorful, and most of the ingredients sit happily in my pantry or can be grabbed from the local grocery store.

In fact, it's John who usually makes these for me—he picked the recipe up on a surfing trip to Nicaragua. There they serve these tacos with the quick chile sauce (page 342), which makes them extra special. But if you are in a hurry, they'll be delicious as they are.

It may look as though there are a lot of ingredients and steps, but this is super quick, and the only real cooking is gently heating the beans. If I am feeling like eating something particularly virtuous, I swap the tortillas for sturdy leaves of tender greens in which to wrap everything. Sometimes I scatter the seeds of a pomegranate into the salad too, for extra crunch.

Black beans hold a secret, which I love: they are packed with a rare combination of protein and fiber. A cup of black beans can contain as much protein as a 4-ounce/100 g serving of chicken, and they have three times more fiber than broccoli. Black beans are also packed with the antioxidants found in other dark purple and deep scarlet foods, like blueberries and grapes.

Heat a frying pan over medium heat, add the garlic and a splash of olive oil, and cook for a minute or so, until the edges of the garlic begin to just brown. Add the cinnamon, cumin, and chipotle paste or chile and stir for another minute to gently toast the spices. Add the beans and their liquid, bring to a simmer, then turn the heat down and cook for 10 to 15 minutes,

CONTINUED

TO SERVE

6 to 8 wheat or corn tortillas

a handful of grated Manchego cheese

optional: hot sauce

optional: all-natural, soy, or coconut milk yogurt

until the liquid has thickened but the beans are still holding their shape. If you need to, add a little hot water to thin. Season with salt and pepper and keep warm.

To make your salsa, chop the tomatoes roughly on a big board. Pile the chile and cilantro on top, season with salt and pepper, and chop all this together. Scrape into a bowl, add the lime juice and a splash of olive oil, and mix well. Set aside.

To make the guacamole, peel the avocado, remove the pit, and mash in a bowl with a little salt and pepper and the lime juice. You can use a potato masher if you like.

Now for the salad. Chop the apple into little shards and put them into a bowl. Squeeze over the lime juice, add the shredded cabbage or lettuce, radishes, and cilantro, season with salt and pepper, and drizzle over a little oil.

Once everything is ready, heat your tortillas. I do this by holding them with tongs over the flame of my gas stove—it's super quick and gives a delicious charred taste—but the oven will do just fine.

Put the beans, salad, guacamole, and salsa in separate bowls on the table, along with the tortillas and grated cheese, and let everyone make their own. Don't forget some hot sauce, and sometimes a little yogurt works well too.

Gado gado

SERVES 4

FOR THE SATAY SAUCE

4 cloves of garlic, peeled

6 small shallots, peeled

1 stalk of lemongrass, crushed and chopped

a thumb-size piece of galangal or ginger

2½ tablespoons sambal oelek chile paste

4 tablespoons vegetable oil

1 cup/200 g roasted peanuts, crushed in a mortar and pestle

2 tablespoons brown sugar or coconut sugar (see page 275)

½ tablespoon sea salt

½ tablespoon paprika

1 tablespoon tamarind paste

⅞ cup/200 ml coconut milk

FOR THE SALAD

10 new potatoes

1 teaspoon ground turmeric

3½ ounces/100 g firm tofu, sliced

sea salt and freshly ground black pepper

olive oil

3½ ounces/100 g French beans, trimmed

3½ ounces/100 g sugar snap peas

7 ounces/200 g broccoli

2 ounces/70 g beansprouts

3 tablespoons fresh cilantro leaves

optional: a handful of crispy fried shallots

A few years ago, when we went to Indonesia, I was amazed at how well the Indonesians take care of vegetarians, with vibrant, fresh, and cleverly spiced tempeh and tofu dishes on every menu. I couldn't help but eat this gado gado for almost every meal.

The satay sauce takes a little time, but you'll see that the layers of flavor are worth it. When I first attempted this sauce, it was against my quick-cooking instincts. Boiling the peanuts in water? Surely just use good jarred peanut butter instead, right? Wrong. I'm all for shortcuts, but sometimes it's worth doing things properly. This satay sauce recipe makes more sauce than you will need, but it's so addictive that you'll be eating it with everything. It will keep well in the fridge for a week or so. I slather it in sandwiches, thin it with a little lime juice for dressing salads, and eat it piled on steamed greens with a bowl of rice. It's good in the tomato and kale salad (page 102) too.

Sambal oelek is an Indonesian chile paste—sort of a smoked sweet chile sauce. You can find it in Asian shops and good supermarkets, but if you can't get your hands on it, try using chipotle paste instead.

I buy fried shallots from my local Asian supermarket and keep a jar for topping noodles and rice. If you can't find them, fry some yourself—just peel and finely slice 2 shallots and shallow fry them in hot oil until crisp.

First make your satay sauce. Put the garlic, shallots, lemongrass, galangal, chile paste, and oil into a food processor and blend until it's a thick paste. Add to a pan and slowly sauté over low heat for 20 minutes, stirring often, taking care not to let it brown too much.

⋮⟩ CONTINUED

Meanwhile, put the crushed peanuts into a pan with ⅞ cup/200 ml of water and simmer for 10 to 15 minutes, until you have quite a thick mixture.

After the lemongrass mixture has had 20 minutes, add the sugar, salt, paprika, and tamarind to the pan and cook for a couple of minutes. Now add the peanut mixture and the coconut milk, stir well, and your satay sauce is done.

To make the salad, bring a large pot of salted water to a boil, add the potatoes and turmeric, and cook until just tender (this should take 10 to 15 minutes). Meanwhile, season the tofu with salt and pepper, then fry in a little olive oil until crisp. Set aside and keep warm.

Just before the potatoes are cooked, throw in the beans, sugar snap peas and broccoli, cook for the last couple of minutes, then drain.

Carefully arrange the potatoes and vegetables on a plate, breaking up the potatoes a little with the back of a spoon so they can absorb the flavors. Top with the beansprouts and tofu, and spoon over a generous amount of the satay sauce (you won't need it all). Finally, scatter over the cilantro leaves and the crispy shallots.

Things to do with satay sauce

· Toss with cooked noodles
· Spread in a tofu sandwich
· Use as a dressing for a tomato salad
· Use as a marinade for grilled tempeh or tofu
· Thin with a little lime juice and use to dress a salad
· Spoon over warm green vegetables

PESTOS

Herb pastes and pestos made with nuts, cheese, herbs, oil, and a host of other ingredients may not be in your daily repertoire, but they're one of the easiest, most effective and labor-saving ways I know to give a dish a flavor boost. All you need is an immersion blender or a mortar and pestle.

Start with a simple herb oil. Blend up a bunch of herbs with a few tablespoons of oil and put in the fridge or in the freezer in ice cube trays to top soups and stews, to dress salads, and to drizzle over roasted vegetables or a poached egg—a good way to use up a lingering bunch of herbs. Just don't add any lemon or vinegar if you want to keep it for a while, as these will turn the herbs black.

Or you can experiment with the flavors here and make herb pestos. Play around and pulse, paste, and pulverize whatever you like. The joy is that these pestos and pastes take only seconds to make but boost the flavor of your food tenfold.

Think about pestos as a family of flavors. I group together ingredients that feel Italian or Middle Eastern, for example, for the most delicious results.

1	2
START WITH A NUT BASE	**ADD AN HERB OR TWO**
about 2 ounces/50 g	a large bunch
↓	↓
ALMONDS	MINT
/	/
PUMPKIN SEEDS	BASIL
/	/
WALNUTS	PARSLEY
/	/
PISTACHIOS	DILL
/	/
HAZELNUTS	CILANTRO
/	/
PINE NUTS	MARJORAM

3	**4**	**5**
ADD SOME ACID KICK	**ADD SOME FAT**	**ADD AN ACCENT/**
about 2 tablespoons	about 4 tablespoons	**FLAVOR**
↓	↓	↓
LIME	AVOCADO	PARMESAN
/	/	/
BALSAMIC VINEGAR	OLIVE OIL	RED CHILE
/	/	/
ORANGE	RAPESEED OIL	GARLIC
/	/	/
RICE VINEGAR	COCONUT MILK	SOY
/	/	/
LEMON	WALNUT OIL	GREEN CHILE
/		/
WHITE WINE VINEGAR		PECORINO
		/
		HONEY/AGAVE

Sweet potato tortilla with almond salsa

Onions and potatoes—there's no greater combination. I crave the tortilla our Spanish friend Carolina would make us when we were growing up. I use sweet potatoes and red onions here for a lighter, brighter tortilla, but the traditional white onions and potatoes work just the same—Carolina's way.

This will seem like quite a lot of oil, but a good bit is poured off after frying, and it is really key to the flavor. Don't be put off by the time it takes to fry the onions and potatoes; you can leave them be and do something else. Just remember to set a timer. Sometimes I add a handful of wilted spinach to the cooked potatoes and eggs for a bit of green.

One terrific thing about tortilla for me is that it becomes even more delicious the next day. Something special seems to happen to the flavors as they mingle and meld. A cold slice of this wrapped in some parchment paper with a couple of tomatoes and some olive oil for drizzling would make a killer packed lunch.

The tortilla is perfect on its own, but to make it into a dinner I like to make the almond salsa too. It fits—tomatoes, almonds, tortilla. It's like you are sitting in the Spanish sunshine with a chilled glass of sherry.

....

In a deep-sided frying pan, heat 3⁄8 inch/1 cm of olive oil until medium hot. Add the sliced onions and fry until soft and sweet so that all the moisture has been absorbed—this will take about 20 to 25 minutes.

Next, add the potatoes to the pan and mix carefully to coat with the onions and olive oil. Season with salt and pepper and cook for another 10 to 15 minutes until the potatoes are softened and just golden brown, turning gently from time to time but taking care not to break them up too much.

SERVES 6

FOR THE TORTILLA
olive oil
1 pound/500 g (about 3 large) red onions, peeled and very finely sliced
1½ pounds/700 g (about 2 medium) sweet potatoes, peeled and very finely sliced
sea salt and freshly ground black pepper
5 large organic or free-range eggs

FOR THE ALMOND SALSA
2 vine-ripened tomatoes
½ a red chile
a handful of skin-on almonds, toasted
a few sprigs of fresh cilantro
a few sprigs of fresh parsley
a pinch of sea salt
extra virgin olive oil

While your potatoes are cooking, make your salsa. Chop the tomatoes into small dice, finely chop the chile, and roughly chop the almonds. Put them into a bowl with the chopped herbs, a pinch of salt, and a bit of extra virgin olive oil. Mix, taste and adjust, then set aside.

Once your onions and potatoes are softened and a light golden brown, drain off the oil, saving it for later, then transfer the potato mixture to a bowl and let cool for 5 minutes.

Now beat the eggs. Add them to the potatoes, season with salt and pepper, and let sit for another 5 minutes.

Heat about 2 tablespoons of the saved oil (you can use the rest another time) in the pan and place over low heat. Allow the pan to heat up a little and then add the potato mixture and quickly flatten it out with a spoon. Cook over low heat for 3 to 4 minutes.

Get a plate just a little bigger than your frying pan. Remove the pan from the heat, cover your hand with a tea towel, then place the plate upside down on the pan and flip it over so the tortilla lands on the plate.

Gently slide the tortilla back into the pan and cook the other side for 3 to 4 minutes. Test with your fingers to see that it is cooked—it should feel quite firm around the outside with a little give in the middle.

Serve cut in thick slices, topped with spoonfuls of almond salsa and some salad greens.

hearty dinners and food to feed a crowd

These are proper meals for proper satisfaction. Vegetarian food has long been mocked for its salad- and beansprout-loving ways. When I stopped eating meat, I found it hard to find dishes that satisfied my hunger (and that of my hollow-legged boyfriend or my brother) and my chef's desire was for something flavor-packed. These are the dishes I make for a crowd on a Sunday, to feed to parties of friends, to put in the middle of my Christmas table, or as a savior on a rainy night when only a good movie and a hearty plate of delicious food will do—delicious, straightforward food that keeps your tummy as happy as your taste buds.

perfect chili · grains · the really hungry burger · butternut squash and kale tart · ricotta, thyme, and sweet potato bake · tomato and coconut cassoulet · beet and bay leaf bourguignon · seeded pistachio and squash galette · cashew and chestnut sausages · double greens and phyllo pie · mushroom and parsnip rösti pie · puy lentil and sweet potato pie · sweet and sticky tomato and onion bake · one-pot mushroom and bay leaf biryani · saffron-spiked ratatouille · black dal · artichoke and fennel seed paella · mac and greens · springtime wild garlic and lemon risotto · mint, pistachio, and zucchini balls · any-night-of-the-week pizza · how to make a killer roast dinner · deep-dish leek and greens pie · goodwill rainbow pie

Perfect chili

My boyfriend John loves chili, and since we moved away from eating meat, I've been trying to put together something that I felt could stand up to the depth of flavor I had come to love about it before the switch. It has been a long time coming, but this is it. Heavily spiced with three types of chiles (and a good heaped tablespoon of cocoa), it packs a flavor punch. The first time we made this, we stood at the pan after dinner taking turns for another spoon.

I find most vegetarian chilis based around lots of beans to be a bit too filling and not very interesting to eat. This one uses lentils, some little beans, and grains that give character and texture and seem to take on the punchy flavors much more readily.

This is a real favorite pantry staple dinner and one I often make for a crowd. Feel free to mix and match the grains as you like—this is a great way to use up those odds and ends left at the bottom of a jar. Pearl barley, farro, and amaranth also work well (but steer clear of couscous; it cooks too quickly).

The amount of stock needed will depend on the type of grain you use, so if you do experiment with different grains (which I would encourage), make sure you watch the liquid levels and add more liquid if needed.

In the UK we seem to think all chili powder is the same, but it's not. Chilis can vary as much as a bottle of wine in taste notes, heat, smokiness, and sweetness. I look for good chili powders wherever I go. Here a chipotle- or ancho-based chili powder would work well, but use whatever you have.

....

First get out your biggest pot and place it over medium heat. Add a splash of olive oil and cook the onion, garlic, ginger, and chile for 10 minutes, until soft and sweet.

Now add the chili powder and cumin seeds and stir for a minute or two. Then add all the other chili ingredients, stirring and mixing as you go—add

SERVES 8 TO 10

FOR THE CHILI
olive or rapeseed oil

1 onion, peeled and finely chopped

4 cloves garlic, peeled and finely chopped

a thumb-size piece of fresh ginger, peeled and finely chopped

1 red or green chile, finely chopped

1 tablespoon good chili powder

1 teaspoon cumin seeds, crushed

1 tablespoon chipotle paste

3 (15-ounce/400 g) cans of chopped tomatoes

1½ cups/300 g lentils

½ cup/100 g bulgur wheat

½ cup/100 g quinoa (I use the red kind here)

1 (15-ounce/400 g) can small beans (navy, black, or black-eyed)

4 to 8 cups/1 to 2 L vegetable stock

1 heaping tablespoon good cocoa powder

sea salt and freshly ground black pepper

TO SERVE
6 tablespoons olive oil

2 green or red chiles, finely chopped

a small bunch of fresh thyme

salted all-natural yogurt

warmed corn tortillas

4¼ cups/1 L of the stock to start with, and keep the rest on hand to add as needed if the chili starts to look a bit dry.

Bring to a gentle boil, then turn the heat down to low and let simmer for 30–35 minutes until the lentils are cooked and the chili is deep and flavorful.

Make a thyme oil by mixing the olive oil, chopped chiles, and thyme with a sprinkling of salt and pepper.

Taste your chili and add a little more salt and pepper if you like. Serve in bowls, topped with a little yogurt, a drizzle of thyme oil, and some warmed corn tortillas for scooping.

GRAINS

Grains are central to my cooking. I like to eat as many grains as possible to broaden my taste and nutritional grain horizons.

Wheat grains, which are used in the majority of carbohydrates we eat, are heavily processed, lack real nutritional value, and can be difficult for a lot of us to digest. They also rank high on the glycemic index, making them less than ideal if you're seeking sustained energy.

So, whether you are sensitive to wheat or not, it will do you good to add these naturally nutritionally packed alternative grains to your diet.

QUINOA

WHAT? Quinoa is often grouped with whole grains, but it is actually the seed of a plant that is a relative of leafy green vegetables such as spinach and Swiss chard. It is really high in both protein and fiber, with the added bonus of containing no gluten and almost no fat. The amino acids in quinoa mean that it is a complete protein and is a really good choice for upping your protein intake.

TASTE AND USES Quinoa tastes great too. It is fluffy and creamy with a tiny bit of crunch and quite subtle, so it works well where you might have rice, pasta, or couscous. It works well in sweet hot cereals for breakfast as well as in more savory lunches and dinners. You can buy it in flakes, which are a great alternative to oats in hot cereal. If you have tried quinoa and disliked it, then you have probably been eating quinoa that is past its best or hasn't been rinsed before cooking—the flavor should be quite neutral.

WHERE TO BUY You can find the most common yellow quinoa in almost all supermarkets these days. The red, pink, and black versions are delicious too and can be found in most health food stores.

HOW TO COOK Rinse your quinoa first: this gets rid of any bitter taste. Wash in a sieve under cold water until the water runs clear. To cook, take 1 part quinoa to 2 parts liquid (water or vegetable stock) and a pinch of salt. Bring to a boil, then reduce the heat to simmer for about 15 minutes until all the water has been absorbed. You will know when it's cooked as the grain will become translucent and the germ will separate into a little coil.

AMARANTH

WHAT? Amaranth is a bit like quinoa—the seed of a cereal-like herb that often gets mistaken for a grain. It was a big deal in Aztec culture. Amaranth packs a serious amount of vitamins into each little grain, as it's really high in protein and calcium, so it's great for people moving toward eating a more vegetarian diet. Amaranth also contains more calcium than milk, and it contains other minerals, which allow the calcium to be absorbed much more easily. Amaranth is naturally gluten free.

TASTE AND USES Amaranth has a gentle, nutty taste with a slightly fresher, subtle grassy flavor. It can be used as you would rice, pasta, or quinoa. It can be thrown into soups and stews or can be made into hot cereal (see page 18).

WHERE TO BUY Amaranth can be found in all health food stores and some supermarkets. It can be a bit pricey, but when you compare it to other foods that you would have to buy to get similar nutritional benefits, it's a bargain. You can even buy puffed amaranth, which makes a great cereal and a great breakfast bar.

HOW TO COOK Amaranth is particularly versatile. For hot cereal, boil with 3 times the amount of water for 20 to 25 minutes, until creamy and thick. You can puff amaranth by popping it in a dry pan and shaking until the grains pop. Remove from the heat and use as a snack or a crispy topping for breakfast or a salad.

TEFF

WHAT? Teff's other name is lovegrass, which I like. It comes from Ethiopia, where it is often used to make sourdough injera breads and in stews. It is the tiniest of grains, the size of a poppy seed, and its name literally means "lost." For a tiny grain it provides a massive amount of nutrition. It is very high in protein and is said to be what fuels Ethiopian distance runners. It is high in calcium and vitamin C and is gluten free.

TASTE AND USES White or ivory teff is the mildest, while darker, brown teff has an earthier taste, but all varieties have a sweet and light flavor. You can use teff flour for baking, pancakes, and flatbreads. The whole grain can be used as a hot cereal or cooked and sprinkled into salads and soups.

WHERE TO BUY Teff is often eaten as a whole grain. It comes in an array of colors from purple to gray, but brown is the most common. Teff can be bought as a flour too.

HOW TO COOK As teff is so small, it cooks quickly. Cook with the same volume of water for 5 minutes, then put a lid on the pan and leave it to steam for sprinkling into salads or soups. You can cook 1 cup of teff with 3 cups of water for 15 minutes or so for a creamy style teff that can be used where you might have mashed potatoes, or it can be sweetened and eaten as hot cereal.

BUCKWHEAT

WHAT? Buckwheat is actually the seed of a plant that is part of the rhubarb family. It has been a staple part of the diet in Eastern Europe, Japan, and China for centuries. Like amaranth and quinoa, it's more of a seed than a true grain, but it's treated like a grain in cooking terms. Buckwheat is high in healthfulness. It has a low GI index, which means it releases energy into your body over a sustained period of time. Buckwheat is really high in protein, so it's a great food for vegetarians. Its unique amino acids mean that it can actually boost the amount of protein we absorb from other foods, such as beans and legumes, that we eat the same day. Buckwheat is naturally free of gluten.

TASTE AND USES Buckwheat has a deep satisfying nutty flavor. It is used to make soba noodles (see page 157) but can be used as you would any other grain in soups, stews, and salads. It can also be mixed with oats as a sustaining and protein-rich hot cereal. The flour makes the most delicious nutty pancakes too.

WHERE TO BUY Buckwheat is usually found roasted and dried. It is available in all good health food stores. Buckwheat soba noodles are widely available in most supermarkets.

HOW TO COOK To cook buckwheat, put 1 part buckwheat to 2 parts water into a pan with a little salt, bring to a boil, and simmer for 15 to 20 minutes, until tender.

MILLET

WHAT? Millet is a versatile grain that originated in Africa but has long been a staple in Eastern Europe as a hot cereal; in India it's ground into flour to make flatbreads called rotis. Apart from quinoa and amaranth, millet has the most complete protein of any grain, which makes it a great choice for vegetarians. It is naturally alkaline and gluten free. It is high in fiber and nutrients such as magnesium and phosphorus.

TASTE AND USES Millet has a mild nutty flavor similar to quinoa but a little drier. Millet can be used in place of rice or any other grain. It makes great hot cereal and can be ground into flour.

WHERE TO BUY Millet seeds are tiny and yellow and are usually bought hulled, that is, with the outer casing removed. You can buy millet in all good heath food stores.

HOW TO COOK To cook, place 1 part millet to 2½ parts cold water in a pan, bring to a boil, and then simmer for 25 to 30 minutes. You can also cook millet with water or milk as a hot cereal. Stir frequently and cook for 40 minutes until creamy.

STORING YOUR GRAINS

Store grains in airtight jars away from moisture and use within a couple of months, or store in the freezer for up to 6 months.

FREEZING TIP

Any leftover cooked grains can, once cool, be stored in a container in the freezer for up to 2 months and can then be quickly thrown into a soup, stew, or sauté for a really quick dinner.

SPROUTING

All these grains can be sprouted, which sends their nutritional value sky high. To sprout, soak them overnight in cold water, then rinse well, place in a sprouter or in a sieve over a mixing bowl, and put in a cool place to sprout—this will take 1 to 2 days. Once sprouted, you will see a little spiral emerging out of each grain. Rinse again and store on parchment paper in the fridge. They will keep for 2 to 3 days.

The really hungry burger

MAKES 8 BURGERS

olive oil

6 big portobello mushrooms, roughly chopped into small pieces

a few sprigs of fresh thyme, leaves picked

sea salt and freshly ground black pepper

1 (15-ounce/400 g) can of white beans, navy or cannellini, well drained

4 fat medjool dates, pitted

2 cloves garlic, peeled and finely chopped

a small bunch of fresh parsley, finely chopped

2 tablespoons tahini

2 tablespoons soy sauce or tamari

1⅓ cup/200 g cooked and cooled brown rice (⅔ cup/100 g uncooked)

⅔ cup/50 g breadcrumbs or oats

grated zest of 1 unwaxed lemon

optional: cheese

TO SERVE

1 to 2 avocados, peeled and sliced

tomato relish or ketchup

pickled cucumber (see above)

a few handfuls of spinach leaves

8 seeded burger buns (I use whole wheat ones)

I had a little fight with myself over this recipe. Does a veggie burger have a place in a modern book about vegetarian food? Something about veggie burgers feels a bit "nut-roast-at-brightly-painted-café-wearing-hemp-pants." However, my love of eating these strode forth, so here they are. Please be assured that this is not the breaded corn and mushroom mush excuse that usually shows up between two white buns. This is a hearty health-packed wonder that makes no apology to anyone.

I've played around with a lot of recipes before settling on this one; some were full of bright herb freshness and grated vegetables, some packed with protein-rich tofu, and all were good, but what I look for in a burger is a deep addictive flavor, savory and complex, so this is the one.

I use brown rice here, but any cooked grain you have will do—quinoa, pearl barley, and farro all work well.

I like to make a quick pickled cucumber to put on top of these. Thinly slice a quarter of a cucumber and place in a bowl with a pinch of salt, a squeeze of honey, and a good tablespoon of white wine vinegar, then scrunch together, and leave to sit while you make your burgers. This is a homemade quick pickle that beats a store-bought one any day.

....

Place a large pan over medium heat and add a splash of olive oil. Once the pan is good and hot, add the mushrooms and thyme and season with salt and pepper. Fry until the mushrooms have dried out and are slightly browned, then set aside to cool.

Next, drain the white beans and put them into a food processor with the dates, garlic, parsley, tahini, and soy sauce. Pulse until you have a smoothish mixture, then transfer to a bowl and add the rice, breadcrumbs, lemon

⋮ CONTINUED

zest, and the cooled mushrooms. Mix well, then put into the fridge for 10 minutes or so to firm up.

Once cooled, divide the mixture into 8 portions and shape into 8 patties. Place them on a baking tray lined with parchment paper and keep in the fridge until needed. (This can be done the day before—and the burgers freeze well at this point.)

Preheat your oven to 450°F/230°C.

Bake the burgers for 15 minutes, until nicely brown. If you like cheese on your burger, put a slice on top a couple of minutes before they come out of the oven.

While your burgers are cooking, get your toppings ready. I go with avocado, tomato relish, and the quick cucumber pickle above, plus a few spinach leaves. Hummus, grated carrot, and sprouts is another favorite combination, but feel free to improvize and try it your own way.

Once the burgers are golden, toast your buns and layer up your burgers. I like to serve them with sweet potato fries (page 242). You can't beat a burger and fries, and these ones are as healthy as they are tasty.

Butternut squash and kale tart

SERVES 6 FOR A MAIN MEAL,
8 AS PART OF A SPREAD

FOR THE PASTRY

¾ cup/125 g all-purpose flour

¾ cup/125 g light spelt or whole wheat flour

1 teaspoon sea salt

a few sprigs of fresh thyme, leaves roughly chopped

9 tablespoons/125 g butter, cold from the fridge

4 to 6 tablespoons ice-cold water

small amount of egg, beaten

FOR THE FILLING

olive oil

1 red onion, peeled and finely sliced

1 butternut squash, peeled, seeded, and grated

7 ounces/200 g kale, stalks removed, leaves shredded

sea salt and freshly ground black pepper

3 organic or free-range eggs

about 1⅔ cups/400 ml whole milk or almond milk

nutmeg, for grating

3½ ounces/100 g Gruyère cheese

This is lighter and brighter than the usual cream-and-cheese-laden quiches and tarts, but still deep and satisfying, with a thyme- and lemon-spiked crust and a lush amber filling. The pastry has some butter, but far less than the traditional kind—it is in every way crumbly, flavorful, and delicious.

I make the pastry with a mixture of spelt and all-purpose flour for a deep-flavored but light, crumbly, and biscuity crust. Buckwheat would work here in place of the spelt if you wanted even more depth.

If you are not a pastry natural (and believe me I wasn't, the first twenty times I made it), think about investing in a food processor—it will make your pastry-making more consistent and crumbly and do a million other useful jobs too. The best pastry tip I ever learned is that hot hands are the enemy. I always find my pastry works really well with the coolness of the food processor. Good store-bought pastry can always be used here if time is short.

For a good gluten-free pastry, use 3½ ounces/100 g of gluten-free flour and 3½ ounces/100 g of buckwheat.

....

You can make the pastry by hand or in a food processor. Start by mixing the flours, salt, and thyme together and pulse in the processor or mix with a wooden spoon. Next, add the butter and either pulse in the processor or rub between your fingers until you have a rough breadcrumb consistency. Now add the water, tablespoon by tablespoon, pulsing or mixing each time, until the mixture comes together as a dough. Shape into a ball, wrap in parchment paper, and place in the fridge for 30 minutes or so.

Preheat the oven to 415°F/210°C and have a cup of tea.

⋮ CONTINUED

Once the pastry is chilled, roll it out on a floured surface into a large circle just bigger than a 9½-inch/24 cm fluted, loose-bottomed tart tin and about ⅛ inch/¼ cm thick. Roll the pastry over your rolling pin and lay it over the tart tin. Use your fingers to push the pastry into the edges of the tin and the scallops around the edge of the tin. Place in the fridge for another 10 minutes if you have the time.

Cover the pastry with parchment paper and use rice or old dried beans to weight it down. No need to trim the sides—I do this at the end, as that way you'll be sure your pastry doesn't shrink down. Bake for 15 minutes, then take it out of the oven, remove the beans and paper, brush with a little beaten egg, and return to the oven for 10 minutes. When it's ready, take it out, leaving the oven on.

Meanwhile, make the filling. Heat a large pan, add a splash of olive oil, then add the onion and cook for 10 minutes, until soft and sweet. Add the grated squash and the shredded kale, plus a good pinch of salt and pepper, and cook for a couple of minutes. Set aside to cool.

Break the eggs into a measuring cup and beat well. Pour milk on top of the eggs until it reaches just over the 2-cup/500 ml mark, then add a good pinch of salt and pepper, a good grating of nutmeg (about a quarter), and the grated cheese. Mix together.

Once the squash is cool, add the egg mixture and mix well. Pour into the prebaked pastry shell and level the top. Bake in the oven for 35 minutes, until just set.

I like to serve this with caramelized leek and potato salad (page 104).

Ricotta, thyme, and sweet potato bake

This warming winter bake features roasted sweet potato, caramelized onions, just-wilted bright green spinach, and a clever creamy sauce that brings it all together. It is the kind of dish that only improves if you can make it in advance and then leave it to sit for a few hours before placing it back into the oven to warm through.

More often than not, I leave out the pasta here and use the roasted sweet potato slices as the intermission between the sweet tomato and spinach layers. But if I feel particularly ravenous, or if it's really cold outside, or if I have a crew of hungry people to feed, I add a little extra energy—a couple of layers of pasta sheets. I'll leave it up to you.

There is no fuss with making a white sauce here—this one takes less than 2 minutes to whip up and tastes out of this world.

Good for a crowd, you can easily double this recipe and make two dishes ahead of time.

....

Preheat the oven to 475°F/240°C.

Place the sweet potatoes in one layer on a couple of baking trays, sprinkle with salt and pepper, drizzle with olive oil, and roast for 30 minutes until just cooked and browning around the edges.

While the potatoes are cooking, make your tomato sauce. Fry the sliced garlic in a little olive oil over medium heat until it begins to brown around the edges, then add the rosemary and stir for a few seconds. Quickly pour in the canned tomatoes, breaking them up a bit with the back of a wooden spoon. Bring to a simmer, then let it simmer for about 10 minutes until the sauce becomes a little thicker and sweet. Season well with salt and pepper and set aside.

SERVES 6

FOR THE LAYERED BAKE
4 medium sweet potatoes, scrubbed and cut into ⅜-inch/1 cm rounds
sea salt and freshly ground black pepper
olive oil
4 cloves garlic, peeled and finely sliced
a couple of sprigs of fresh rosemary, leaves picked
2 (15-ounce/400 g) cans of good chopped tomatoes
2 red onions, peeled and roughly sliced
a small bunch of fresh thyme
2 (8-ounce/200 g) bags of spinach, washed
8 ounces/200 g ricotta cheese
3½ ounces/100 g Parmesan or pecorino cheese (see page 136)
optional: 8 no-cook lasagne sheets

FOR THE LIMA BEAN SAUCE
1 (15-ounce/400 g) can lima beans
grated zest and juice of 1 unwaxed lemon
3 tablespoons olive oil

Sauté the onions in a little olive oil with the thyme over medium heat until soft and sweet; this will take about 10 minutes. Then add the spinach and let it wilt (I usually put in a third of the spinach first, let it wilt down, then add the rest; otherwise it's too much for the pan). When the sweet potatoes are ready, take them out of the oven and turn the heat down to 425°F/220°C.

Now make the lima bean sauce. Put the lima beans into a blender with the liquid from their can, the lemon juice and zest, the olive oil, and some salt and pepper and blend to a sauce that will be smooth and thin enough to spread over the top of the bake. If it's too thick, add a couple of tablespoons of water and blend again.

Once everything is ready, you can start layering in a big ovenproof dish. Put a layer of the tomato sauce on the bottom, top with a layer of spinach, dot over half the ricotta, and grate over a thick layer of Parmesan. Add a layer of pasta here, then top this with some sweet potatoes. Finish with half the lima bean sauce, then repeat the layers, finishing with a second layer of lima bean sauce and a final grating of Parmesan. Drizzle with olive oil and sprinkle with more thyme leaves.

Bake in the oven for 30 minutes until golden brown on top. Serve with a crisp green salad.

Tomato and coconut cassoulet

This delicious recipe brings together so many of my favorite things. Carmelized roasted tomatoes, the soothing creaminess of coconut milk, and sweet little white beans, topped with a crust of sourdough bread. Don't be put off by the coconut milk—it adds a gentle creamy note and brings everything together (and what you don't use can be frozen and used in a curry another day).

If fresh tomatoes are not at their best, a second can of chopped tomatoes will do just fine. In the winter I swap the basil for some thyme too.

I love sourdough bread. If you haven't tried it before, search it out. It's made from a natural fermented starter dough. When I worked as a baker I loved that someone fed it every couple of days and kept it alive. Because of the starter it's actually easier for our bodies to digest. So everyone's a winner.

SERVES 4 TO 6

olive oil

1 leek, washed, trimmed, and roughly sliced

1 clove of garlic, peeled and finely chopped

1 red chile, seeded and finely chopped

a ⅜ inch/1 cm thick piece of fresh ginger, peeled and roughly chopped

sea salt and freshly ground black pepper

1 (15-ounce/400 g) can of chopped tomatoes

4 tablespoons coconut milk

1 (15-ounce/400 g) can navy beans, drained

1 pound/500 g vine-ripened or cherry tomatoes, halved

a bunch of fresh basil

4 slices of sourdough bread

Preheat the oven to 400°F/200°C.

First heat an ovenproof pan over medium heat and add a splash of olive oil. Add the leek, garlic, chile, ginger, and a pinch of salt and some pepper, then turn the heat down and cook for 10 minutes until the leeks are soft and sweet. Next, add the canned tomatoes, coconut milk, and beans, simmer for a couple of minutes, and then take off the heat. Check the seasoning and add a little more salt and pepper if needed.

Add the fresh tomatoes, followed by the basil. Then tear the slices of bread into chunks and push them into the gaps between the tomatoes. You are looking for a covering of tomatoes and chunks of bread.

Drizzle with olive oil and bake for 30 minutes until the tomatoes have shrunk and sweetened and the bread is crisp and golden. Allow to sit for a few minutes before piling on to plates with lemony green salad.

Beet and bay leaf bourguignon

I am often faced with feeding my strapping meathead friends a hearty dinner. Some think a meal without meat isn't worth the plate it's served on. I have always liked a challenge and I relish feeding reluctant vegetable eaters, especially working up something that calls for excited rounds of seconds and thirds.

This is now the dish for such a crowd, and it has found its way into my weeknight dinners too, as it is really super easy—just 20 minutes' work getting everything into the pan and then it simmers away happily on its own. This is a bolstering winter dish and sits well on some crushed olive-oil-dressed potatoes with a good glass of wintry red.

I also eat it when things warm up too. I swap the deep red beets for more cheerful candy cane (Chioggia) beets and use carrots in place of the parsnips, and I pair it with a zippy green salad and some bread for mopping up the neon-pink juices.

SERVES 4 TO 6

olive or rapeseed oil

2 medium onions, peeled and roughly chopped

4 cloves garlic, peeled and roughly chopped

8 small to medium beets, peeled and quartered

4 parsnips, peeled and cut into finger-length pieces

4 bay leaves

a few bushy sprigs of fresh thyme

1 cup/250 ml good red wine (Bordeaux if you have it)

4¼ cups/1 L good vegetable stock

2 tablespoons tomato purée

¼ cup/50 g pearl barley

6 shallots or small onions, peeled and halved

3 large portobello mushrooms, roughly sliced

Place a big pot on the heat, add a glug of oil, and cook the onions and garlic over medium heat for 10 minutes until soft and sweet.

Add the beets and parsnips and stir for a couple of minutes, then add the herbs, wine, stock, tomato purée, and pearl barley. Bring to a gentle simmer for 30 minutes or so, until the beets are soft. Turn the heat off and cover with a lid.

Heat another splash of oil in a large frying pan and add the shallots. Cook them for 10 minutes over medium-high heat, until they have softened and are beginning to brown, then add the mushrooms and cook for another few minutes, allowing the mushrooms to brown on all sides.

Add the shallots and mushrooms to the stew and serve with crushed potatoes and some perky greens—oh, and more red wine.

Seeded pistachio and squash galette

SERVES 6

FOR THE SQUASH

½ a small butternut squash, seeded and cut into ¼-inch/½ cm slices

sea salt and freshly ground pepper

olive oil

FOR THE GALETTE CRUST

¾ cups/100 g shelled pistachio nuts

¾ cups/100 g sunflower or pumpkin seeds

4 ounces/100 g vacuum-packed chestnuts

2 tablespoons olive oil

1 tablespoon maple syrup

grated zest of 1 unwaxed lemon

a small bunch of fresh thyme, leaves picked

sea salt and freshly ground black pepper

FOR THE SPINACH TOPPING

½ cup/75 g cashew nuts, soaked overnight if you remember to do it (see page 340 for why)

1 ripe avocado, halved and pitted

2 big handfuls of spinach

juice of ½ a lemon

TO FINISH

1 red onion, peeled and finely sliced

1 red chile, sliced

This is what I make on a Sunday for a crowd. A galette is somewhere between a tart and a pizza, but this galette base is much kinder in terms of time and far less fussy than pastry or a dough. You will need a food processor, though.

Using this crust, I vary the toppings throughout the year. In spring I use wild garlic instead of spinach, char some asparagus on the griddle, and top the galette with those instead of the butternut squash. In summer I add a bright bunch of basil in place of a quarter of the spinach and add some roasted tomatoes in place of the squash.

The final secret is that even though this tastes amazing, it is all incredibly healthy—no dairy, gluten, or sugar—shhhh.

....

Preheat the oven to 400°F/ 200°C.

Spread the squash on a baking tray with some salt and pepper and a drizzle of olive oil and roast in the oven for 30 minutes, until golden.

While the squash is roasting, make the galette crust: put the pistachios and sunflower or pumpkin seeds on a baking tray and roast in the hot oven alongside the squash for 5 minutes.

Remove the tray of nuts and seeds (leaving the squash to finish roasting) and add them to a food processor with the chestnuts, olive oil, maple syrup, lemon zest, thyme, and a good pinch of salt and pepper. Blend until you have a fine crumbly paste that comes together when you squeeze it. If it is too crumbly, add a touch more oil until it comes together into a solid piece when you scrunch it in your hands.

CONTINUED

Lay a sheet of parchment paper on your work surface, then turn out the paste and pat it into a circle with your hands. Place another sheet of parchment paper on top and use a rolling pin to roll it out into a pizza-sized circle about ¼ inch/½ cm thick. Put it on a baking tray and take off the top sheet of paper, then prick the dough with a fork and bake in the oven alongside the squash for 15 to 20 minutes, until golden around the edges. Take it out and let it cool a little. If the squash is ready before the crust, take it out and set it aside.

Meanwhile, fry the red onion in a little oil with a pinch of salt until deep violet, sweet, and just starting to color (this will take about 10 minutes).

Now put all of the topping ingredients—soaked cashews, avocado, spinach, and lemon juice—into a blender with a good amount of salt and pepper and blend until you have a smooth, whipped, grass-green paste.

Once the galette base has cooled a little, spread it with the spinach topping and scatter over the red onion, squash, and red chile. I sometimes sprinkle over a bit of feta too.

In summer I serve this with a bowl of crisp salad and some roasted new potatoes, and in winter, with roasted root vegetables and flash-fried lemony kale.

Cashew and chestnut sausages

This is perfect for weekend breakfasts or perched on top of a pile of mashed root vegetables and gravy (page 249 and 343). And it's a great way to be able to join in at barbecues where meat is king. Cashews, tofu, winter herbs, and a little scattering of Cheddar come together to make a really good vegetarian sausage. Or you could even leave out the cheese and use a grated carrot.

This is a deeply easy recipe and makes enough for you to freeze at least half. Satisfyingly, they freeze really well and amazingly will cook well over low heat from frozen—they will just take a bit longer.

Tofu is a hard sell for most people. There has been bad press about soy. But soy holds a whole host of health benefits, and I think including a little bit of good tofu is the way to go. A lot of people are also put off by tofu as there is a perception that it's hard to cook. Not the case—you need to choose the right one for the job. Milky soft is good for making puddings and custards, but trying to fry it is a disaster no matter how good a cook you are. Firmer tofu is good for frying and to bind patties and fritters. The even firmer smoked stuff you can slice and put straight into sandwiches, or fry and add to noodles, rice, or soups.

Most supermarkets stock it. I make sure I buy organic tofu from a company I am familiar with at my local natural foods store.

....

First, put the cashew nuts and chestnuts into a food processor and grind to a fine breadcrumb texture. Mash up the tofu in a large mixing bowl, add the nuts, and then add all of the other ingredients except the olive oil and mix really well.

Wet your hands, take golfball-sized pieces of the mixture, and shape them into 16 sausages or patties, or whatever shape you like. Lay them on

MAKES 16

1⅓ cup/200 g unsalted cashews, soaked overnight if you have time (see page 340)

7 ounces/200 g cooked vacuum-packed chestnuts

9 ounces/250 g firm tofu

1 small red onion, peeled and grated

1 red chile, seeded and roughly chopped

grated zest and juice of 1 unwaxed lemon

2 cups/150 g breadcrumbs (I use whole wheat)

several sprigs of fresh thyme, leaves picked and roughly chopped

3½ ounces/100 g Cheddar cheese, grated

1 tablespoon soy sauce or tamari

1 organic or free-range egg, beaten (or see note on chia, page 42)

olive oil, for frying

⁘ CONTINUED

a baking tray lined with parchment paper and place them in the freezer to firm up for 5 minutes or so.

Heat a little olive oil in a frying pan over low heat and fry the sausages for 5 to 7 minutes, turning them until they are brown all over. They can also be baked in the oven at 425°F/220°C for 12 minutes or barbecued for a few minutes on each side.

Eat with a poached egg for breakfast or on top of a pile of mashed root vegetables and greens for dinner. Or sandwich them between 2 good slices of seeded bread with some tomato ketchup at a barbecue.

Double greens and phyllo pie

This pie is loosely based on the Greek spanakopita but is much quicker and easier to put together. This recipe was one of the first that satisfied my boyfriend John's unstoppable appetite after we gave up eating meat.

Using some clever shortcuts, you can have this on the table in half an hour.

I use collard greens and chard here instead of all spinach, as they stand up a little more robustly in the pie and I like their lemony freshness against the feta. Spinach on its own would work too, though. I vary the greens depending on what's in season.

I love using sheep's milk cheese and for the most part prefer its taste to cow's milk cheese. Feta is a favorite—it works well with the food that I cook and I always have a package in the fridge to crumble over roasted carrots or on top of a quick avocado salad. Sheep's milk has twice as much calcium as cow's milk, and feta is actually suitable for people who have a sensitivity to cow's milk, as most of the lactose is in the whey, which is not eaten after the feta has formed.

Try Greek and Turkish shops for the best feta. My local shop has a big barrel of it in the fridge, and I go in and scoop out beautiful clean white rounds that are much softer and creamier than the kind you buy in packages.

....

Preheat your oven to 425°F/220°C.

Put a 10-inch/26 cm nonstick ovenproof frying pan over medium heat and add a little olive oil, then add the scallions with a pinch of salt and fry for a few minutes, until softened.

SERVES 4 TO 6

olive oil

1 bunch of scallions (about 8), trimmed and roughly chopped

sea salt and freshly ground black pepper

9 ounces/250 g collard greens or kale, leaves shredded, stalks removed

9 ounces/205 g chard or spinach, leaves shredded, chard stalks chopped

grated zest of ½ an unwaxed lemon

3 organic or free-range eggs

7 oz/200 g feta cheese

a small bunch of fresh parsley, picked and roughly chopped

a small bunch of fresh dill, picked and roughly chopped

4 large sheets of phyllo pastry or 8 smaller ones

1 tablespoon poppy seeds

⁙ CONTINUED

Next, add a couple of handfuls of collard greens or kale and cook until they have shrunk down a little. Keep adding like this until all the greens are in the pan, then cook until just wilted. Add the chard or spinach and let that wilt too. Sprinkle over the lemon zest and season with more salt if needed and a bit of pepper. Transfer to a bowl and set aside to cool a little.

Crack the eggs into a mixing bowl, crumble in the feta, and add the chopped herbs. Once the greens are cool, add these too. Wipe out the frying pan with some paper towels.

Get a large sheet of parchment paper, about 20 inches/50 cm long, and lay it on your work surface. Drizzle it with a little olive oil, then scrunch it up into a ball so it's all coated (this will keep it from burning in the oven). Now lay it flat again.

Lay the phyllo over the parchment paper in two layers—it will overlap here and there but that's okay. Drizzle with a bit more oil. Now carefully lift the paper to rest on top of the frying pan, with the excess hanging evenly round the edges.

Pour the egg and greens mixture into the middle and level out with a spoon. Fold the excess layers of pastry over the top to cover the top of the greens mixture. No need to be too neat here, as some movement and texture looks beautiful. Sprinkle over the poppy seeds and place in the oven to bake for 20 minutes.

I like to serve this with a cucumber salad, simply dressed with dill and lemon, and some green leaves.

Mushroom and parsnip rösti pie

This unfussy, hearty, warming winter pie would satisfy the richest and most lavish tastebuds, but is light enough that it won't send you to sleep.

Frying the mushrooms separately makes sure they stay crisp, woody, and golden as the pie cooks. The parsnip topping is a little lighter, with more crunch and texture than a traditional mashed potato topping, but sometimes after a long walk, I top it off with a 50/50 parsnip/potato and olive oil mash—a really filling dinner that will serve nearer to eight. I often make this without the crème fraîche—you'll need to simmer for a couple of minutes extra to thicken.

SERVES 6

olive or rapeseed oil

1⅔ pounds/750 g mushrooms (I use a mixture of portobello, cremini, or wild mushrooms, if I can get them), roughly chopped into chunky pieces

sea salt and freshly ground black pepper

3 cloves garlic, peeled and sliced

a small bunch of thyme, leaves picked

2 red onions, peeled and sliced

2 carrots, peeled and finely chopped

½ a rutabaga (9 ounces/250 g), peeled and finely chopped

⅞ cup/200 ml white wine or vegetable stock

1 tablespoon vegetarian Worcestershire sauce

1 tablespoon Dijon mustard

2 tablespoons whole grain mustard

a small bunch of fresh flat-leaf parsley, roughly chopped

optional: 2 to 4 tablespoons crème fraîche

4 parsnips, scrubbed clean

Place your biggest frying pan over high heat (I use a large cast-iron sauté pan that can go into the oven) and add a good glug of oil. Add enough mushrooms to cover the base of the pan, season with salt and pepper, and sauté until nicely brown and beginning to crisp at the edges. Transfer to a bowl and keep frying the rest in batches until all the mushrooms are golden.

When all the mushrooms are in the bowl, put the pan back on the heat and add another glug of oil. Add the garlic, thyme, onions, carrots, and rutabaga, season with a good pinch of salt and pepper, and cook over medium heat for 10 minutes until softened and starting to brown. Preheat your oven to 400°F/200°C.

Next, add the cooked mushrooms and the wine or stock, and simmer until almost all the liquid has evaporated. Now add the Worcestershire sauce, mustards, parsley, and crème fraîche, and cook gently for a few more minutes until you have a rich gravy. Taste and add more salt and pepper if needed. Grate the parsnips into a bowl and season with salt and pepper.

Transfer your mushroom mixture to an oven proof dish if necessary, then pile the parsnips on top, leaving a little gap around the edge. Drizzle generously with oil and bake for 40 minutes, until golden brown and crispy. Serve with some cheerful greens—I sauté some chard with a little chile and lemon zest.

Puy lentil and sweet potato pie

This is a warming, filling, super-easy-to-put-together pie. A vivid orange crown of sweet potatoes tops a layer of lentils slow-cooked with melting sweet garlic and upfront spices. There is an Indian tone to the lentils, which I love. It warms on a cold winter day.

This is a great supper for a crowd, as it feeds quite a few and can be made in advance and warmed up. It is pretty much a one-pot meal, and I serve it with a simple bowl of peas or some winter greens.

I use Puy lentils here. Puy lentils are also known as poor man's caviar, and there is something quite sophisticated about their sweet, almost earthy taste. They hold up very well in cooking and hold their shape, unlike red, green, or brown lentils. They pack a punch in the nutritional department too—they are super high in folate, which helps our bones and nervous system, and they are particularly good for pregnant ladies.

....

Preheat your oven to 425°F/220°C.

Cook the sweet potatoes in boiling salted water for 15 to 20 minutes until cooked through. I keep the skins on but you can peel them if you like.

While they are cooking, make the lentils. Heat a large heavy-bottomed pan (I like to use a shallow cast-iron pan that can go straight into the oven, to save clean up time). Place it over medium heat and add a good glug of olive oil, then add the carrots, celery, onions, and garlic and let them sauté for 10 minutes until everything has softened a little.

Now add all the spices and the thyme leaves and cook for another few minutes. Pour in the tomatoes, then add 2 empty tomato cans full of cold water, along with the lentils.

SERVES 6

FOR THE MASHED SWEET POTATOES
5 medium sweet potatoes, scrubbed clean
2 tablespoons olive oil
4 scallions, finely sliced
grated zest of ½ an unwaxed lemon

FOR THE LENTIL MIXTURE
olive oil
2 carrots, roughly chopped
2 stalks of celery, roughly chopped
2 red onions, peeled and roughly chopped
2 cloves garlic, peeled and roughly chopped
1 teaspoon cumin seeds, crushed
1 teaspoon ground cinnamon
½ teaspoon ground allspice
a small bunch of fresh thyme, leaves picked
1 (15-ounce/400 g) can of tomatoes
2 cups/400 g Puy lentils
sea salt and freshly ground black pepper

Simmer for 15 minutes, until the lentils are cooked and the sauce has thickened. Add a little hot water from time to time if needed, making sure to taste and season with salt and pepper.

Once the sweet potatoes are ready, drain and mash them with the olive oil, scallions, lemon zest, and a good pinch of salt and pepper. Spoon them on top of the lentil mixture, scatter with a little more thyme, and bake in the oven for 25 to 30 minutes until the top is golden brown.

Sweet and sticky tomato and onion bake

This is a dish that is more than the sum of its parts. Something amazing happens to onions and tomatoes when they are roasted: the tomatoes become juicy, burnt-red orbs of sweet and sour, and the once harsh little onions are mellowed to milky sweetness. The real star of this dish is the rich sweet gravy from the onions and tomatoes that bastes the roasting potatoes and beans, making sure not a drop is lost. Trust me, this is a dinner in its own right. Just a perky, lemon-dressed green salad on the side will do.

This is a great way to make the most of end-of-season tomatoes, as roasting them in this way brings out their very best. In winter I have made it with a couple of cans of drained tomatoes, and it was also delicious.

....

Preheat your oven to 415°F/210°C.

Put the onions into a bowl and cover them with boiling water. Use a slotted spoon to fish them out and peel back the skins, which will have been helpfully loosened by the hot water. Cut any larger ones in half.

Spread the peeled onions on to your biggest roasting tray and add the tomatoes and the halved potatoes. It might be a squeeze, but everything will shrink a bit as it cooks, so don't worry. Squishing it all into one tray is what's needed here, so that the tomatoes will baste the potatoes in their juices. Season generously with salt and pepper and pour over some olive oil. Toss to coat, then roast in the oven for 1 hour, tossing everything every 15 minutes or so.

After an hour, it should be smelling delicious, the onions should be soft and slightly browned in places, and the tomatoes blistered and burnished. Remove the tray from the oven and add the drained beans and the basil, then put back in and roast for another 15 minutes.

Spoon onto warm plates and make sure not to miss a drop of those juices.

SERVES 4

1 pound/500 g baby onions

1⅔ pounds/750 g large cherry tomatoes

1⅔ pounds/750 g new potatoes, washed and halved

sea salt and freshly ground black pepper

olive oil

1 (15-ounce/400 g) can cannellini beans, drained

a small bunch of fresh basil

One-pot mushroom and bay leaf biryani

FOR THE MUSHROOMS

1 pound/500 g mushrooms, roughly chopped (I use a mixture of cremini or black poplar and portobello, with a few wild ones if I can get them)

2 cloves garlic, peeled and roughly chopped

a thumb-size piece of fresh ginger, peeled and roughly chopped

½ teaspoon ground turmeric

½ teaspoon ground cilantro

½ teaspoon ground cumin

2 tablespoons oil (I use cold-pressed rapeseed; ghee works as well)

½ a bunch of fresh cilantro, leaves picked and roughly chopped

sea salt and freshly ground black pepper

FOR THE BIRYANI

1½ cups/300 g basmati rice

ghee or oil, for cooking

2 onions, peeled and finely sliced

3 bay leaves

5 cloves

5 cardamom pods, split

1 cinnamon stick

1 teaspoon cumin seeds

1 to 2 green chiles

½ a bunch of fresh cilantro

2 tomatoes or ½ (15-ounce/400 g) can of chopped tomatoes

1 lemon, zest and juice

Deeply scented with cinnamon, bay leaf, cloves, and cardamom, this biryani is a super-easy one-pot dinner.

I eat this simply with some raita, mango chutney, and a chapati or two, but it makes a great rice dish for a feast of curries too. I sometimes finish it with pomegranate seeds—not traditional, but the crunch and freshness of the seeds are a perfect foil for the spices. Leftovers are really good fried until starting to crisp, then topped with a fried egg and more chopped cilantro.

First, put the mushrooms into a bowl, add all the other mushroom ingredients, and a good pinch of salt. Set aside for half an hour or so.

Next, soak the rice in cold water. Place a large pan over medium heat and add a teaspoon of ghee or oil. Add the onions and sauté for 10 minutes until just golden; then add the bay leaves, cloves, cardamom pods, cinnamon stick, and cumin seeds and sauté for another couple of minutes.

Blend the green chiles, cilantro, and tomatoes in a food processor and add to the pan. Cook for 5 minutes, until almost all the moisture has evaporated, and then add the mushrooms and cook over high heat for 5 minutes until they have softened a little.

Fill a kettle with cold water and bring to a boil. Drain the rice and rinse in cold water, then add to the pan, and gently stir to fry the rice a little—be gentle, you don't want to break up the grains. Now add boiling water from the kettle until it is ⅜ inches/1 cm above the level of the rice. Put the lid on and cook over high heat for 2 minutes, then turn the heat down and cook on low for 5 minutes—without taking the lid off to peek. Now turn the heat off, leaving the lid on, and let it sit for 10 minutes.

After 10 minutes, take the lid off and use a fork to carefully fluff up the rice. Grate over the zest of the lemon and squeeze over the juice.

Saffron-spiked ratatouille

Ratatouille has been banished to the sidelines since its heyday, and I want to put it back, center stage, on menus across the land—when it's done well, it's hard to beat. My mama has been flying the flag for ratatouille weekly for as long as I can remember, and she makes a mean one—this is hers with the addition of a little sunshine saffron, which transports me from Hackney to Antibes in August in a mouthful.

I fry all the vegetables separately in olive oil to give extra flavor and so that they hold their shape nicely. I then roast them in the oven—it's not the original Provençal way, but I find it much easier. The great thing about ratatouille is it just gets better—I make a batch and, if I can, I wait until the day after to eat it, when the flavors have mingled and intensified.

SERVES 4

2 red peppers, seeded and cut into eighths

olive oil, for frying

sea salt and freshly ground black pepper

2 onions, peeled and sliced

2 cloves garlic, peeled and finely sliced

6 sprigs of fresh thyme, leaves picked

6 ripe red tomatoes, roughly chopped, or 1 (15-ounce/400 g) can of good tomatoes

a good pinch of saffron

1 tablespoon red wine vinegar or sherry vinegar

2 eggplants, cut into ⅜-inch/1 cm slices

3 zucchini, cut into ⅜-inch/1 cm slices

a small bunch of fresh basil

Preheat your oven to 400°F/200°C.

Put the red peppers on a baking tray, drizzle over a little olive oil, sprinkle them with salt and pepper, and then put them into the oven to roast for 25 minutes.

Next, heat a glug of olive oil in a large frying pan and add the onions and a pinch of salt. Cook for 10 minutes, until soft and golden, then add the garlic and thyme and cook for another couple of minutes.

Add the tomatoes and saffron and vinegar and cook for a few minutes more, until almost all the liquid has evaporated. Put this sauce into a deep baking dish or tray.

Put the frying pan back on the heat, add a little more olive oil, and fry the eggplants in batches until golden on both sides, adding more oil as needed—the eggplants tend to soak it up. Once cooked, pile the eggplant

CONTINUED

slices on top of the tomato and onion sauce. Fry the zucchini the same way and add these to the dish too.

Once the peppers have had their time in the oven and are burnished around the edges, add them to the dish. Stir the peppers, eggplant, and zucchini together on top of the sauce, season with a little more salt and pepper, and return to the oven for 40 minutes to cook through.

Once ready, stir to mix it all together, then tear over the basil, add more salt and pepper if needed, and drizzle with olive oil.

I like to serve my ratatouille with a fried egg on top and a good chunk of bread or flatbread.

Black dal

Black dal is one of my all-time favorite things to eat. Deeply spiced, creamy, almost smoky, to me it seems like half Boston baked beans and half creamy spiced masala.

There is a restaurant near me called Dishoom that makes a really good one, which as far as I can tell is finished with a generous drizzle of cream. No cream in sight here—I mash the lentils, which makes for a naturally creamy dal—but if you are feeling decadent, you could add a spoonful of cream or thick yogurt.

This is really easy to make at home—though it does cook for a couple of hours, it takes just 10 minutes to get going, and then it's just a case of adding water and stirring from time to time. My mom's old friend the pressure cooker works amazingly well when cooking legumes. If you have one, use it here. You can follow the recipe in exactly the same way, then, once you have added the lentils and beans, bring the cooker to pressure and cook for 20 minutes, until the beans and lentils are cooked through.

The black lentils can be bought from any Indian shop or large supermarket. It helps to soak the lentils and beans overnight in water, but if you forget, don't worry—they will just take a little longer to cook.

....

First soak your lentils and beans in a deep bowl of cold water—overnight is ideal, but a few hours will do.

Next, heat a little oil in a large pan and gently fry the onions for 10 to 15 minutes until sweet, soft, and lightly browned. Add the cumin seeds, cardamom pods, turmeric, chile powder, fennel seeds, garlic, ginger, and tomato purée and stir for a couple of minutes.

SERVES 4 TO 6

1 cup/200 g whole dried black lentils (also called urad dal or black gram)

½ cup/100 g dried kidney beans

peanut oil, coconut oil, or ghee, for frying

2 onions, peeled and finely chopped

1 teaspoon cumin seeds

2 cardamom pods, split

1 teaspoon ground turmeric

½ teaspoon red chile powder

1 teaspoon fennel seeds

3 cloves garlic, peeled and finely chopped

a thumb-size piece of fresh ginger, peeled and finely chopped

2 tablespoons tomato purée

2 tomatoes, finely chopped

a small bunch of fresh cilantro, leaves picked and roughly chopped

Drain the lentils and beans and add to the pan with the chopped tomatoes and 8½ cups/2 L of cold water. Bring to a boil, then turn the heat down to a fairly gentle simmer, put the lid on, and cook for 2 to 2½ hours until the lentils and beans are cooked and the liquor is thick, dark, and deeply flavored. Stir the dal from time to time while it cooks, and add a little hot water if it looks too dry.

Once the lentils and beans are cooked through, mash about half of them to a paste, using a potato masher in the pan, then stir together to make the dal super creamy.

Scoop the dal into bowls and finish with a little yogurt, if you like, and a good pile of chopped cilantro. Serve warm, with soft, fluffy naans or chapatis.

Artichoke and fennel seed paella

I find myself making this in deep winter, when the big flavors of the sunshine-soaked saffron and smoked paprika seem to cut through the cold and sometimes gray London days. It would be great in summer too. I like to serve it with a shaved fennel salad.

This is a very quick one-pot dinner. Most of it comes from the pantry, so it is a great thing to have on standby if you can't summon the energy to make it to the supermarket.

The trick with paella is to be brave and resist the urge to stir the rice once you have poured the stock in. The rice will settle in the pan, and the stock will bubble up in little channels through the rice, making sure it all cooks evenly—clever.

....

Put a large sauté pan over medium heat. Add a little olive oil and the onions and peppers and allow to cook for 10 minutes, until soft and sweet.

Next, add the garlic and fennel seeds and sauté for another 5 minutes, until the onions begin to brown a little. While that's cooking, stir the saffron into the vegetable stock and leave to infuse.

Add a little more oil to the pan and turn the heat up. Add the rice and fry for a couple of minutes, until it is completely coated in the oil, then pour in the sherry or wine and continue to cook until the alcohol evaporates. Add half the chopped parsley, the smoked paprika, season with salt and pepper, and stir.

Now pour in the stock and turn the heat down to medium. Leave your paella alone now—try not to stir it, as it will settle and the stock will find little channels through the rice. Stirring the rice will keep it from cooking evenly.

CONTINUED

SERVES 4

olive oil

2 onions (the sweet Spanish kind are best), peeled and finely chopped

2 green peppers, seeded and finely chopped

4 cloves garlic, peeled and finely chopped

½ teaspoon fennel seeds

1 teaspoon saffron

4¼ cups/1 L vegetable stock

1¼ cup/250 g paella rice (Bomba, also called Calasparra)

⅞ cup/200 ml dry sherry or white wine

a small bunch of fresh parsley, leaves picked and roughly chopped

1 teaspoon smoked paprika

sea salt and freshly ground black pepper

1 (12-ounce/300 g) jar of artichoke hearts, each one quartered

2 big handfuls of spinach, washed

8 ounces/220 g piquillo peppers

1 lemon

Cook for 10 minutes, until there is about ⅜ inch/1 cm of liquid bubbling on top of the rice. Scatter the artichokes on top and push them down into the liquid to warm them through. Lay the spinach on top and push this down into the liquid too. Cook without stirring for another 5 minutes, then turn off the heat and cover with a lid or some foil and let sit for 5 minutes.

Finish by stirring in the piquillo peppers, the rest of the parsley, and the juice of the lemon.

Serve with some bright salad and a glass of sherry.

Mac and greens

This is my version of beloved mac and cheese. I make a creamy pesto of cherry tomatoes, toasted almonds, and basil, inspired by the Sicilian pesto alla trapanese, which coats the squash-studded macaroni. Sometimes I add a little cheese to the tomato mixture before I stir in the pasta—1 cup/125 g of Manchego, pecorino, or Parmesan works well—but it is by no means needed. A broccoli crumb adds crunch and interest.

This works particularly well with gluten-free pasta as there is a good amount of sauce to ensure that the pasta is not too dry.

....

Preheat your oven to 400°F/200°C and put a large pan of well-salted water on to boil.

Meanwhile, put half the basil, the oats, broccoli, a good glug of olive oil, and seasoning into a food processor and pulse until you've got fine crumbs. It'll be a bit damp, but that's okay. Transfer to a small bowl and rinse the processor. Put the cherry tomatoes and almonds into the clean food processor with the remaining basil and 2 tablespoons of olive oil. Blend to a nearly smooth paste, then season well with salt and pepper and blend again.

When the water is boiling, add the pasta and the sliced squash and cook together for half the time the package suggests—you want it to be fairly undercooked. Drain, reserving a big cup of the pasta water for later.

Return the drained pasta to the pan, then add the tomato mixture and stir. Add the reserved pasta water bit by bit, using enough to thin the sauce to the consistency of heavy cream. You want it a bit runny, as the pasta will soak it all up in the oven.

Transfer everything to a large baking dish or casserole. Sprinkle the green crumbs evenly across the top and bake for 20 to 25 minutes or until the topping is crunchy. Remove from the oven and wait 10 minutes before serving.

SERVES 6

1 large bunch of fresh basil

½ cup/50 g oats

7 ounces/200 g (½ a head) broccoli, roughly chopped

olive oil

sea salt and freshly ground black pepper

11 ounces/300 g cherry tomatoes

1 cup/150 g toasted blanched almonds

11 ounces/300 g macaroni (I use organic gluten-free macaroni, but regular macaroni and whole wheat work well too)

14 ounces/400 g squash (butternut, delicata, or other winter squash), peeled, seeded, and cut into thin slices

Springtime wild garlic and lemon risotto

All the best new spring vegetables come together in this recipe to tell us spring is here. I love it that with spring comes a whole new palette of flavors and colors, and cleverly hidden in there are nutrients we need to adapt to the change in seasons.

The problem with most risottos is that they are loaded with cheese and butter to make them creamy, but I find them over-rich and cloying at times and not something that I can enjoy every day of the week.

This risotto is different—it uses a quick purée of wild garlic or spinach and slow-cooked onions in place of the butter and cheese. The idea came from a delicious risotto I ate at Daylesford, a farm cafe. So this is a risotto to eat any time.

I sometimes use pearl barley here—it does take a bit longer than rice to cook, but it's really worth the wait. You'll need to increase the cooking time to 40 minutes and add water as needed.

....

Fry the onion slowly in a drizzle of olive oil over low heat until soft but not too brown. Add a ladleful of hot stock, stir in the wild garlic or spinach, allowing it to wilt, then take off the heat. Allow to cool a little and then blend in a food processor. Set aside for later.

Next, heat a little oil in a large pan and cook the celery, leek, and garlic for 10 to 15 minutes, until the vegetables are soft and sweet. Add the sliced asparagus stalks and cook for a minute or so. Then turn up the heat, add the rice, and stir for a couple of minutes. Add the wine and cook until it is absorbed.

Once all the wine is gone, turn the heat down to medium-low and start adding the stock a ladleful at a time, allowing each ladleful to be absorbed as you stir. Keep adding stock until the rice is almost cooked—this will take

SERVES 4

FOR THE WILD GARLIC PURÉE
1 onion, peeled and roughly chopped
olive oil
1 ladleful of hot vegetable stock (see risotto below)
a couple of handfuls of wild garlic or spinach

FOR THE RISOTTO
1 stalk celery, finely diced
1 leek, washed, trimmed, and finely diced
2 cloves garlic, peeled and roughly chopped
a bunch of asparagus, woody ends snapped off, tips kept whole, stalks finely sliced
1 cup/200 g risotto rice
1 wineglass of white wine
6⅓ cups/1½ L hot vegetable stock
2 large handfuls fresh peas
2 large handfuls fresh fava beans

TO SERVE
grated zest and juice of 1 unwaxed lemon
a good grating of pecorino cheese
a bunch of fresh mint, leaves picked and roughly chopped
a couple of handfuls pea shoots or other spring leaves

about 25 minutes.

Once the rice is just about cooked, add the asparagus tips, peas, and fava beans and cook for another 5 minutes, until they are tender.

Take the risotto off the heat and add the wild garlic purée and the lemon juice, stirring vigorously to mix it through. Put the lid on and leave the risotto to rest for a couple of minutes.

Serve with lemon zest and pecorino grated over the top and add a scattering of chopped mint and a little pile of pea shoots.

Mint, pistachio, and zucchini balls

These little cloud-like rounds are somewhere in falafel territory—much lighter but no less satisfying. They could easily be eaten with spaghetti and a tomato sauce, or stuffed into a pita with pickled beets, hummus, and some caper berries for a filling lunch.

Once formed, the balls freeze well, and can be slowly fried from frozen in a pan with a little olive oil. Here they are baked for ease and to make their load a little lighter.

If you don't have a food processor, a potato masher will have the same effect on the lentils—and a mortar and pestle will make a mighty pesto.

....

Pulse the lentils in a food processor a few times until you have a textured mush. Place in a bowl and grate in the zucchini, then add all the other zucchini ball ingredients (keeping half the mint for later) and mix well. Season with salt and pepper—this mixture needs a good seasoning as it seems to soak it all up in the oven. Let sit for 20 minutes or so. Meanwhile, preheat your oven to 425°F/220°C.

Divide the mixture into 4 portions and roll each one into 6 little balls, to get 24 polpette. Place them on a baking tray and drizzle well with olive oil (if you want to be really precise, brush them all over for a perfectly crispy outside). Bake them in the hot oven for 20 minutes, until they have a golden crust.

While they are in the oven, pop all the pesto ingredients as well as the reserved mint into your food processor. Add 2 tablespoons of water and blend to a chunky paste. If you like a little more oil in your pesto, add some more here—I like the freshness of it without too much oil. Taste and adjust the levels of lemon, salt and pepper, and pecorino, as you need.

Take the polpette out of the oven. Serve them on a pile of quinoa, topped with a healthy spoonful of pesto and some leaves for a proper meal.

SERVES 4

FOR THE ZUCCHINI BALLS
1¼ cups/250 g cooked Puy lentils
2 zucchini
1 cup/100 g breadcrumbs (I use whole wheat)
4½ ounces/125 g ricotta cheese
1 clove garlic, peeled and finely chopped
grated zest of 1 unwaxed lemon
1½ ounces/40 g pecorino or Parmesan cheese, finely grated (see note on Parmesan, page 136)
1 red chile, chopped, or a pinch of crushed red pepper flakes
a few sprigs of fresh parsley, leaves picked and roughly chopped
a bunch of fresh mint, leaves picked and roughly chopped
olive oil

FOR THE PISTACHIO PESTO
a handful of pistachio nuts
a small bunch of fresh basil, leaves picked
4 tablespoons olive oil
juice of ½ a lemon
a couple of tablespoons of water
optional: a handful of grated pecorino cheese
sea salt and freshly ground black pepper

Any-night-of-the-week pizza

This is not a run-of-the-mill pizza—the base is made from cauliflower, oats, and almond flour and makes a crispy, hearty, and delicious vehicle for the mozzarella, tomato, and fennel that sit on top of it.

I'm not trying to pretend it's a normal pizza and that you won't ever want a delicious sourdough margherita again—you will, because those are unstoppably delicious. But a good pizza dough can mean a little too much work for a weeknight. This base is so very easy and healthy, you could eat it any night of the week with glee. Sounds weird, tastes genius—give it a try.

....

Preheat the oven to 425°F°/220°C and line a baking tray with baking paper.

Blend the cauliflower in a food processor until it has a fine, rice-like texture. Put it into a mixing bowl, add the almond flour, oats, oregano, salt, and pepper, and mix with your hands. Make a well in the center and add the eggs. Mix it all together, then use your hands to form the lot into a ball. It won't look like a traditional pizza dough—it will be a little wetter and less firm.

Rub the baking paper with some olive oil, put the dough in the middle of the baking tray, and use your hands to flatten it out until it is about ¼ inch/ ½ cm thick, slightly thicker around the edges. Bake for 20 minutes, until just golden. Meanwhile, blend up the tomatoes in the food processor with half the basil, a good pinch of salt and pepper, and a good drizzle of olive oil.

Once the base is golden, remove it from the oven and turn the oven up to 450°F/240°C. Spread over the tomato sauce, top with the mozzarella, greens, and shaved fennel, drizzle with a little more oil, then put back into the oven for another 8 minutes to cook the toppings.

Once cooked, finish the pizza with the remaining basil, some more oil, and a little grating of pecorino.

MAKES 1 PIZZA, TO SERVE 2 TO 3

FOR THE PIZZA BASE

1 medium cauliflower, cut into big chunks

1 cup/100 g almond flour

1 cup/100 g oats

a good pinch of dried oregano

sea salt and freshly ground black pepper

2 organic or free-range eggs, beaten

olive oil

FOR THE TOPPING

½ (15-ounce/400 g) can of chopped tomatoes

a big bunch of fresh basil

1(5-ounce/125 g) ball of organic mozzarella cheese

2 big handfuls of leafy greens (I use spinach or arugula)

½ a bulb of fennel, shaved into thin slices with a vegetable peeler

pecorino cheese, for grating

HOW TO MAKE
A KILLER ROAST DINNER

Roast dinners are all about timing and juggling everything in the oven. This is my Sunday dinner of choice. I've picked out the recipes I use and put them together into an easy-to-use timed chart so you know what to do, when. There is even time for a cup of tea. Although the roasted vegetables are ideally done at different temperatures, a 400°F/200°C oven will work.

THIS AMOUNT WILL SERVE 6 PEOPLE

YOU'LL NEED THESE RECIPES

ROASTED SQUASH (PAGE 250)

ROASTED BEETS (PAGE 250)

SWEET AND SALTY TAHINI CRUNCH GREENS (PAGE 246)

SEEDED YORKSHIRE PUDDING (PAGE 317)

AND HERE ARE A COUPLE OF QUICK ADD-ONS

Quick horseradish sauce:
Mix 6 tablespoons of grated horseradish (fresh or jarred) with 2 tablespoons of olive oil and a good pinch of salt and pepper. Add a little yogurt or crème fraîche if you like.

Roasted potatoes:
Peel and halve 2¼ pounds/1 kg of russet potatoes. Blanch for 12 minutes until almost cooked. Drain and shake in a colander to rough up. Put into a roasting tray with 2 tablespoons of olive oil, salt and pepper, 6 smashed cloves of garlic, and 2 sprigs of rosemary. Roast at 400°F/200°C for 1 hour 30 minutes.

2 HOURS BEFORE DINNER

2H	prepare roasted potatoes
	prepare roasted beets
	prepare roasted squash
1H 45M	roasted potatoes > oven
	roasted beets > oven
	roasted squash > oven
1H 30M	make Yorkshire batter
	prepare greens
	make horseradish sauce
1H 15M	set the table and get plates ready
	check roasting vegetables and turn

1 HOUR BEFORE DINNER

45M	relax a little and have a cup of tea
30M	take potatoes out > keep warm
	take beets out > keep warm
	take squash out > keep warm
	warm plates
15M	heat Yorkshire tray
	put Yorkshires in oven
	finish greens
	take out Yorkshires

GET EVERYONE AROUND THE TABLE AND SERVE

Deep-dish leek and greens pie

This is the kind of hearty dinner for which I have spent years scouring vegetarian cookbooks—something stand-out that will feed my hollow-legged boyfriend as happily as my health-conscious sister. It's hearty, creamy, tasty, and very British. In the spring and summer, I make this with leeks, asparagus, and peas; in the colder months, it's red onions, sprouting broccoli, and greens.

The pastry couldn't be easier. I love spelt flour for the nutty savoriness it gives, but whole wheat flour works too. I use olive oil in the pastry here, as it gives a lighter crust than butter. The topping is akin to a savory crumble and means there's no fussy rolling of pastry for the top.

SERVES 6

FOR THE PASTRY

1¼ cups/200 g whole wheat or light spelt flour

a few sprigs of fresh thyme or marjoram

grated zest of 1 unwaxed lemon

a pinch of salt

3 tablespoons plus 1 teaspoon olive oil

FOR THE FILLING

a good glug of olive oil

3 big leeks, washed, trimmed, and sliced

2 bunches of asparagus, woody ends snapped off, tips left whole, stalks chopped

7 ounces/200 g frozen peas

1 tablespoon whole wheat or light spelt flour

1⅔ cups/400 ml vegetable stock

optional: 3 tablespoons ricotta cheese

grated zest of ½ an unwaxed lemon

sea salt and freshly ground black pepper

FOR THE CRUMBLE TOPPING

2 handfuls of oats

1 handful of pumpkin seeds

grated zest of the other ½ lemon

a good pinch of salt

1 tablespoon olive oil

Preheat the oven to 415°F/210°C.

Now make your pastry. Put the flour, herbs, lemon zest, and salt into a food processor. Pulse a few times and then add the oil and pulse again until you have breadcrumbs. Add about 5 tablespoons of cold water until it comes together in a ball. (If you don't have a food processor, you can do this just as easily by hand.)

Get a 9-inch/22 cm pie dish or even a deep loose-bottomed tart pan. Scoop the pastry out of the food processor and place it on a floured work surface. Roll it out until it is just bigger than your pie dish, then carefully wrap it round your rolling pin and lower it into the pie dish. Gently press it in so the pastry takes the shape of the dish. Prick with a fork and blind bake in the oven for 12 minutes (no need to use baking beans for this pastry).

While your crust is baking, make your filling. Heat a splash of olive oil in a pan, add the leeks, and cook slowly over low heat for 15 minutes or so until they are soft and sweet. Add the asparagus and peas and cook for another 5 minutes until the peas have defrosted and the asparagus has lost its rawness.

Next, add a spoonful of flour and stir for a minute or so, then add the stock and simmer until you have a thick gravy. Take off the heat, stir in the ricotta and lemon zest, then taste and season with salt and pepper. Allow to cool while you make the topping.

Put all the topping ingredients into a food processor and pulse until crumbly.

Take the crust out of the oven and allow to cool a little, leaving the oven on. Then pile your asparagus filling into the crust and scatter the oaty topping over it. Bake for 20 minutes in the hot oven.

Serve in hearty slices with mashed potatoes and steamed greens.

Goodwill rainbow pie

The winter-herb-spiked pastry hugs the carefully flavored and individually celebrated layers of winter vegetables, while a grating of crumbly Lancashire cheese ties them together. If you can't get Lancashire, substitute white cheddar. This is a show-stopping pie that tastes even better than it looks.

This goodwill pie requires a bit of time and love—it's something I make for special occasions and holidays and it's almost always the centerpiece of our Christmas dinner. It may seem like there's a lot to do, but everything can happen at once—all the roasting can be done while you make the leeks and greens.

The pastry is made with a little butter and a good bit of cold water, so it's light and crispy. If you are really short of time, a good-quality store-bought crust could stand in here.

I often make this for my vegan brother and sister. I use vegetable shortening or coconut oil instead of butter, and omit the cheese. The pastry uses baking powder, so you don't need an egg. You can use soy milk to brush the pastry.

....

First make the pastry. Sift the flour, salt, and baking powder into a bowl and add the chopped thyme. Cut the butter or shortening into small bits and rub these into the dry ingredients until you have a breadcrumb-like mix. Add the water and knead until you have a smooth dough, but don't overwork it. You could also use a food processor: pulse to breadcrumbs, then add the water and pulse until it just comes together. Wrap the pastry in plastic wrap and chill while you make everything else.

Preheat the oven to 425°F/220°C.

SERVES 8 TO 10

7 ounces/200 g Lancashire or white cheddar cheese

1 organic or free-range egg, beaten, or soy milk for brushing

FOR THE PASTRY

3¾ cups/600 g all-purpose flour, plus extra for rolling

1 teaspoon fine sea salt

½ teaspoon baking powder

a small bunch of fresh thyme, leaves picked and very finely chopped

13 tablespoons/200 g butter or vegetable shortening

up to 1 generous cup/250 ml ice-cold water

FOR THE SWEET POTATOES

3 sweet potatoes, scrubbed clean

a little butter or olive oil

a good few gratings of fresh nutmeg

FOR THE BEETS

5 medium beets, peeled and cut into rough cubes

olive oil

splash of red wine vinegar

2 sprigs of fresh marjoram or oregano, leaves picked

sea salt and freshly ground black pepper

INGREDIENTS CONTINUED →

CONTINUED

FOR THE PARSNIPS

4 parsnips, peeled and cut into little fingers

a couple of sprigs of fresh sage, leaves picked

zest of 1 unwaxed orange

1 tablespoon honey

olive oil

FOR THE LEEKS

2 tablespoons butter or olive oil

2 good-sized leeks, washed, trimmed, and sliced

3 sprigs of fresh thyme, leaves picked

FOR THE GREENS

2 heads of chard, collard greens, or kale, stalks removed, roughly shredded

grated zest and juice of ½ an unwaxed lemon

1 red chile, finely chopped

Roast the sweet potatoes for 1 hour until soft. Meanwhile, prepare the beets and parsnips.

Place the beets into a roasting pan with a splash of olive oil and the vinegar, add the marjoram or oregano, and season. Cover with foil and roast alongside the sweet potatoes for 1 hour, removing the foil for the last 15 minutes.

Put the parsnips into a roasting dish with the sage, orange zest, honey, and a drizzle of olive oil, mix to coat, then cover with foil. Roast with the other vegetables for 45 minutes, until golden, removing the foil for the last 5 to 10 minutes. When all the vegetables are cooked, remove from the oven and turn the temperature down to 400°F/200°C.

Meanwhile, cook the leeks. Heat the butter or oil in a large nonstick frying pan. Add the leeks and thyme and cook over low heat for 20 minutes, until sweet and softened, then set aside.

Add a little more olive oil to the pan, add the greens, and cook over low heat for a few minutes, until just wilted. Season, then add the lemon zest and chili. Set aside.

Once the sweet potatoes are cool enough to handle, scoop out the flesh and mash with a pat of butter or 1 tablespoon of olive oil and a good grating of nutmeg. Adjust the seasoning for all the vegetable mixtures, if needed.

Take your pastry from the fridge and let it sit for a few minutes. Then roll it out on a lightly floured surface to ⅛ inch/¼ cm thick and use it to line an 8-inch/20 cm springform pan, leaving the excess hanging over the edges.

Now it's time to start layering the pie. Start with all the leeks, then a grating of Lancashire or cheddar cheese, then the beets, the greens, and another layer of cheese, then the parsnips, and finally the sweet potato mash.

Finish by bringing the excess pastry over the top of the sweet potatoes, twisting the ends, and laying them on top in a haphazard fashion—the little rough bits of pastry will crisp up and look beautiful. The pastry may not cover the whole top, but a little vivid orange sweet potato poking through is okay. Brush with the beaten egg or some soy milk.

Bake the pie on the bottom rack of the oven for 35 to 40 minutes, until golden brown. Let cool for 15 to 20 minutes, then remove from the pan and place in the middle of the table. Serve with gravy on the side (page 343).

vegetables to go with things

Red, yellow, purple, orange, and green—these are vegetables in all their glory. Every recipe in this book is loaded with vegetables, but here I have stripped back my favorites to serve alongside other dishes. Whether a dish served with a pizza or a pie or just one of a host of colorful bowls of vegetables, these are some of my favorite simple ways to make vegetables shine. From the underdogs of the vegetable world to my go-to favorites, there is no sidelining here.

honey-roasted radishes · bay leaf and saffron-roasted cauliflower · crispy sweet potato fries with chipotle dipping sauce · smoked paprika oven-baked fries · vegetable underdogs · sweet and salty tahini crunch greens · favorite roasted roots · sweet balsamic grilled chicory · mashed root vegetables · roasted root vegetables · super-sweet slow-cooked fennel · sage, pumpkin, and potato bake · my top vegetables · roasted squash with chile, dukka, and lime

Honey-roasted radishes

Radishes are one of my favorites. I love their shock of pink in a salad, and, just straight up, their peppery crunch is so good with a little sea salt. Roasting radishes turns them into something new—it mellows their punch, and they turn the most beautiful reddish pink color. I roast mine with honey and some lemon juice.

Radishes are the unsung heroes of the kitchen. They have made a mini-comeback in recent years, showing up on restaurant plates with good butter and salt as a fresh start to a meal. I almost always have them in my fridge. Their tops can be eaten too and contain even more vitamins than the roots. I sauté them with spinach, lemon, and olive oil or toss them into a green salad. My favorites are two-toned breakfast radishes, but any variety will do well here.

Don't waste the tops, as they can be tossed with the roasted radishes to pep them up and provide a beautiful contrast to the neon pink. Be sure to wash well first, though.

....

Preheat your oven to 425°F/220°C.

Trim the leaves from the radishes and wash both leaves and radishes well. Set the leaves aside. Halve the radishes and spread on to a baking tray with a good pinch of salt and some olive oil, then drizzle over the honey or syrup and squeeze over the lemon juice. Roast in the oven for 15 minutes, until just softened and starting to brown.

Take the radishes out of the oven and toss them with the radish tops and a little more good olive oil, then taste and add a little more salt and pepper if needed.

They are perfect alongside a summer tart.

SERVES 4

2 bunches of radishes, with their tops

a good pinch of sea salt

olive oil

1 tablespoon honey or agave syrup

juice of 1 lemon

Bay leaf and saffron-roasted cauliflower

Something magical happens to a cauliflower when you roast it. I usually turn to pungent Indian spices when I think of cauliflower, but one bright May Day, I turned to the sunshine warmth of saffron. My bay tree was in full bloom, and so this mellow but cheerfully flavored dish found its way into my oven.

I throw in a handful of golden raisins for some sweetness and some almonds for crunch. Leftovers are delicious stirred into pasta with a little extra olive oil—*conchiglie* (shells) work well.

I love the sight of a cauliflower—it's a pretty vegetable to me, with its milky curds wrapped in pale leaves and the tiny green leaves that cling to the sides in an act of complete protection. Keep those little leaves on—they are bright and tasty and look so pretty. If you can get your hands on a colored cauliflower (vivid purple and orange are my favorites), then you've got added antioxidants too, and your dinner will be colorful. I make this with spiky romanesco, too, when it's in season—its pale green looks amazing against the saffron.

....

Preheat your oven to 400°F/200°C.

Put the saffron into a little bowl, cover it with a couple of teaspoons of boiling water and let steep.

Get a large deep baking tray; add the cauliflower, onions, chile flakes, and bay leaves, and season with salt and pepper. Once the saffron has steeped, pour in the saffron strands and their liquid, add the raisins and almonds, toss everything together, then cover the tray with foil and bake in the oven for 20 minutes.

Remove the foil and bake for a further 10 to 15 minutes until the tips are burnished and the cauliflower is tender. Add the chopped parsley, toss, and serve.

SERVES 4

2 pinches of saffron strands

1 large or 2 small (approx. 2¼ pounds/ 1 kg) cauliflowers, leaves broken off, head broken into medium florets, stalk roughly chopped

2 medium onions, peeled and finely sliced

1 tablespoon Turkish chile flakes (see page 22) or a good pinch of crushed red pepper flakes

3 bay leaves

sea salt and freshly ground black pepper

a handful of raisins (I use golden ones)

a handful of almonds, roughly chopped

a bunch of fresh parsley, roughly chopped

Crispy sweet potato fries with chipotle dipping sauce

I am a sucker for sweet potato fries and all their orange crispness. To get them really crispy here, I use a little trick some people use to get roasted potatoes crisp—polenta. Personally, I don't love it with roasted potatoes but I do like it with sweet potatoes as there is something about corn and sweet potatoes together that just tastes right.

Using the polenta means that you get a super-crispy potato fry in the oven, no parboiling. I like to pair them with this chipotle dip, but they are wonderful with a fiery salsa (page 64), or simply with some ketchup and a bit of mayo.

Sweet potatoes contain a lot of something called storage proteins, which means that they are full of their own antioxidants and can actually use those to help our bodies heal. They are also really high in beta-carotene and vitamins, which is why I often eat them instead of white potatoes. So these are technically the healthiest fries on the planet.

SERVES 4

FOR THE FRIES

3 large or 4 small sweet potatoes, scrubbed and cut into long ⅜-inch/1 cm thick chips

2 tablespoons fine polenta

sea salt and freshly ground black pepper

olive or rapeseed oil

FOR THE CHIPOTLE DIPPING SAUCE

4 tablespoons thick Greek yogurt (or coconut yogurt)

1 tablespoon chipotle paste

a handful of sun-dried tomatoes, roughly chopped

1 tablespoon maple syrup

Preheat your oven to 425°F/220°C.

Put the sweet potato fries into a colander and run cold water over them to remove some of the starch. Pat them dry with a tea towel and spread them out over two baking trays.

Scatter the polenta evenly over the trays, then add a couple of pinches of salt and a good grinding of pepper to each. Drizzle with oil and toss everything in both trays until coated. Bake for 30 to 40 minutes, until the polenta has crisped and the fries are starting to turn golden brown.

Mix all the dipping sauce ingredients together, then taste and add a little salt and pepper if needed.

These fries can be served with pretty much anything.

Smoked paprika oven-baked fries

I like an underdog. Here I wanted to make the most of one of the unsung heroes of the vegetable world. Every trip I made to the supermarket, a few dumpy rutabagas or some turnips would turn up in my basket. I sort of feel sorry for them, as they don't get the love that they used to. I try to use them in interesting ways to give them a new lease on life.

This was one of those experiments that really worked. A few unlikely but simple ingredients came together to make something miles better than expected. The sweetness of the roasted rutabaga with its deep savory tones is backed up by some punchy chile. These really are good.

The joy of these fries is that with no parboiling you still get the crispiest edges and fluffy insides. I eat these as a side with a wrap or sandwich for a light dinner or Saturday lunch or with ketchup and mayo for a night in front of the fire with a good movie.

I often make these with sweet potatoes and even white potatoes too—white potatoes will need parboiling for a couple of minutes first, though.

....

Preheat your oven to 425°F/220°C.

Put the rutabaga fries into a sieve and run cold water over them, then pat dry with paper towels (this will get rid of some of the starch and help them to crisp up). Lay them on a baking tray and season well with salt and pepper, then shake over the smoked paprika, drizzle over a bit of oil, and toss together to coat everything in the oil and paprika.

Bake for 25 minutes, until the fries are golden around the edges and soft inside. I like mine with ketchup and good mayo, or with the burger recipe (page 186).

SERVES 4

3 medium or 2 large rutabagas, thickly peeled and cut into long ⅜-inch/1 cm thick fries

a good pinch of sea salt and freshly ground black pepper

1 teaspoon sweet smoked paprika

a couple of tablespoons olive or rapeseed oil

VEGETABLE UNDERDOGS

WHAT TO DO WITH ALL THE WEIRD STUFF

TURNIPS

GOOD WITH
thyme, rosemary, bay leaf, garlic, parsley, watercress, carrots, leeks, potatoes, Cheddar, blue cheese

IN A SALAD
Slice young baby turnips thinly and dress with lemon and oil for an unusual salad.

IN A SOUP
Peel and cook in a soup with leeks, thyme, and bay leaves; top with parsley and Gorgonzola.

ROASTED
Peel and chop into equal chunks, roast with salt, pepper, oil, garlic, and lemon for 45 minutes at 350°F/180°C.

A QUICK PICKLE
Slice thinly and pickle with cider, vinegar, fennel seeds, and a good drizzle of honey.

TIP
Old ones need to be peeled; young ones are okay with skins on and can be eaten raw.

CHARD—RAINBOW, SWISS

GOOD WITH
white beans, lentils, pasta, garlic, thyme, lemon, cumin, nutmeg, vinegar, tahini, Parmesan

QUICK SAUTÉED
Separate stalk and leaves; sauté stalks with garlic and oil for 3 minutes, add leaves, season, and serve.

IN A SOUP
Add to any soup near the end of cooking as you would spinach; the stalks need longer than the leaves.

JUST THE STEMS
Cut into 3 inch/8 cm lengths, blanch for 4 minutes; then dress with 2 tablespoons tahini and juice of ½ a lemon.

QUICK FRITTERS
Fold blanched leaves and stalks into leftover mashed potatoes and then make into little cakes and fry on both sides; serve with yogurt and lemon.

TIP
The stalks and leaves need treating separately as the leaves cook more quickly.

CAULIFLOWER, ROMANESCO

GOOD WITH
butter, mustard, horseradish, garlic, green olives, parsley, cumin, cilantro, saffron, caraway, coconut milk, curry

IN A SALAD
Blanch cauliflower; dress with lemon, oil, mustard, and capers; and finish with parsley and goats' cheese.

IN A SOUP
Follow soup recipe (page 78) adding turmeric and coconut milk in place of ½ of the stock.

ROASTED
See recipe on page 240. Leftovers are good stirred into pasta.

RAW
Slice very finely and dress with toasted cumin, chile, and lime.

TIP
Pick a clean white cauliflower—no brown spots. Florets should be tightly packed.

BRUSSELS SPROUTS

GOOD WITH
smoked paprika, juniper, mustard, potatoes, dates, vinegar, chestnuts, walnuts

MASHED
Boil, then finely chop, and mix with salt, pepper, nutmeg, and oil or butter.

ROASTED
Roast halved or quartered sprouts at 400°F/200°C for 20 to 30 minutes with oil, salt, and pepper. Dress with an herb and mustard vinaigrette.

RAW
Trim and finely slice and then toss with olive oil and salt.

LEFTOVERS
Slice leftover cooked sprouts and sauté with cooked potatoes in oil; season and squeeze over lemon. Serve with pickles and some Cheddar.

TIP
Don't overcook—that's why sprouts have a bad rep. You want them just soft and vibrant green.

CELERIAC

GOOD WITH

parsley, thyme, tarragon, lemon, truffles, hazelnuts, sage, butter, watercress, apples, pears

IN A SALAD

Chop into fine matchsticks and add to apple and shredded kale. Dress with lemon, oil, and mustard. Season.

HASH BROWNS

Use instead of potato in a rösti or hash brown. Grate and use ½ and ½ with potatoes in hash with onions.

MASHED

Mash with coconut milk or regular milk and lots of black pepper; stir in celery leaves to finish.

IN A SOUP

See celeriac soup recipe (page 88), switching up herbs for a change (see herbs in list above).

TIP

Peel well and keep in lemon water once cut to prevent discoloring.

JERUSALEM ARTICHOKES

GOOD WITH

butter, seeds, walnuts, lemon, radicchio, celeriac, artichokes, bay leaves, thyme, rosemary, parsley

IN A SALAD

See sunchoke salad recipe (page 108).

IN A SOUP

Follow soup recipe (page 78). Use bay leaves to season and finish with pumpkin seeds and croutons.

ROASTED

Peel if needed and roast at 350°F/180°C with rosemary, lemon, salt, and pepper for 40 to 50 minutes until tender.

MASHED

Boil for 20–30 minutes until tender and mash with tarragon, lemon, and a splash of vinegar and oil or butter.

TIP

They don't cook evenly: Some are hard and some are soft. That is their nature—don't worry!

RADISHES

GOOD WITH

bread, butter, salt, thyme, vinegar, sesame, chile, soy, seeds

IN A SALAD

Mix thinly sliced radishes, turnips, and carrots and dress with lemon, dill, or chives.

IN A SPRING DISH

Add a few quartered radishes to a pot of simmering peas for the last few minutes. Dress with oil and serve with mint and salt and pepper.

IN A COLESLAW

Stir them into a coleslaw of cabbage, apple, and carrot; finish with lime and cilantro.

USE THE TOPS

Sauté the tops with garlic, salt and pepper, and olive oil to make the most of every bit.

TIP

Pick smaller radishes. They will be sweeter.

RUTABAGA

GOOD WITH

nutmeg, parsley, smoked paprika, caraway, bay leaves, rosemary, apples, potatoes, carrots, turnips

IN A SOUP

Use in place of celeriac in the soup recipe (page 88). Swap sage for rosemary.

FRIES

See recipe (page 243) for rutabaga fries—in my opinion, the best way to eat rutabaga.

ROASTED

Roast at 350°F/180°C with salt, pepper, olive oil, and caraway seeds until soft inside and browned outside. Leftovers are good stirred into pasta.

MASHED

Cook until tender then mash with parsley and toasted caraway.

STEW

Use in place of sweet potatoes in the stew on page 85.

TIP

Peel thickly, as the tough outside is not good to eat.

Sweet and salty tahini crunch greens

This is a recipe that changes as the seasons roll by. I like to have a plate of greens on the table most evenings. Ordinarily they are quickly blanched and simply dressed with lemon zest, olive oil, salt, and pepper.

Here, spritely greens are bright, sweet, and salty; nuts and seeds bring layers of flavor and crunch, while the dressing is a happy blend of deep earthy tahini, zippy lemon, and warm woody maple sweetness. This is a dish that delivers on every level. I often make a double batch of the seeds and keep some for snacking on throughout the day because they are so good.

Below I've suggested greens to use through the year, but feel free to switch things up. I like to keep my greens vivid green with a bit of crunch—to me, cooking them for longer than a minute spoils their character. This way fewer of the nutrients seep into the water too. Follow the timings given below for different greens.

....

Preheat your oven to 400°F/200°C.

Put the seeds and nuts on a baking tray, pour over the maple syrup, and season with a good pinch of salt and pepper. Toss so that everything is coated in the syrup, then roast in the oven for 10 minutes. Take out of the oven and allow to cool a little.

While the seeds and nuts are roasting, make your dressing by mixing all the ingredients together in a little bowl or jar with a good pinch of salt and pepper.

Next, blanch your greens in a big pot of boiling water. See the timings (to the left) for each one.

Once your greens are blanched, drain them and place in a serving bowl or on a platter. Pour over the dressing and toss everything to coat, then top with the roasted seeds and nuts and serve immediately.

SERVES 4

FOR THE GREENS

4 tablespoons pumpkin seeds

4 tablespoons pistachio nuts

1 tablespoon maple syrup

sea salt and freshly ground black pepper

1 pound/500 g mixed seasonal green vegetables (see seasonal options below)

FOR THE TAHINI DRESSING

2 tablespoons tahini

juice of 1 lemon

2 teaspoons maple syrup

1 tablespoon extra virgin olive oil

SEASONAL OPTIONS

Spring · purple sprouting broccoli (40 seconds) and asparagus (60 seconds)

Summer · green beans (40 seconds) and broccoli (40 seconds)

Autumn · shredded sprouts (30 seconds) and winter greens (30 seconds)

Winter · purple sprouting broccoli (40 seconds) and kale (30 seconds)

Favorite roasted roots

This is my favorite way to eat root vegetables and works really well as part of a roast dinner. This all cooks in one big tray too, so there's no fuss. In winter a few sprigs of chopped thyme or rosemary work in place of the bunch of summery mint.

....

Preheat your oven to 425°F/220°C.

Cut the ends off the squash, then cut it in half and scoop out the seeds. Slice it into chunky strips lengthwise. You can leave the skin on for this, as it tastes wonderful roasted. Give the rest of the vegetables a good scrub, then cut off the ends. Cut the beets and parsnips into quarters and the carrots in half lengthwise.

Put all of the vegetables into a big roasting tray with the garlic cloves (no need to peel them either). Add the thyme, drizzle with olive oil, and season well. Toss together until lightly coated, then put the tray into the oven and roast for 50 minutes until the vegetables are golden.

While the vegetables are roasting, make the dressing. Finely chop the mint and mix it in a bowl with the rest of the ingredients.

Once the vegetables are ready, take them out of the oven and remove the garlic cloves from the tray. Let the garlic cool a little, then squeeze it out of its skins into the dressing. Mix well and then pour the dressing over the roast vegetables and stir.

Serve a pile of roast vegetables topped with a couple of spoonfuls of yogurt, a scattering of pumpkin seeds, and some toasted bread, if you like, to mop it all up with.

A little sprinkling of crumbled feta or goats' cheese works really well too.

SERVES 4

FOR THE VEGETABLES
1 butternut squash
4 fresh beets
2 parsnips
8 carrots
8 cloves of garlic
a few sprigs of fresh thyme
olive oil
sea salt and freshly ground
black pepper

FOR THE DRESSING
a small bunch of fresh mint
1 tablespoon red wine vinegar
2 tablespoons honey
½ a red chile, finely chopped
4 tablespoons olive oil

TO SERVE
all-natural yogurt
a handful of pumpkin seeds,
toasted

Sweet balsamic grilled chicory

I love this dressing—it pretty much works with any sturdy salad or vegetable and is really welcome here against the flame-tamed bitterness of the chicory. Sweet balsamic, citrus pop, and mellow sweet heat from the chile make this simple and delicious dressing unusual.

......

Put the chopped rosemary into a bowl with the chiles, balsamic vinegar, orange juice, oil, and salt and pepper, and stir to combine.

Heat a griddle pan until smoking hot and grill the chicory or radicchio on all sides until charred and just soft.

Toss the chicory in the dressing and serve immediately. This is great with some grilled halloumi or on top of a thick slice of toasted sourdough slathered in soft goats' cheese.

SERVES 4

a sprig of fresh rosemary, leaves picked and chopped

2 red chiles, deseeded and finely chopped

2 tablespoons good balsamic vinegar

juice of ½ an orange

2 tablespoons extra virgin olive oil

sea salt and freshly ground black pepper

8 heads of red chicory or 4 small radicchio

Mashed root vegetables

Everyone loves mashed potatoes. This one is colorful and full of goodness, and doesn't leave me snoozing on the sofa in the way a bowl of mashed potatoes might.

......

You know this one, but I'll tell you anyway. Put your vegetables into a pan, cover with boiling water, and simmer for 10 to 15 minutes until they are soft all the way through (check them with the point of a knife). Remove from the heat and drain in a colander, then let steam for a couple of minutes.

Put the vegetables back in the pan and mash with the oil and lemon zest. Season with a little salt and pepper. I like to use a spatula to mix—this way it'll look nice and smooth.

SERVES 4

14 ounces/400 g parsnips or turnips, peeled

14 ounces/400 g sweet potatoes, peeled

2 carrots, peeled

a good glug of olive oil

grated zest of 1 unwaxed lemon

sea salt and freshly ground black pepper

ROASTED ROOT VEGETABLES

All these roasted root vegetables can be mixed and matched together and finished with any of the dressings. Just make sure if you are roasting them together to be aware of different cooking times. Cutting longer-cooking vegetables smaller works!

BEETS

PREP
Peel and cut into halves or quarters depending on size.

ROAST
Put into tray with oil, salt, pepper, and a splash of vinegar, cover with foil for 1 hour and then without for 30 minutes at 350˚F/180˚C.

ROAST WITH
thyme, marjoram, or oregano

SQUASH

PREP
Cut in half and scoop out seeds. Cut into 1¼-inch/3 cm pieces.

ROAST
Put into tray with oil, salt, and pepper, cover with foil, and roast for 1 hour. Uncover and roast for 20 minutes at 350˚F/180˚C.

ROAST WITH
rosemary, cinnamon, chile, cilantro, or sage

PARSNIPS

PREP
Peel and cut into halves or quarters. Keep in water until ready.

ROAST
Blanch for 5 minutes and then roast for 45 minutes with oil, salt, pepper, and a little honey at 400˚F/200˚C.

ROAST WITH
honey, thyme, rosemary, cumin, or smoked paprika

POTATOES

PREP
Peel and cut into halves or quarters. Keep in water until ready.

ROAST
Blanch for 12 minutes until nearly cooked. Shake in colander and then roast with oil, salt, and pepper for 1 hour and 20 minutes at 400˚F/200˚C.

ROAST WITH
smoked paprika, cumin, chipotle, thyme, or lime

SWEET POTATOES

PREP
Scrub and cut into wedges.

ROAST
Season with salt and pepper and drizzle with oil. Roast for 1 hour until golden at 400˚F/200˚C.

ROAST WITH
smoked paprika, cumin, chipotle, thyme, or lime

CARROTS

PREP
Peel and cut lengthwise into halves.

ROAST
Roast with salt, pepper, and oil for 45 minutes until brown at edges.

ROAST WITH
honey, thyme, miso, orange, cumin, or cilantro

5 DRESSINGS

CHILE AND MINT

Chop a small bunch of mint and mix it with 1 tablespoon of red wine vinegar,
2 tablespoons of honey, ½ a chopped red chile, and 4 tablespoons of olive oil.
Season and drizzle.

TARRAGON AND LEMON

Chop a small bunch of tarragon, add a pinch of salt and pepper, and mix in the juice
of a lemon and 4 tablespoons of olive oil. Season and drizzle.

CUMIN, THYME, AND SMOKE

Toast 2 tablespoons of cumin seeds in a frying pan. Add the leaves from a small
bunch of thyme, 1 tablespoon of sweet smoked paprika, and 4 tablespoons of olive
oil. Heat the mixture until the thyme begins to crisp, then remove and drizzle.

HONEY, ORANGE, AND ROSEMARY

Finely chop a few sprigs of rosemary. Add 1 tablespoon of honey,
the juice of 1 orange, and 4 tablespoons of olive oil. Mix well and season
with salt and pepper. Drizzle.

SOY, MISO, AND SEEDS

Toast 2 tablespoons of sesame seeds. Mix in a bowl with
1 tablespoon of miso, 1 tablespoon of soy, and 3 tablespoons
of olive oil. Drizzle.

Super-sweet slow-cooked fennel

I am a big fan of fennel. Depending on how you treat it, it can be like two completely different vegetables. Shaved thin when raw, it is fresh and cleansing, with a clean aniseed flavor. Sliced more thickly and cooked, it is deeply sweet, soft, and comforting. When slow-cooked this way, it's delicious stirred into pasta, too, and great on toast with a spoonful of goats' cheese for a starter or a snack.

This makes me think of Italy and was something I often made in the kitchen at Fifteen. I'm sure it's not the most groundbreaking recipe, but every time I make it, it meets with riots of approval and high-fives across the table (even from people who claim to be fennel haters).

Start with the fennel bulbs. First, cut off the leafy top, reserving a few fronds for later. Next, slice off the bottom of the root and remove the tough outer layer, making sure the base is still holding everything together; then cut each bulb lengthwise into ¾-inch/2 cm slices.

Heat the olive oil in a large frying pan over high heat and add a layer of sliced fennel. Don't overcrowd the pan; just leave it for a few minutes until one side has turned golden brown. Use tongs to turn the slices over and cook on the other side for a few minutes, until golden, and then remove from the pan. Add a bit more olive oil if needed and repeat the process with the rest of the fennel.

Once all the fennel is golden and has been removed from the pan, reduce the heat and put in the fennel seeds, dried chile, and plenty of salt and pepper. Add the agave syrup or sugar and allow to cook, stirring for a minute or two and adding a little more oil if needed. Now put all the cooked fennel back into the pan and cook over medium heat to caramelize gently. Once the fennel is caramelized and tender (this will take about 5 minutes), turn off the heat and stir in the garlic.

Place on a serving plate and scatter the dill, fennel tops, and lemon zest.

SERVES 4

4 small fennel bulbs

4 tablespoons olive oil

1 teaspoon fennel seeds

a good pinch of crushed red pepper flakes or ½ a crumbled dried chile

sea salt and freshly ground black pepper

1 tablespoon agave syrup or unrefined sugar

1 clove garlic, peeled and very finely chopped

a small bunch of fresh dill or fennel tops, roughly chopped

grated zest of 1 unwaxed lemon

Sage, pumpkin, and potato bake

This potato and pumpkin bake reminds me of trips to the River Café in London as a young chef, when food was glossy, new, and what I lived for … not much has changed. We'd save up our wages and go for a set lunch on a weekday, when it was cheapest, and we thought we had it made. My favorite time to go to the River Café is late autumn, when pumpkins and wild mushrooms dot the menu.

In the summer, I make this with a head of radicchio instead of the squash, and in spring, with a bunch of asparagus. I love this as a simple supper with some sweet balsamic-dressed leaves, but to make it a hearty meal, I bake some ricotta in the oven for the last 20 minutes, with salt, pepper, chile, and crushed fennel seeds.

....

Preheat your oven to 400°F/200°C.

Cut the potatoes into ¼-inch/½ cm slices. I do this carefully using a mandoline or, if I am in a rush, in my food processor using the wide slicing attachment. Put the sliced potatoes straight into a big bowl of cold water and let soak for 10 minutes to get rid of some of the starch. Cut the pumpkin or squash into slices about the same thickness.

Drain the potatoes and pat them dry with paper towels, then place them in a large roasting tray with the pumpkin, garlic, sage, and a generous sprinkling of salt and pepper. Add a couple tablespoons of olive oil and toss everything together. Push the layers down to flatten them out, pour in the hot stock, and then cover with foil and bake in the oven for 40 minutes.

Remove the foil and then put back into the oven for another 25 minutes, until golden brown and everything is soft and cooked through.

Serve with a crisp salad or some green beans for a light supper or alongside a pie or tart for a more filling dinner.

SERVES 4 AS A MAIN, 6 AS A SIDE

3½ pounds/1½ kg waxy potatoes

2¼-pound/1 kg piece of pumpkin or 1 butternut squash, peeled and seeded

3 cloves garlic, peeled and finely sliced

a small bunch of fresh sage, leaves picked

sea salt and freshly ground black pepper

olive oil

4¼ cups/1 L hot vegetable stock

MY TOP VEGETABLES

PURPLE SPROUTING BROCCOLI

GOOD WITH butter, olive oil, garlic, lemon, mustard, capers, olives, ginger, soy milk, feta, blue cheese

PREP Trim ends and cut any larger stalks in half lengthwise. Chop up thick stalks to even cooking time.

IN A SOUP Follow soup recipe (page 78) using broccoli and potatoes. Finish with pumpkin seeds and, if you like, a crumble of feta or blue cheese.

FOR A QUICK PASTA Slice stalks and sauté with sliced garlic, chile, and olive oil; add florets and leaves, then stir into cooked orecchiette and finish with lemon zest and pecorino.

QUICK GINGER DINNER Steam broccoli until tender. Fry 2 cloves of garlic with 1 thumb-size piece of ginger, sliced. Add 1 chopped chile, 2 tablespoons of soy milk, 1 tablespoon of honey, and the juice of 1 lime. Pour over broccoli and serve with brown rice.

TIP Don't overcook—renders it mushy and tasteless. Boil for 3 minutes only.

ASPARAGUS

GOOD WITH fennel, eggs, mint, potatoes, peas, fava beans, peanuts, lemon, tarragon, Parmesan

PREP Snap off the woody ends as they are too tough to eat. You can use them to flavor a vegetable stock.

IN A SALAD See page 116.

WITH NOODLES Serve sliced blanched asparagus with just-cooked egg noodles and spoonfuls of the quick satay sauce (page 173).

WITH A SOFT-BOILED EGG Blanch stems and serve with a soft-boiled egg and sourdough bread, butter, and salt.

IN A POTATO BAKE Replace the pumpkin (page 253).

SPRING VEGETABLES Blanch and toss with blanched peas and fava beans, chopped mint, lemon and salt and pepper.

CHARRED Heat a griddle pan and grill on each side for 2 minutes, toss in lemon juice and olive oil and serve with mozzarella.

PEAS

GOOD WITH mint, lemon, feta, mozzarella, paneer, lettuce, watercress, basil, asparagus, fava beans, tarragon, parsley

PREP Frozen peas need a few minutes covered in boiling water; fresh just need to be removed from pod. Early sweet ones are good raw; larger ones need blanching for 2 minutes.

SMASHED ON TOAST Mash blanched or young raw peas with a handful of basil and mint, zest and juice of 1 lemon, and a good glug of olive oil. Serve next to mozzarella with grilled bread. Can be served warm too.

SAUTÉED WITH PANEER Cut paneer into cubes and toast cumin and cilantro seeds in a pan. Crush, then sprinkle on the paneer. Fry until golden. Add blanched peas and cilantro and finish with a squeeze of lemon.

SUPER QUICK SOUP Follow the soup recipe (page 78) using leeks and peas. Add spinach or sorrel (if you can get it) at the end. Top with raw peas, herbs, oil, and some quick croutons.

TIP Buy fresh peas and cook within a day or two.

KALE

GOOD WITH garlic, almonds, raisins, lemon, vinegar, radishes, breadcrumbs, poached eggs, potatoes, chile, white beans

PREP Young leaves can be shredded, stalks and all, but remove the central stalk from bigger, older leaves as they toughen as the plant ages.

FLASH-FRIED Heat oil in a pan. Add kale and sauté until shiny and crisp. Squeeze over the juice of a lemon to soften and eat with rice or a poached egg and some chile.

RAW IN A SALAD Raw kale is great. Put into a bowl with the juice of ½ a lemon and pinch of salt and scrunch until soft. Add toasted almonds, raisins, and red wine vinegar.

BAKED EGGS Fill a baking dish with kale. Dot over with yogurt. Top with lemon zest, break in 4 eggs, scatter over chopped red chile, and bake for 15 minutes in a medium oven. Serve with flatbread.

TIP Avoid all yellowing leaves—they will be bitter.

ZUCCHINI

GOOD WITH basil, lemon, garlic, eggs, tomato, oregano, dill, mint, capers, olives, olive oil, pine nuts, pistachios

PREP Young small ones need to be washed, ends trimmed, and chopped. Larger ones may need core removed as it can become foamy and bitter.

RAW WITH GOATS' CHEESE Peel into strips, dress with olive oil, lemon, and chile and serve next to a pile of toast and some soft goats' cheese.

QUICK SAUTÉED Cut zucchini into coins and sauté them with olive oil until the edges are golden. Squeeze over lemon and oil and season. Tear over mint or dill and serve with pasta or brown rice for a quick supper.

FAST FRITTERS Mix grated zucchini with ricotta and season. Add crushed cilantro seeds, lemon zest, and a little cilantro and fry in olive oil until crisp on both sides. Serve with dill and other herbs scattered over.

TIP Try to get zucchini with flowers. Stir the leaves into pasta or use to top pizza.

CARROTS

GOOD WITH cilantro, cumin, mustard seeds, orange, tomato, fennel, apple, celery, cinnamon, coconut, parsley, peanuts

IN A SALAD Shave thinly with a peeler and toss with toasted cumin seeds, a squeeze of orange juice, olive oil, and salt and pepper.

QUICK INDIAN FRY Grate 2 carrots and sauté them with shredded napa or savoy cabbage and some mustard seeds, a pinch of brown sugar, a good squeeze of lemon, salt, and pepper.

A SOUP Make a carrot and tomato soup and add a can of coconut milk (page 78).

MASHED CARROTS Boil carrots until tender and mash with a little orange juice and some olive oil. Serve in place of mashed potato.

TIP Look out for purple, white, and yellow carrots as well as orange ones.

ARTICHOKES

GOOD WITH mint, lemon, potatoes, peas, Parmesan, olive oil, pasta, chile, almonds, parsley

PREP Peel baby artichokes back to their pale, light leaves. Halve them and remove the hairy chokes with a teaspoon. Place the artichoke in a pan with just enough water to cover them. Add a couple of garlic cloves and a little squeeze of lemon juice and cook until the stalks are tender.

IN A SALAD Shave raw artichokes on a mandoline. Dress with lemon and olive oil, salt, and pepper and toss with arugula and grated Parmesan.

ARTICHOKE DIP Blend a jar of artichokes with a can of fava beans, some lemon juice, a little olive oil, parsley, a grating of Parmesan, and salt and pepper, until smooth.

QUICK SUMMER VEGETABLES Mix cooked artichokes with peas, fava beans, lemon juice, oil, salt and pepper.

BRUSCHETTA Pile cooked artichokes onto toasted slices of bread; top with chopped mint, olive oil, and pecorino or Parmesan.

EGGPLANT

GOOD WITH pepper, chile, ginger, garlic, nutmeg, soft cheese, tomato, pomegranate, smoked paprika

BABA GHANOUSH See page 166.

JAPANESE Fry cubed eggplant for a couple of minutes in peanut oil and then add a tablespoon each of chopped ginger, soy sauce, miso paste, and a little water. Cover and simmer for 30 minutes.

BRUSCHETTA Grill thin slices of eggplant until charred and cooked through, toss with basil and chopped tomatoes, and eat with good bread and some mozzarella.

NUTMEG SALTED Fry slices of eggplant in olive oil until cooked through and golden; grate fresh nutmeg over and sprinkle with salt. Eat immediately.

TIP Most eggplants are grown so they don't need salting before you cook them. Avoid any really seedy pieces.

Roasted squash with chile, dukka, and lime

This is, hands down, my favorite way to eat squash. The dukka recipe makes more than you will need for the squash, so save it in a jar and use it to scatter over charred flatbread with olive oil or to sprinkle on pretty much any roast vegetable.

Preheat your oven to 425°F/220°C.

Put your squash on a tray with a good pinch of salt and pepper and a drizzle of olive oil, toss to coat, and put into the oven to roast for 25 to 30 minutes.

Meanwhile, make your dukka. Put the hazelnuts, cilantro seeds, sesame seeds, cumin seeds, fennel seeds, and peppercorns on a baking tray and roast in the oven alongside the squash for 10 minutes. Once the hazelnuts have browned and it's all smelling wonderful, remove from the oven and allow to cool.

Once cool, mix with the dried mint and salt and then pulse in a food processor or crush in a mortar and pestle until you have a chunky paste.

Once the squash is roasted, lay it on a serving plate and sprinkle over the dukka and the chopped chile. Grate over the zest of 1 lime and squeeze over the juice of 2.

Things to do with dukka
- Scatter over soup with a tablespoon of yogurt
- Sprinkle on warm flatbread with olive oil
- Roast with any root vegetables
- Use as a rub to marinate vegetables or tofu before grilling
- Scatter over a hearty salad
- Sprinkle on top of hummus

SERVES 4

1 butternut squash or
2 smaller squash such as acorn, halved, seeded, and cut into ⅜-inch/1 cm thick pieces
sea salt and freshly ground black pepper
olive oil
1 red chile, chopped
grated zest and juice of 2 unwaxed limes

FOR THE DUKKA
a handful of hazelnuts
4 tablespoons cilantro seeds
3 tablespoons sesame seeds
2 tablespoons cumin seeds
1 teaspoon fennel seeds
1 tablespoon black peppercorns
1 teaspoon dried mint
1 teaspoon sea salt

sweet endings

Desserts are when I am most excited. From mint chocolate chip ice cream to banana cream pie, I have always been a dessert girl. While my sweet tooth has grown up with me, so has my desire to make a show-stopping, delicious, and quietly nutritious treat. These desserts use unrefined sugars, honey, maple syrup, grains, and fruit, which makes their load a little lighter and their taste even better.

molten maple chocolate cakes · strawberry poppy seed crisp · brown sugar meringues with sticky apples and pears · banana, toffee, and coconut cream pie · brown sugar tart · cherry and rosewater macaroon tart · granola and milk tart · the sweet stuff · strawberry elderflower sherbert · roasted banana and coconut ice cream · mint stracciatella frozen yogurt · blood orange and chocolate chip sorbetto

Molten maple chocolate cakes

It takes a lot to beat molten chocolate. If there is an oozy chocolate dessert on the menu in a restaurant I struggle to order anything else. I spent my first few years living close to the Cadbury's chocolate factory in Bournville. We were a Cadbury's family: of my dad's eleven brothers and sisters, at least six of them worked there.

My uncles and aunts would come home with big bags of chocolate from the chocolate shop, always the slightly misshapen bars that didn't make the final cut. I liked them all the more for their peculiarities. Dinners at my grandmother's were merely killing time until we were allowed into the old teak sideboard and let loose on the chocolate stash. I am well and truly a chocolate lover, and these oozy cakes hit the spot.

Preheat your oven to 400°F/200°C.

Put the butter or coconut oil into a pan over medium heat and let it melt. Take the pan off the heat and add the cocoa, salt, vanilla, and maple syrup. Then stir to combine and let cool. When cool, put into a mixing bowl.

Separate the eggs, putting the whites aside. Add the yolks to the cooled chocolate mixture—it will thicken up a little.

In a clean bowl, whisk the egg whites until they form soft peaks, then gently fold into the chocolate mixture (a spatula works well for this). Don't overmix as you still want to keep the lightness of the egg whites.

Butter four little ovenproof dishes or ramekins and divide the mixture among them. Put them on a baking tray and place in the hot oven for 12 minutes exactly.

Serve with a spoonful of yogurt (I like coconut yogurt) and a scattering of seasonal fruit.

MAKES 4 PUDDINGS

5 tablespoons/75 g butter or coconut oil

4 tablespoons cocoa powder (I like to use raw cacao powder)

a pinch of sea salt

seeds from 1 vanilla pod

3 tablespoons maple syrup

3 organic or free-range eggs, at room temperature

Strawberry poppy seed crisp

This is kind of a crumble: a super-light, crisped oat polenta and poppy seed crumble that sits on top of jammy lemon and vanilla-baked strawberries. A crisp, which I love, is an American take on a crumble as it has a lighter, more summery feel than a buttery crumble (though there is space in my kitchen for both).

I make this all year round and trade strawberries for peaches, plums, rhubarb, and pears throughout the year, adjusting the amount of sugar to the acidity of the fruit as I go.

Preheat your oven to 400°F/200°C.

Put the strawberries into an ovenproof dish with the 3 tablespoons of sugar, the lemon zest, and the vanilla seeds.

Mix the almond flour, oats, poppy seeds, and the rest of the sugar in a bowl and add the orange zest.

Break the butter into little chunks and add it to th–e bowl or pour in the coconut oil and then use your fingers to rub the mixture together, lifting them out of the bowl to get some air into the crisp topping. Once the mixture looks like fine breadcrumbs and there are no big lumps of butter, you're ready to go.

Pile the mixture on top of the strawberries and bake in the hot oven for 25 minutes, until the top is golden and the strawberries have shrunk and started to caramelize around the edges.

I like to serve this with a big spoonful of coconut yogurt, but cream, ice cream, or custard work too.

SERVES 4

1¾ pounds/800 g hulled strawberries, cut into halves and quarters

½ cup/100 g plus 3 tablespoons unrefined light brown sugar

grated zest of 1 unwaxed lemon

seeds from 1 vanilla pod

1 cup/100 g almond flour

1 cup/100 g steel-cut oats

2 tablespoons poppy seeds

grated zest of 1 unwaxed orange

7 tablespoons/100 g cold unsalted butter or coconut oil

Brown sugar meringues with sticky apples and pears

I love these meringues—I use brown sugar, which is pretty unusual for a meringue, but it really works. Granted they won't be quite as peaky as the ones made with white sugar, but the trade-off is that you get more good chewiness and a light caramel flavor.

In the summer, I serve these with raspberries and some Greek yogurt sweetened with honey, sometimes with a little basil or mint stirred in. Sometimes I fold a little melted chocolate (2 ounces/50 g) or a tablespoon of cocoa into the meringues to make them chocolatey.

....

Preheat the oven to 300°F/150°C and line a baking tray with parchment paper.

Put the egg whites into a squeaky clean bowl and whisk with an electric mixer (or in an electric stand mixer on medium speed) until stiff peaks form. Gradually add the sugar while mixing on high speed until the mixture is thick and glossy. It's ready when you can pinch the mixture and not feel any granules of sugar. Fold in 2 tablespoons of the runny honey, leaving some ripples through the mixture.

Spoon into 8 mounds on the baking tray and bake for 1½ to 2 hours (depending on how chewy you like your meringues—less time means chewier middles). The meringues are ready when they are set and light to pick up. Set aside to cool.

For the fruit, put the sugar into a pan with the wine and place over medium heat. Once it's bubbling, add the fruit, bay leaf, spices, and lime zest. Reduce the heat to low and simmer for 10 minutes, or until soft. Set aside to cool completely.

Fold the lime zest and remaining honey into the yogurt. Serve the meringues piled with yogurt, fruit, and the syrup from the fruit.

SERVES 8

4 organic or free-range egg whites

scant 1 cup/200 g soft light brown sugar

3 tablespoons runny honey

grated zest of 1 unwaxed lime

1 cup/250 ml Greek yogurt or coconut yogurt

FOR THE STICKY APPLES AND PEARS

½ cup/100 g unrefined soft light brown sugar

scant ½ cup/100 ml red wine

3 apples, peeled, cored, and cut into 8 pieces

3 Bartlett pears, peeled, cored, and cut into 8 pieces

1 bay leaf

1 cinnamon stick

1 star anise

zest of 1 unwaxed lime, peeled into strips with a vegetable peeler

Banana, toffee, and coconut cream pie

SERVES 6 TO 8

FOR THE CRUST

½ cup/75 g almonds

½ cup/75 g pecans

120 g medjool dates
(6 fat ones), pitted

1 tablespoon creamed honey
or agave nectar

a good pinch ground ginger

FOR THE BANANA CARAMEL

12 tablespoons unrefined light
demerara sugar

3 ripe bananas, peeled and
mashed well

FOR THE COCONUT
CLOUD CREAM

2 (15-ounce/400 g) cans of
full-fat coconut milk

1 tablespoon creamed honey or
agave nectar

seeds from 1 vanilla pod

TO FINISH

2 bananas

juice of 1 lime

Banana . . . toffee . . . whipped coconut cream—this is half tart, half pie, and half cake, which by my calculation adds up to one and a half, which seems suitable for a dessert like this—it's pretty spectacular.

When I ask my brother what he wants for his birthday each year I get the same answer—"Your banoffee pie." Owen chose to be a vegan before any of the rest of our family had come around to the importance of conscious eating.

So by its nature, this pie is vegan and all the better for it. Cloying sweetness and heavy whipped cream are replaced by a quick no-bake crust, a foolproof banana caramel, and a cloudy whipped coconut topping that I could eat with everything. I think it's the stuff dreams are made of: a banoffee pie that's all good for you.

For the topping you will need a can of full-fat coconut milk; the half-fat stuff just won't work. You'll need to put it into the fridge a good hour or so before you want to make the topping, as this allows the coconut milk to separate—the thick coconut cream settles at the top of the can, while the coconut water stays at the bottom. The top is scooped off, whipped up like cream, and tastes like a combination between marshmallows and clouds. The water left over is good for using in smoothies and soups, so it won't go to waste.

If you don't have medjool dates, use other pitted ones—soak them in hot water first and use a couple extra.

First of all, make sure that your coconut milk is in the fridge chilling.

CONTINUED

Next, make your crust. Put the nuts into a food processor and pulse until you have a chunky crumble. Add the dates, honey, and ginger and pulse a few more times until it comes together.

Place the mixture into an 8-inch/20 cm springform pan and use your fingers to press it all over the base, making a lip around the sides about ⅜ inch/1 cm deep. Put into the fridge to chill.

Now make your banana caramel. Put the sugar into a pan with the mashed banana, place over medium heat, and simmer until the caramel has thickened and is a deep brown color. This will take 3 to 5 minutes.

Peel the bananas and slice them into thin rounds. Toss them in the juice of the lime, then lay them evenly on top of the crust.

Once the caramel is cool, pour it over the bananas, spread it evenly, and put into the fridge to chill.

Scoop the thick white top layer from your cans of coconut milk and put it into a bowl. Add the honey and vanilla seeds and whisk until thick, like whipped heavy cream. Put into the fridge to chill for 20 minutes.

When you are ready to eat, give the coconut cream a final stir, spoon it on top of the caramel, and use the back of a spoon to create pretty swirls.

If you like, top with some grated dark chocolate or, if you are feeling fancy, some chocolate curls.

Brown sugar tart

The brown sugar filling is somewhere between a treacle tart and a pecan pie and it is in every way as delicious as both.

I serve this with seasonal fruit and a scoop of yogurt, crème fraîche, or ice cream—nothing too sweet.

....

Preheat the oven to 375°F/190°C.

To make the crust, first blend the oats in a food processor on high speed until you have a roughly blended flour. Put it into a large mixing bowl and combine with the spelt flour and salt.

Put the butter or coconut oil and honey into a small pan and melt together over a low heat. Pour into the bowl of flour and mix with a spoon until everything is incorporated. You may need to use your hands to knead the dough a little at this point, to bring it all together.

Press the dough over the base of an 8-inch/20 cm springform pan and to come halfway up the sides—the thinner the better—so make sure you press it down well. Bake the crust in the oven for 10 minutes until just turning a light golden color on the edges, then set aside to cool.

Meanwhile, make the filling. Melt the butter or heat the coconut oil in a small pan over low heat and add the seeds from the vanilla pod. Put the sugar and honey into a medium mixing bowl, pour in the melted butter or coconut oil, then add the cornstarch, baking powder, and salt and whisk well. Once well whisked, fold in the pecans. Spoon the filling into the tart shell and bake in the oven for 20 minutes. As the tart cooks, the filling will bubble up and caramelize, which looks beautiful (it will firm as it cools).

Once the tart is cooled, run a knife around the edge to loosen it before you release the springform pan. Serve with a little crème fraîche.

SERVES 8

FOR THE CRUST

1⅓ cup/130 g rolled oats

⅔ cup/100 g spelt flour

¼ teaspoon sea salt

3 tablespoons butter or coconut oil, melted

4 tablespoons honey or agave syrup

FOR THE FILLING

2 tablespoons unsalted butter or coconut oil

seeds from 1 vanilla pod

½ cup plus 1 tablespoon/125 g unrefined dark brown sugar

2 tablespoons honey

1 tablespoon cornstarch

a pinch of baking powder

a couple of pinches of sea salt

¾ cup/100 g pecans, roughly chopped

Cherry and rosewater macaroon tart

This tart has the lightness and freshness that's key in a summer dessert. The coconut crust is topped with a macaroon filling and scattered with cherries.

You can make this all year round, swapping out the cherries for what's in season: strawberries in summer, slices of ripe pear in autumn, blood oranges and orange blossom water in winter.

....

Preheat the oven to 400°F/200°C.

Butter a 9-inch/23 cm springform and line it with parchment paper.

To make the crust, combine the flour and sugar in a large bowl, then stir in the melted butter or coconut oil and mix until crumble-like. Press the mixture into the prepared pan, making sure you work all the way around the sides, and bake for 10 minutes. Then set aside and allow to cool completely.

While the crust is baking, prepare the macaroon filling. Whisk the egg whites with the sugar and rosewater until fluffy, either by hand or using an electric mixer. Once they have formed stiff peaks, fold in the dried coconut, being careful not to flatten all the air out.

Scatter most of the halved cherries across the tart base and spoon the macaroon filling over them, pushing it to the edges of the tin. Be sure to let at least a few of the colorful cherries pop through.

Bake for about 15 minutes, or until the peaks of the macaroon topping are deeply golden. Let the tart cool and garnish by sprinkling with the remaining cherries and the crushed pistachios.

SERVES 8 TO 10

FOR THE COCONUT
PASTRY CRUST

1¼ cups/200 g flour (I use a 50/50 mix of coconut flour and spelt flour, but all-purpose flour will do fine)

½ cup/100 g unrefined superfine sugar

11 tablespoons butter or coconut oil, melted

FOR THE FILLING

4 extra-large organic or free-range egg whites

⅓ cup/70 g unrefined superfine sugar

2 teaspoons rosewater

1 cup/140 g dried coconut

11 ounces/300 g cherries, washed, pitted and halved

½ cup/50 g pistachio nuts, crushed

Granola and milk tart

This crumbly pastry has a clean, quick-and-easy vanilla milk center, topped off with maple granola and toasted fruit, nuts, and oats.

As I was making this, I realized that I'd made a dessert that sounds like breakfast: my two favorites—breakfast and dessert—coming together.

This is great for when you have visitors, as it can be made ahead of time and sits just fine at room temperature without spoiling.

....

Rub the flour, confectioners' sugar, and butter or coconut oil together in a bowl until it resembles breadcrumbs (you can do this in a food processor if you have one). Add 2 to 3 tablespoons of ice-cold water and pulse or knead until the pastry comes together in a ball. Wrap in plastic wrap and chill for 30 minutes.

Meanwhile, make your granola topping: mix the oats with the fruit, chopped nuts, maple syrup, and cinnamon, then scatter over a baking tray and set aside.

Preheat the oven to 375°F/190°C.

Once it's had enough time to chill, take the pastry out of the fridge and allow it to soften slightly. Shape it into a rough circle, then put it in an 8-inch/ 20 cm loose-bottomed round tart pan. Gently push the pastry out so that it covers the bottom and sides of the pan. Carefully press the pastry down into the corners, then place in the fridge to chill for another 20 minutes.

Once the crust has chilled, use a fork to prick the crust all over. Line it with parchment paper and pour in some dried beans. Put into the oven along with the tray of granola topping and bake both for 15 minutes.

When the 15 minutes are up, take both the crust and the granola out of the

SERVES 6

¾ cup/125 g light spelt flour

⅓ cup/50 g unrefined confectioners' sugar

7 tablespoons/100 g unsalted butter or coconut oil (from the fridge)

½ cup/50 g rolled oats

½ cup/100 g raisins

⅓ cup/50 g chopped hazelnuts or pecans

2 tablespoons maple syrup

½ teaspoon ground cinnamon

½ cup/100 g light brown sugar

4 organic or free-range eggs, beaten

seeds from 1 vanilla pod

1 cup plus 1 tablespoon/250 ml whole milk or coconut milk

4 tablespoons finely ground corn meal

oven. Remove the dried beans from the crust and return to the oven for another 10 minutes. Let the granola cool.

Have your sugar, eggs, and vanilla ready in a large bowl. Put the milk and corn meal into a pan and whisk together. Place over medium heat and bring to a boil, whisking all the time. It will start to thicken quite quickly.

Once the milk and corn starch mix has thickened, remove from the heat and slowly pour it onto the sugar and eggs, whisking all the time.

Pour this mixture into the crust, bake for 35 minutes, and then sprinkle on the granola and bake for another 5 minutes until golden brown on top.

Serve this with a scoop of ice cream and some berries in summer, poached apples or pears in autumn or winter.

THE SWEET STUFF

Eating just refined white sugar is a bit like eating sliced white bread every day. You would miss the depth of a sourdough loaf, the malty richness of a slice of rye, the buttery chiffon layers of a warm croissant. Natural sweeteners, like flours, spices, salts, and fats, come in all colors, flavors, and dimensions. While these sweeteners are still sugars, they are absorbed by your body more slowly and have the added bonus of lots of other nutrients that come along with the sweetness.

Cooking with a variety of natural sweeteners opens up your cooking to a completely new plane. By pairing these more natural sugars with whole grain and nut flours, I find that a slice of cake is more satisfying, has a more developed and individual flavor, and is closer to the food I like to eat.

AGAVE

Light and clean-tasting agave is a neutral sweetener that's made from the juice of the agave plant, which is also used to make tequila. It comes in dark and light varieties. I mostly use the light one, but the dark one is good in rich, darker baking and actually has more nutrients. I love to use agave in cocktails and dressings as well as hot drinks. It is a particularly good alternative to honey for vegans. Buy it in any supermarket.

HONEY

I love honey, and a jar lasts just a few days in our house. I love it in teas, in baking, on toast, stirred into yogurt—any way I can involve it in my day is a good thing. What I love about it most is the fact that each honey is so different and reflects the character of the plants and flowers by which the bees were surrounded. I have a few honeys on hand at any time: a creamed honey for toast and to stir into icings, a mild honey for teas and dressings, and a darker, thicker honey for eating with cheese. Look for raw honey if you can—it retains the most nutrients as it hasn't been heated and tastes incredible. As a rule, the darker the honey, the higher it will be in antioxidants. Try not to stir honey into boiling water. I like to use honey in cakes and icings (see the honey butter icing on page 287), in dressings and marinades, and to spread on good toasted bread for my favorite and the simplest ever breakfast.

MAPLE SYRUP

Amber nectar   I love maple syrup; it tastes of childhood trips to American diners for towering stacks of maple-laced pancakes. Maple syrup is high in nutrients and minerals such as zinc. It comes from boiling down the sap of the maple tree. Be on the lookout for pure maple syrup, as many are a blend and have very little maple at all. There are different grades of maple syrup, and the flavor and darkness depend on when in the season the sap is harvested. In the United States, maple syrup is usually sold with a grade letter denoting the strength and depth of the syrup; generally grade A has a lighter flavor and grade B has a deeper and more maple-y flavor. I like to use maple syrup in cakes, dressings, and cookies and to sweeten fruit compotes. It does particularly well with apples, pears, and any berries.

UNREFINED AND NATURAL SUGARS

Unrefined sugar to me means sugar that is as unprocessed as possible and retains many of its nutrients and much of its natural character. It is of course still sugar, but in the rawest, most untreated form. My favorite natural sugars are muscovado and demerara, and I use unbleached superfine sugar sometimes too. Natural brown sugars retain their brown color from the natural color of the sugar cane, whereas other brown sugars are just refined white sugar mixed with low-quality molasses. You can use brown sugar in place of white in most baking, though the stronger flavor of dark molasses doesn't work in all baking (try the muscovado chocolate chip cookies on page 294).

BLACKSTRAP MOLASSES

This stuff is other-worldly—thick and black like tar. It is a full-bodied, dark, thick sweetener. It is made from successive boiling down of the sugar cane, which preserves a lot of the nutrients. It's particularly high in calcium and iron, which are both difficult to come by for vegetarians. Look for blackstrap molasses, which comes from the last boiling and is richest in nutrients. It works well with deep rich baking, winter fruits, and ginger (try the apple molasses cake on page 287).

COCONUT SUGAR

Coconut sugar has a round, caramely flavor and a mellow sweetness. Coconut sugar comes from coconut palm trees. The sap of the tree is boiled, then dehydrated. It is much lower in fructose than traditional sugar and so it's lower on the gylcemic index. As it is a dry sweetener, you can use it ounce for ounce as you would sugar, in most recipes.

Strawberry elderflower sherbet

I make this when strawberries are at their best, as that way this sherbet has a deep bubblegum flavor that you only get from super-ripe strawberries at the height of their sweetness. It may seem a little over the top to pulverize a whole lemon in a blender, but it adds an amazing sherbet freshness.

I make a version of this with plums in the autumn, replacing the lemon with an orange and the elderflower cordial with sloe gin or damson cordial. That's also insanely delicious. An ice-cream machine is useful here if you have one—if not, a plastic tub, a sturdy whisk, and a bit of patience will suffice.

For my elderflower cordial, see page 325.

....

Put the lemon into a food processor and pulse until you have a fine pulp. Add the strawberries, blend to a slushy crimson purée, and then mix in the cordial.

If you have an ice-cream machine, pour the mixture into the machine and churn until frozen. Transfer to a freezerproof container and freeze. Take it out of the freezer about 15 minutes before you want to serve it, to allow it to soften a little.

If you don't have an ice-cream machine, pour the mixture into a large freezerproof container and put into the freezer for an hour and a half. Then take it out and use a whisk to break up the crystals that are starting to freeze. Do this every half hour until it is almost frozen.

It is best eaten within a couple of weeks.

MAKES A DECENT TUB

1 unwaxed lemon, cut into chunks and seeded

2¼ pound/1 kg sweet summer strawberries, hulled

1¼ cups/300 ml elderflower cordial

Roasted banana and coconut ice cream

I was always envious of my parents' dinner parties. Everything seemed so decadent and grown-up. I used to help cook and then shyly sneak upstairs with my sister when guests started arriving. We loved the roar of laughter and the dancing that always came after dessert: Motown music mixed with squeals and giggles. One of the most grown-up and mesmerizing things I remember from those dinner parties was dessert: lemon mousse, brown bread ice cream, banana cake, and homemade ice cream. They were the tastiest and most magical things I had ever eaten.

This is a cheat's ice cream that you can make easily without an ice-cream machine—no sugar, no dairy, no making complicated custards. The roasted bananas form the base, topped off with the creamy cloudiness of coconut milk. You will need a food processor or a blender. I make this the night before it's needed and make sure I take it out of the freezer just before serving to soften up a little.

Preheat oven to 350°F/180°C.

Slice the bananas into ½- to ¾-inch/1 to 2 cm pieces and toss them with the honey in a baking tray. Bake for 30 to 40 minutes, stirring once during baking, until the bananas are browned and cooked through. Scrape the bananas and any syrup in the baking dish into a blender or food processor. Add the coconut milk, vanilla, lemon juice, and salt, and purée until smooth.

Chill the mixture in the fridge until cool, then freeze it in your ice-cream maker or place in a shallow baking tray, then into the freezer, and stir with a spatula every 20 minutes or so until it is almost completely frozen.

If you like a softer, more mousse-like texture, serve it immediately. Otherwise freeze for 30 minutes to 1 hour, to firm up.

Serve as is or with some toasted coconut shavings or crushed pistachios.

MAKES 1 PINT

3 medium, ripe bananas

drizzle of honey

1 (15-ounce/400 g) can of coconut milk

1 teaspoon vanilla extract or the seeds from a vanilla pod

juice of ½ a lemon

pinch of salt

Mint stracciatella
frozen yogurt

Anyone who knows me will know about my infatuation with mint chocolate chip and stracciatella cream, which luckily is shared by John. I may have taken it a step too far.

Second to mint chocolate chip comes my love of frozen yogurt, a passion born of a childhood spent in California, where a cup of chocolate frozen yogurt heralded a sunny day. Here my fascinations come together. I urge you to make this—it's really easy, really healthy (for ice cream), and really, really good.

I have used just fresh mint here because I like the gentle sweetness. For a more classic mint taste, add a ½ teaspoon of natural mint extract. This also works well with coconut yogurt (though it's a bit more expensive). If you don't have an ice-cream machine, see page 276.

....

First, put the milk into a pan and add most of the mint leaves, keeping a couple of sprigs back. Bring to a boil and then immediately turn off the heat. Stir well, add the agave syrup, and allow to steep for at least 30 minutes.

After 30 minutes or so, your milk should be cool and will have taken on the flavor of the mint. Pour through a sieve into a large bowl and throw away the mint leaves—they have done their job.

Stir in the yogurt, then cover the bowl and let sit for 30 minutes in the fridge for all the flavors to meld. Taste for sweetness and add a little more agave syrup if needed, remembering that once it's frozen it will taste less sweet.

Pour into your ice-cream maker and churn for 30 minutes or until it is well frozen. Then chop the remaining mint leaves very finely and stir them into the mixture with the chopped chocolate. Scoop into a freezer-proof container, cover, and freeze for an hour before eating. If your ice cream is frozen hard, leave it out for 10 to 15 minutes before eating.

MAKES A DECENT TUB

1 cup plus 1 tablespoon/250 ml whole milk or coconut milk

a large bunch of fresh mint

1 cup plus 1 tablespoon/250 ml agave syrup

2 (pint/500 ml) containers of good Greek yogurt or coconut yogurt

2 ounces/50 g good dark chocolate, chopped up small

Blood orange and chocolate chip sorbetto

One of my favorite things to do is to go out for dinner on a whim. Whenever John and I find ourselves with a night to spare, we start in Soho with a big bowl of udon noodles and some sake and we always end up at Gelupo, a little place on Archer Street that has the best ice cream I have ever tasted. The few minutes before I walk through the door are always filled with ice-cream-choice anxiety. If it's quiet, we'll taste a bunch of flavors—avocado and rhubarb ices, almond or bergamot granita.

Despite the sampling, I always go for exactly the same thing in the end; a clear cup of sherbet-pink blood orange sorbet with a slick of bitter chocolate sorbet to cap it off. It is always incredible as the spoon dips through the piercingly dark chocolate to the candy ice shards of bubblegum blood orange.

So this is how I make it happen at home. I am sure it has none of the technique or finesse of the Gelupo masters, but the flavor is pretty special nonetheless. I make this with clementines or regular oranges when blood oranges are not around. I use 70 percent Green & Black's chocolate here, which works well—don't be tempted to use higher than 70 percent, though, as it gets too hard in the freezer.

....

In a large bowl, mix the blood orange juice with the agave syrup.

Turn on your ice-cream machine, pour in the blood orange mixture, and churn until you have a lovely smooth-set ice cream (my machine takes 20 to 30 minutes). If you don't have an ice-cream machine, see page 276.

Once it's ready, use a spatula to scoop out the sorbet into a freezerproof container. Stir in the chopped chocolate and put into the freezer for another few minutes before serving.

This needs to be eaten within a couple of weeks for it to be at its best.

MAKES 1 QUART OR SO

1 quart/1 L blood orange juice, which is the juice from about 15 blood oranges

⅞ cup/200 ml light agave syrup

4 ounces/100 g good dark chocolate, chopped

cakes, bread, and a few other things

Nothing makes me happier than a well-baked treat—a thickly iced cake, a warm seeded crusty loaf, a stack of gooey caramel brownies. Any of these freshly baked treats in the middle of my table—with a big pot of tea and hands diving from every angle and resounding appreciation—is what I love best. A home-baked cake or loaf of bread is a way to make new friends, show old ones you love them, and be the focus of a great big celebration. These cakes and breads won't have you spinning from sugar highs because they use honey, maple syrup, and natural sugars, along with all kinds of interesting flours and grains that are easier to digest.

double chocolate cloud cake · apple molasses cake with honey icing · flours and milling · cardamom and carrot cake with maple icing · muscovado chocolate chip cookies (and ice-cream sandwiches) · seeded banana bread with lemon sesame glaze · super raw brownies · salted caramel crack brownies · lady grey fig rolls · pistachio and elderflower cordial cake · butterscotch chocolate chip blondies · coconut oatmeal cookies · cardamom lemon glaze cake · carrot and black pepper soda bread · coconut vanilla loaf · never superseeded loaf · seeded yorkshire pudding

Double chocolate cloud cake

**MAKES ONE BIG DOUBLE-
LAYERED CAKE**

FOR THE CAKE

½ cup/125 g coconut oil

⅔ cup/150 ml maple syrup

2 teaspoons vanilla extract

⅔ cup/100 g white spelt flour

1¼ cup/150 g almond flour

1 cup/100 g good unsweetened cocoa powder

2 teaspoons baking powder

a good pinch of salt

1 ripe banana

⅞ cup/200 ml milk (I use almond milk or ready-to-drink coconut milk; see page 39)

FOR THE ICING

1 (15-ounce/400 g) can full-fat coconut milk

3 tablespoons creamed honey

3 tablespoons cocoa powder

1 tablespoon vanilla extract

FOR THE CHOCOLATE GLAZE

¼ cup/60 ml milk (I use almond milk or ready-to-drink coconut milk; see page 39)

4 ounces/100 g good-quality dark chocolate, chopped into small pieces

TO DECORATE

a couple of handfuls of berries (I use blueberries and blackberries, but raspberries and strawberries look good too)

This is everything you want in a chocolate cake: rich, bouncy, and well rounded, with a chewy brownie outside, cloud-light chocolate icing, and a dreamy chocolate glaze to top everything off.

But wait, there is a secret here. This cake is not only really tasty but really good for you too: no butter, refined sugar, or white flour but still over-the-top delicious. I let people take a couple of big chocolatey bites and then tell them just how good for them it actually is.

It's not that I don't have a good old-fashioned slice of cake every now and then, but I love that it's possible to have a slice of cake that is as nourishing as it is delicious. One of the things I love about cooking, and particularly baking, is that there is always an opportunity to take something classic and make it in a way that suits how you like to eat. And I have to say that the first time I tried a slice of this, I was very proud.

I use light spelt flour here, as I prefer its more flavorful character and it is much easier on your body than white flour—however, if you can't get your hands on it, all-purpose flour would work. Likewise, if you can't get coconut oil, you can use melted butter. Half-fat coconut milk doesn't work here, though.

....

Preheat your oven to 350°F/180°C.

Grease a 9-inch/23 cm springform cake pan and line the bottom with parchment paper. Put your can of coconut milk into the fridge to chill.

Put the coconut oil into a small pan and let it melt over low heat. Add the maple syrup and vanilla extract and mix well.

CONTINUED

Put the spelt flour, almond flour, cocoa, baking powder, and salt into a bowl and mix well. Mash the banana and add it to the milk. Make a well in the center of the dry ingredients and slowly pour in the melted coconut oil mixture and the banana and milk. Mix well.

Pour the mixture into the lined pan and level the top using the back of a spoon. Bake in the oven for 35 to 40 minutes until it feels firm to the touch and a skewer comes out clean. Don't worry if the cake has cracked on the top, as this will all get covered by the chocolate glaze.

Remove the cake from the oven and let cool in its pan for 10 minutes. Then carefully transfer to a cooling rack and let cool completely.

Once it has had an hour in the fridge, open the can of coconut milk and scoop the thick, creamy white top layer into a bowl, leaving behind the watery stuff (you can keep this to use in smoothies). Add the honey, cocoa powder, and vanilla extract, then use an electric mixer or a whisk and a bit of elbow grease to quickly whisk it together, breaking down the coconut cream and whisking it into a smooth fluff. Transfer immediately to the fridge and let chill.

For the chocolate glaze, pour the milk into a small pan, bring to a simmer, then remove from the heat. Put the chopped chocolate into a medium bowl and pour over the hot milk, stirring until melted and glossy.

Once the cake has cooled, use a bread knife to gently slice it horizontally into two layers. Remove the top layer and set aside. Spread the chocolate-coconut icing over the bottom layer and put the top layer on. Now put the cake back on the cooling rack and place a plate underneath.

Pour the glaze all over the top of the cake, letting it drip down the sides (the plate underneath should catch all the drips). Pile the fruit on top and place in the fridge to chill for 10 minutes, allowing the chocolate on top to set.

Apple molasses cake with honey icing

When the apples fall from the trees, it seems the right time of year for some comforting filling sweetness: filling in the best sense, dark bronzy brown with a comforting addictive flavor. This cake is perfect for those days when you need a heavy sweater and a never-ending supply of tea.

I use molasses and brown sugar to sweeten this cake. Blackstrap molasses is pretty amazing stuff. It's a by-product of the sugar-making process and holds on to all the nutrients from the sugar cane that don't show up in refined white sugar. Molasses is high in iron and calcium, so it's really good for vegetarian diets. I buy it from my health food store and I try to get the organic or unsulfured kind if I can get it.

I try to use unrefined confectioners' sugar for the icing—it has a caramelly note. If it's hard to find, regular confectioners' sugar will work. Perfect comfort deserves perfect icing.

This is a particularly moist cake so it works well if you replace the spelt flour with a gluten-free one.

....

Preheat the oven to 400°F/200°C.

Sift your flour into a bowl with the cinnamon, allspice, baking powder, and baking soda.

In another big bowl, mix the molasses, sugar or syrup, eggs, and olive oil until you have a deep, dark, even mixture. Stir in the flour mixture and mix again until evenly combined. The mixture should be quite thick. Grate in the apples and ginger and mix well.

Butter and line a standard 8 by 4-inch/450 g loaf pan, pour the cake mix in, and smooth out the top with the back of a spoon.

SERVES 10 TO 12

FOR THE CAKE

1½ cups/250 g light spelt flour

1 teaspoon ground cinnamon

a pinch of ground allspice

1 teaspoon baking powder

1 teaspoon baking soda

1 tablespoon molasses

⅔ cup/150 g soft light brown sugar or ⅔ cup/150 ml maple syrup

2 extra-large organic or free-range eggs, at room temperature (or see note on chia, page 42)

⅔ cup/150 ml olive oil

3 apples, grated

a thumb-size piece of fresh ginger, peeled and finely grated

FOR THE ICING

9 tablespoons/125 g butter, at room temperature

2 tablespoons honey

1½ cups/200 g unrefined confectioners' sugar

a small handful of almonds, roughly chopped

Bake for 45 to 50 minutes, until a skewer inserted into the cake comes out clean. Check from time to time by peering through the oven door. If the top looks like it's browning too quickly, cover loosely with foil.

Once golden, remove from the oven and cool in the pan for 5 minutes before turning out onto a wire rack to cool completely.

To make the icing, beat the butter, honey, and confectioners' sugar together in a bowl until fluffy. An electric mixer would be helpful here, but start off slow or you'll cover yourself in confectioners' sugar. If you only have a wooden spoon, that'll do—it'll just take a bit longer.

Spread the icing thickly all over the top of the cake, sprinkle over the crushed almonds, and serve with a cup of tea.

FLOURS AND MILLING

While I love a loaf of sourdough or the occasional treat made with all-purpose white flour, I try to use variety in all my cooking and baking. You'll find jars of these favorites on my shelf.

SPELT FLOUR

I adore the nuttier, more rounded taste of spelt flour, and it is my grain of choice for most baking and pastry. It's an ancient grain eaten by the Romans that is making its way back into our kitchens. It's a more nutrition-packed cousin of wheat and is higher in protein and lower in gluten than wheat flour (but it still has a good amount of gluten, so it's not okay for anyone who has an intolerance). Buy it at any supermarket. Light spelt flour is the one to use in baking.

OAT FLOUR

I love the creamy note that oat flour adds to baking and the sustaining power of oats. Using oat flour in baking means that the energy from a piece of cake will be released into your body a bit more slowly and more gently. I usually grind my own oat flour (see opposite page, it's really easy) as oats have a higher oil content than most other grains and so the flour loses its freshness very quickly. Buy it at any supermarket or grind some up yourself.

CHESTNUT FLOUR

Chestnut flour has a delicate, nutty, light caramel flavor and is known in Italy as *farina dolce*, sweet flour. It's made from dried milled chestnuts. It works well in most cakes and particularly well with chocolate—try swapping half your all-purpose flour for chestnut in the chocolate cake (page 284). Chestnut flour is completely gluten free. Buy it in any good heath food store.

COCONUT FLOUR

Coconut flour is a soft powdery flour made from dried coconut. It adds a very subtle coconut flavor to baking, which I love. It is high in protein and healthy fats. Coconut flour is obviously not grain based, so it's completely gluten free. But coconut flour absorbs much more liquid than regular grain-based flours, so it's hard to substitute. Instead, look for recipes that specify coconut flour, such as the coconut loaf (page 313) and the macaroon tart (page 270). Buy it at any good health food store.

BUCKWHEAT FLOUR

I adore the strong nutty flavor of buckwheat in baking. Buckwheat is in fact not wheat at all but a relative of two of my very favorite things: rhubarb and sorrel. It works so well in pancakes and blinis. I like it in bread too and sometimes swap it for a third of the spelt flour in the never superseded loaf (page 314). Buy it at your local natural foods store.

RYE FLOUR

Rye flour has a deep, almost malty character. I am fond of using rye flour in chocolate cakes and cookies and especially in brownies (page 300). I often mix ¼ rye with ¾ spelt in the bread recipe (page 314). Rye is high in a special type of fiber that helps you feel satisfied, which I find particularly useful when trying not to reach for another brownie. Rye flour is available at most supermarkets.

NUT FLOURS

I bake using a lot of nuts. I like the way they keep cakes from drying out and that they bring their own healthy fats and nutrients with them, allowing you to use a little less of the less healthy fats like butter. I don't buy preground nuts as I find them lacking in flavor; I grind my own in the food processor as needed for each cake. Pistachios, almonds, pecans, macadamias, hazelnuts, walnuts, and pine nuts all work well in cakes, pancakes, and muffins.

A WORD ON STORING FLOURS

Don't store them for too long; buy in smallish quantities—enough to keep you going for a month or so—and store, well-sealed, in a cool, dry place. Whole grain flours, in particular, should be sealed and refrigerated if you're not using them within a few weeks, because their natural oils can turn rancid quickly in a warm kitchen.

SOMETIMES I MAKE MY OWN FLOUR

All you need is a standard home food processor and a couple of minutes. I find making a jar of something you thought you had to buy from a store so satisfying. You can make your own flour from pretty much any grain or dried legume or nut. The ones that work best for me and that I like the taste of the most are oats, quinoa flakes, dried lentils, dried chickpeas, brown rice, and any kind of nut.

To make your own flour at home, put about 14 ounces/ 400 g of grains or dried legumes into your food processor. It's important to put a decent amount in; otherwise the grains just fly around the bowl. You can get away with doing smaller batches of nuts, though. Put the food processor on high and blend until the flour has formed a little wall around the sides and is no longer falling back into the center. Remove the flour and sift it through a medium sieve, for slightly more textured flour, or a fine sieve, for fine flour for lighter cakes and sauces.

Here's why I like to make my own flour: It will be truly whole grain. Most commercial flours are made with the germ of the grain removed. The germ is where most of the nutrition is stored. It is taken out in milling as it contains oils and, without it, flour has a longer shelf life. The nutrients in flour also quickly deplete after milling, so freshly milled flour will allow your body to get the very best from the grain.

It'll taste better too, just as freshly ground whole almonds do, and will smell and feel different from the flours you might buy in a package. Freshly milled flour will taste miles better than stuff that's been sitting on a shelf for weeks.

It's really easy to make unusual flours at home. Interesting flours can be expensive and hard to find, so milling your own in the food processor saves time and is easier on the pocket.

You can also make unusual flours with dried beans and lentils, which add incredible flavor and healthy proteins as well.

Cardamom and carrot cakes with maple icing

I haven't met anyone who doesn't like these. They are a crowd-pleaser, loved by old, young, boys, girls, junk-food lovers, and health-food freaks alike. This is as close to a cupcake as I get—super-buttery sugary cupcakes don't really do it for me. I like something with character and depth. These are what I make if I am taking cakes to a party or to a friend's for tea. They work well at any time of day, stay super moist, and are packed with goodness.

These are free of refined sugar and sweetened with maple syrup and banana (though you can't taste it). You can easily make them dairy and gluten free with no compromise on flavor. My favorite version uses coconut oil (instead of butter) and chickpea flour, but you can use butter and all-purpose or spelt flour, if you prefer. Soy cream cheese or very thick yogurt works for the icing too.

I sometimes swap the carrot for butternut squash or even a parsnip, so in that sense, this is a very wonderful way to use up any lingering root vegetables.

....

Preheat your oven to 400°F/200°C. Line a 12-cup muffin pan with cupcake liners and set aside.

Put the butter or coconut oil and maple syrup into a pan with the spices and let it melt over low heat. Set aside to cool.

Now put the almond flour, flour, pumpkin seeds, and baking powder into a bowl. Add the grated carrot, mashed banana, and eggs, pour in the cooled maple mixture, and mix well. Spoon into the cupcake liners. Bake for 25 minutes until golden on top and a skewer inserted into the cakes comes out clean.

While the cakes are cooking, make your icing. Put the cream cheese into a bowl with the maple syrup and spices and beat until light and fluffy. I like to do this with an electric hand mixer, but a wooden spoon works just fine too. Once the cakes are out of the oven and have cooled down, thickly spread each one with the icing and finish off with a grating of lime zest.

MAKES 12 LITTLE CAKES

FOR THE CAKES
6 tablespoons/80 g butter or coconut oil

4 tablespoons maple syrup

seeds from 4 cardamom pods, finely ground in a mortar and pestle

1 teaspoon ground cinnamon

½ teaspoon ground ginger

1¼ cups/150 g almond flour

⅔ cups/100 g light spelt or chickpea flour

⅓ cup/50 g pumpkin seeds

2 teaspoons baking powder

2 medium carrots, grated

1 banana, peeled and mashed

3 organic or free-range eggs, beaten (or see note on chia, page 42)

FOR THE ICING
1 (8-ounce/200 g) package cream cheese

4 tablespoons maple syrup

a pinch of ground cinnamon

a pinch of ground ginger

TO DECORATE
grated zest of 1 unwaxed lime

Muscovado chocolate chip cookies (and ice-cream sandwiches)

As a child I was insistent that when I grew up, I would have a room in my house filled only with marshmallows—I'm still hopeful. I guess one of the joys of a childhood in post-hippy San Francisco was feeding a fascination with over-the-top American sweets, be it the Mars bar rainbow ice-cream cake I had for my fourth birthday, the pop-tarts I eyed during every trip to the supermarket, or, of course, the mighty ice-cream sandwich.

These cookies are a little better than the ones I grew up eating because they contain brown sugar and whole wheat flour, and peanut butter replaces most of the butter here (I even make a version with 14 ounces/200 g of peanut butter and no butter at all). Sandwich them with good vanilla-bean-flecked ice cream, frozen yogurt, or dairy-free ice cream. Use dark or milk chocolate as desired (I use a good 70 percent dark).

I use a mixture of half light brown sugar and half dark brown sugar, but either will do. All light gives a straight-up chocolate chip cookie; all dark gives something richer and maltier.

MAKES ABOUT 24 COOKIES

1 cup/100 g oats

⅔ cup/100 g whole wheat or spelt flour

½ teaspoon baking powder

4 ounces/100 g chocolate, roughly chopped into good chunks

6 tablespoons/100 g butter, at room temperature

6 tablespoons/100 g smooth peanut or almond butter (page 340 shows you how to make your own)

⅔ cup/150 g light muscovado sugar

⅔ cup/150 g dark muscovado sugar

1 teaspoon vanilla extract

2 organic or free-range eggs, beaten

Preheat the oven to 400°F/200°C and line two baking trays with parchment paper.

First grind the oats in a food processor until they are a fine powder. Put them into a bowl, combine with the flour, baking powder, and chopped chocolate.

Put the butter, peanut butter or almond butter, sugars, and vanilla extract into another bowl and beat together until whipped and creamy. I use my electric hand mixer or a food processor here, but a strong arm and a wooden spoon will do.

CONTINUED

Mix the eggs into the sugar and butter, mixture and then add the dry ingredients, mixing well with a wooden spoon until everything is evenly combined. The dough will be quite stiff.

Use a teaspoon to scoop the dough onto the lined baking trays, leaving about a 1¼-inch/3 cm gap between them (I get 6 to 8 on a 12 by 8-inch/30 by 20 cm baking tray). Bake for 8 to 10 minutes until they have spread out and turned a little golden around the edges.

Eat hot from the tray or let them cool and make sandwiches with your favorite ice cream. Make sure the ice cream is slightly soft so it's just spreadable—then put the sandwiches back into the freezer to harden for 5 minutes before eating. If you want to keep them in the freezer, wrap them in parchment paper—they will keep for a couple of weeks.

Note: If you don't want to make all 24 cookies, roll the dough into a log, wrap it in parchment paper, and freeze. You can cut ⅜-inch/1 cm slices off the frozen log for instant cookies (they will take a couple of minutes longer to bake).

Seeded banana bread with lemon sesame glaze

One cold January week I just couldn't get away from banana bread. A loaf packed up in string and brown paper arrived in the mail from a baker friend; another emailed me asking for my ultimate banana bread recipe; I arrived at a third friend's house to the smell of a loaf in the oven. The signs were there: it was a week for banana bread and a quest for the best loaf I could make.

This was the result. Deeply seeded, it's a blend of all the good things from the different loaves I made. Trust me on the brave use of seeds—they make the bread. I use the same mixture every time—⅓ cup/50 g of golden flaxseeds, ⅓ cup/50 g of poppy seeds, and ⅓ cup/50 g of black sesame seeds—but any tiny seeds would work.

Banana bread is brilliant, as there is so little sugar needed to make something that feels like a real treat. I like to keep the bananas quite chunky so you can see some bits in the cake, but mash them up completely if you prefer. The cake stays very moist because of the bananas, so don't worry if it looks quite soft as you slice into it—that's what makes it so delicious. It's also a good opportunity for swapping in gluten-free flour.

The seeds in this cake contain a long list of vitamins and minerals and hence have amazing health benefits. Flaxseeds are the richest plant source of omega-3s, which helps our brains, joints, and immune systems—they can also help level out hormones and are packed with fiber. So eat your cake and know it's doing you some serious good. Having your cake and eating it is what that's called.

....

Preheat your oven to 400°F/200°C.

MAKES 1 GOOD-SIZED LOAF

FOR THE CAKE

¾ cup/125 g all-purpose flour (I use unbleached)

¾ cup/125 g whole wheat or spelt flour

generous ½ cup/125 g light brown sugar

1 cup/150 g little seeds

a good pinch of sea salt

1 teaspoon baking powder

3 medium ripe bananas, peeled

grated zest and juice of 1 unwaxed lemon

2 tablespoons olive oil

2 tablespoons all-natural or unsweetened soy yogurt or coconut yogurt

2 organic or free-range eggs, beaten (or see note on chia, page 42)

FOR THE LEMON SESAME GLAZE

1 tablespoon tahini

3 tablespoons unrefined confectioners' sugar or creamed honey

juice of 1 lemon

⁘ CONTINUED

Butter and flour a nonstick 8 by 4-inch/450 g loaf pan (if your loaf pan is not nonstick, line it with baking paper too).

Put all the dry ingredients into a mixing bowl—the flours, sugar, seeds, salt, and baking powder—and mix well.

In another bowl, mash the bananas with a fork (I like to keep them quite chunky), then add the lemon juice and zest, olive oil, yogurt, and eggs, and mix well.

Mix the wet ingredients into the bowl of dry ingredients, taking care not to overmix—just do enough to make sure it is all combined. Spoon into the loaf pan and bake for 40 to 45 minutes, until a skewer comes out clean.

While your loaf is baking, make the lemon glaze. Beat the tahini and onfectioners' sugar in a bowl until smooth, squeeze in the lemon juice, and mix well.

Take your loaf out of the oven and leave it in the pan until it is cool enough to move to a cooling rack. While the loaf is still warm, place a large plate under the rack, then skewer the cake all over, pour over the glaze and leave it to sink in.

This is delicious on its own, thickly sliced, with a cup of coffee, but sometimes I like to spread the slices with a thick layer of almond or peanut butter.

Super raw brownies

These brownies taste like you shouldn't be eating them—chewy, caramel squares of dense chocolatey goodness. But when you look a little closer, you realize that everything in them is insanely good for you. It's a win-win and then win again. They are flavored with sea salt and the deep caramelly taste of medjool dates, and if I had to pack my desert island lunchbox, these would be in it.

An added bonus is that these brownies are completely raw (if you use raw honey and cocoa, that is). What's the big deal with raw food? I hear you say. Raw foods are foods that have not been heated to above 108°F/42°C. Most foods in their natural state contain everything we need to digest them. When we heat foods, we destroy some of their natural digestive enzymes, making them harder to digest, which is why we often feel lethargic after eating. As raw foods are "live," they keep your energy levels high. So to me, including a bit of raw food in my day is a great thing to do, and what better way to start than with a brownie?

Put the almonds into a food processor and grind until you have a coarse powder. Add the dates, honey, cocoa, and salt and blend again for about a minute until it comes together into a dough-like ball. Transfer the brownie mixture into a bowl, add the chopped pecans, and knead to bring them into the dough.

Line an 8-inch/20 cm square baking pan with parchment paper and turn the mixture into it, pressing it down with your fingers until you have an even layer. Cover with plastic wrap and place in the fridge to chill for 15 minutes before cutting up. I cut these into about 20 small squares as they are good and rich, but cut them bigger if you are planning on serving them as a dessert. Top with a dusting of cocoa. These will keep for up to a week—if it's hot outside, it's best to keep them in the fridge.

**MAKES ABOUT
20 MINI BROWNIES**

⅔ cup/100 g almonds, skin on

9 ounces/250 g medjool dates, pitted (about 12)

2 tablespoons creamed honey (raw honey if you can get it)

3 ounces/75 g cocoa powder (the raw stuff is best), plus extra for dusting

½ teaspoon salt

2 ounces/50 g pecans, chopped

Salted caramel crack brownies

Find me someone who doesn't like these, and I'll deliver you a batch myself. These are deeply chocolatey brownies with a burst of melting salted caramel. I make a super simple and speedy caramel that cools quickly and gets chopped up and sunk into the top of the brownie mixture. The caramel melts into the brownie as it cooks and leaves little pools of chewy warm fudgy caramel throughout the perfectly crusted brownies. Sounds delicious . . . and I can assure you they are. The first time I made these, I had to make a second batch the same afternoon, as they were eaten in a flash (not all by me). We all have a vice. These are mine.

I have tried to keep these a little lighter here by using rye flour (see note on page 290) and suggesting coconut oil as an alternative to butter—it will give a slight coconut taste, which I like. I use unrefined sugar, either light brown for a dense super-fudgy effect, or coconut sugar (see page 275), which works too, though not for the caramel. But let's not pretend: these are the treat they should be.

....

First make the caramel. Lay a piece of parchment paper over a shallow tray and rub the upper surface of the paper with oil. Put the sugar into a pan and place over medium heat. Watch it carefully, letting it heat and melt until almost all the sugar grains have gone. Then quickly pull the pan off the heat, add your butter or coconut oil, and beat with the pan off the heat for a minute or so. Add the salt and coconut milk and beat again. Place back on the heat for 2 to 3 minutes and beat vigorously until the mixture has darkened and thickened and any sugary lumps have gone. Pour onto the greased paper and place in the freezer to harden for 30 minutes.

Preheat your oven to 350°F/180°C

**MAKES 12
GOOD-SIZED BROWNIES**

FOR THE SALTED CARAMEL

3½ tablespoons/50 g unsalted butter or coconut oil, plus a little for greasing

½ cup/100 g unrefined superfine sugar

a hearty pinch of flaky sea salt

3 tablespoons milk (I use coconut or almond)

FOR THE BROWNIES

5 ounces/150 g dark chocolate (70 percent)

10 tablespoons/150 g unsalted butter or coconut oil

1¼ cup/250 g unrefined superfine sugar or light muscovado sugar

3 organic or free-range eggs

1 teaspoon vanilla extract or the seeds from 1 vanilla pod

⅔ cup/100 g rye flour or light spelt or all-purpose flour

CONTINUED

Butter and line a small brownie pan with parchment paper (mine is 8 by 8-inches/20 by 20 cm, but anything around that will do).

While the caramel is chilling, make your brownie mix. Place a heatproof bowl over a pan of gently simmering water, making sure the bowl doesn't touch the water. Add the chocolate and the butter or coconut oil and let them melt, stirring from time to time. Once melted, take the bowl off the heat and stir in the sugar, followed by the eggs (one by one) and finally the vanilla and the flour.

Once your caramel has hardened, take it out of the freezer. Chop a third of it into small pieces and stir into the brownie mix. Chop the rest into chunky ⅜-inch/1 cm pieces.

Pour the brownie mix into the lined pan and scatter over the larger chunks of salted caramel. Bake for 25 minutes, until just cooked—a crust will have formed on top and the caramel will have melted into deep amber pools. Let cool for at least 20 minutes before cutting. I know this will be hard to do, but the caramel will be very hot.

These will keep for 4 days in an airtight container. I dare you to make them last an afternoon.

Lady Grey fig rolls

Lady Grey tea is my favorite tea—I drink a cup a day. The stylish sister of the Earl, she has his floral character pepped up with a little backnote of lemon. Earl Grey or your own favorite tea would work well here too.

We all know figs are good for you, but I didn't realize just how good. They are a great source of calcium, which is really good news for those of us reducing the amount of dairy in our diet. They are also high in fiber, which helps control blood sugar and lowers cholesterol. And in Chinese medicine they are valued for their detoxifying properties. Look for sulfite-free dried figs if you can.

MAKES 14

1¼ cup/125 g oats

¼ cup/50 g brown sugar or coconut sugar (see page 275)

½ teaspoon baking powder

a pinch of sea salt

1 teaspoon ground cinnamon

1 tablespoon maple syrup

1 organic or free-range egg, (or see note on chia, page 42)

5 tablespoons/70 g butter or coconut oil

⅔ cup/150 ml super-strong Lady Grey tea (I used 4 bags)

7 ounces/200 g dried figs, stems removed, roughly chopped

seeds from 1 vanilla pod, plus the pod

grated zest and juice of ½ an unwaxed orange

grated zest and juice of ½ an unwaxed lemon

Put the oats into a food processor and grind until you have a roughly mixed flour. Add the sugar, baking powder, salt, and cinnamon and mix well. Now add the maple syrup, the egg, and the butter or coconut oil. Pulse until the dough forms a ball, then wrap it in parchment paper and place in the fridge to chill a little.

Brew the tea for at least 20 minutes, then discard the tea bags and pour the tea into a pan with the chopped figs, vanilla seeds and pod, and the citrus zest and juice. Place over low heat and simmer until the figs are soft and all the liquid has gone. Remove the vanilla pod and blend the mixture in a food processor until you have fig jam.

Preheat your oven to 400°F/200°C.

Place the dough between two sheets of parchment paper and roll it out into a long rectangle (it should be about 12 by 6-inches/30 by 15 cm once you are done). Spoon the jammy figs down the middle, then fold the sides over to encase the filling. Cut into 14 little rolls, place them on a baking sheet, and bake for 15 to 20 minutes, or until crisp and golden. Serve with a big cup of Lady Grey.

Pistachio and elderflower cordial cake

I live in Hackney, where it can be a little rough around the edges, but I like it that way. Once a year the elderflowers spring up all over Hackney in parks and marshes, and no one seems to even notice they are there. So I head out with my blue stepladder to pick as many of the flowers as I can.

I make cordial, gallons of it (see page 325 for my recipe), and I always make this cake. Instead of flour, I use pistachios and polenta, which gives the cake a dense baklava feeling. You really need a food processor to grind the pistachios up, so if you don't have one, use almond flour instead.

One friend said she was going to name her firstborn after this cake. I am not sure there could be higher praise.

MAKES 1 DEEP 8-INCH CAKE

FOR THE CAKE

9 tablespoons/125 g butter, at room temperature

½ cup/125 g Greek yogurt

1¼ cup/250 g unrefined light brown sugar or coconut sugar (see page 275)

2 cups/250 g pistachio nuts

1¼ cup/200 g polenta

1 teaspoon baking powder

grated zest and juice of 1 unwaxed lemon

3 organic or free-range eggs

⅔ cup/150 ml elderflower cordial

FOR THE ELDERFLOWER ICING

4 ounces/100 g thick Greek yogurt or cream cheese

4 tablespoons unrefined confectioners' sugar or creamed honey

1 tablespoon elderflower cordial

a handful of pistachio nuts, crushed

Preheat your oven to 400°F/200°C. Grease and line the bottom of an 8-inch/20 cm springform cake tin.

Put the butter, yogurt, and sugar into a bowl and cream together until light and fluffy.

Now grind the pistachios to dust in a food processor—don't grind them too much, though, or they will turn to butter. Add the ground pistachios, polenta, baking powder, and lemon zest and juice to the butter mixture and mix well. Then crack in the eggs and mix in, one by one.

Pour into the cake pan and bake for 45 to 50 minutes until a skewer comes out clean. Remove from the oven and let cool in the pan. Make a few holes in the warm cake with a skewer, then gently pour the elderflower cordial slowly over the cake, allowing it time to seep in. Leave the cake in the pan until cool enough to transfer to a cooling rack.

For the icing, mix the yogurt, sugar or honey, and elderflower cordial until smooth. Spread over the cooled cake and sprinkle with the pistachios.

Butterscotch chocolate chip blondies

These lie somewhere between a chocolate chip cookie and a brownie—a dense caramelly sugar-crusted blondie, studded with melting pools of chocolate. They take less than 5 minutes to get into the oven and about 30 seconds to eat.

If you can get it, butterscotch chocolate works well here. It will have a bit of extra sugar in it, though, and if you'd rather something less sweet, 70 percent cacao chocolate will do.

I often make a dairy-free version, using soy or coconut yogurt and coconut oil—I like the lightness you get without dairy. All-natural plain yogurt works too.

....

Preheat the oven to 375°F/190°C.

Grease a square brownie pan, line with parchment paper, and set aside.

Put the butter or coconut oil and sugar into a large bowl and mix well with an electric mixer or by hand. Add the vanilla seeds and the yogurt and beat well until everything is combined. Add the honey or agave syrup and beat this in too.

Put the flour, baking powder, and salt into a mixing bowl and mix well.

Add the dry ingredients to the wet ingredients and mix thoroughly until well combined. Bit by bit, add the milk, and then fold in the chopped chocolate.

Pour the batter into the brownie pan and spread with a spoon or spatula. Bake for 35 to 40 minutes, until the top is firm and brown.

Allow to cool completely, then cut into little squares. The yogurt in these means they will stay gooey and fresh for at least a week.

MAKES 12 BLONDIES

7 tablespoons/100 g coconut oil or butter, at room temperature

½ cup/100 g light brown sugar

seeds from 1 vanilla pod

4 ounces/100 g soy or all-natural coconut yogurt

2 tablespoons honey or agave syrup

1½ cups/250 g all-purpose flour

2 teaspoons baking powder

a large pinch of sea salt

6 tablespoons/90 ml milk (cow's, coconut, almond, or soy)

5 ounces/150 g dark chocolate or butterscotch chocolate, roughly chopped

Coconut oatmeal cookies

I like coconut macaroons. I like chewy oatmeal and raisin cookies. I like Anzac cookies. These cookies are my way of having all three at once. Some may call it greed; I call it clever cooking.

These are chewy in the best sense and can be whipped up in a flash. They are low on sugar levels too, so they are a pretty healthy snack, and if you want you could swap the brown sugar for coconut sugar for an even healthier treat.

I make these both as big hearty cookies and as daintier little bites depending on my mood—I have given timings and instructions for both. If you don't have coconut oil, melted butter will work here in its place.

....

Preheat your oven to 400°F/200°C.

Line two baking trays with parchment paper.

Weigh out all the dry ingredients into a bowl—flour, oats, coconut, raisins, sugar, and baking soda.

Next, melt the coconut oil in a small pan, allow to cool a little, then add the maple syrup. Stir the warm mixture into the bowl of dry ingredients and mix well—the dough will look a bit crumbly but it will come together when you squeeze it.

Using a spoon and your hands, form the dough into balls. For larger cookies, make them just over tablespoon size; for smaller ones, make them a generous teaspoon size. Place them on the prepared baking trays, leaving a little space for them to spread.

Bake the bigger cookies for 12 minutes and the smaller ones for 8 to 10 minutes, until lightly golden and even in color. Allow to cool for about 5 minutes on the trays before transferring them to a cooling rack to cool completely.

MAKES ABOUT 14 BIG OR 24 LITTLE COOKIES

¾ cup/125 g light spelt flour or coconut flour

½ cup/50 g oats

½ cup/50 g unsweetened coconut flakes or dried coconut

½ cup/100 g raisins

⅓ cup/75 g unrefined soft brown sugar

¼ teaspoon baking soda

9 tablespoons/125 g coconut oil

3 tablespoons maple syrup

Cardamom lemon glaze cake

Lemon glaze cake is without question my favorite. I love its upfront lemon zing. This is my version: half afternoon tea at your grandmother's and half mint tea at the café.

I use almond flour here, which keeps the cake moist and lovely and also has more to offer nutritionally than all-purpose flour. Instead of loading this cake with butter and sugar, I use yogurt in place of butter—it means the cake doesn't dry out and is a bit lighter too. Honey sweetens it instead of sugar. Limes can be used instead of lemons—just use 1½ limes to each lemon in the recipe.

Honey is a completely natural sugar. I love the variations of flavor you get with honey and the way you can taste the flowers from which the bees have taken the pollen. Sure, it's still a sugar, but it's not been messed around with in the way refined sugar has. I think orange blossom honey works really well here if you can get it. In summer I mix a teaspoon of local Hackney honey into my morning hot water—a little honey from your local area is supposed to help with allergies like hay fever.

....

Preheat your oven to 350°F/180°C.

Put the eggs into a mixing bowl and whisk until they have fluffed up a bit. Fold in the yogurt, honey, and olive oil, and then grate in the zest of both lemons.

Now put all your dry ingredients into another bowl and mix well. Gently beat this dry mixture into the yogurt mix.

Grease an 8-inch/20 cm springform cake pan with olive oil, then line the bottom with parchment paper. Pour the cake mixture into the pan and level

MAKES A DEEP 8-INCH CAKE

FOR THE CAKE

3 organic or free-range eggs (or see note on chia, page 42)

4 ounces/100 g Greek yogurt or coconut yogurt

⅔ cup/150 ml runny honey

⅔ cup/150 ml light olive oil, plus extra for greasing

2 unwaxed lemons

2 cups/200 g almond flour

1¼ cups/200 g light spelt flour

1 teaspoon baking powder

1 tablespoon poppy seeds

seeds from 4 cardamom pods, crushed to a powder in a mortar and pestle

FOR THE GLAZE

1 unwaxed lemon

6 tablespoons plus 2 teaspoons/100 ml honey

seeds from 8 cardamom pods, crushed to a powder in a mortar and pestle

CONTINUED

out the top with the back of a spoon. Bake in the oven for 30 minutes, until golden on top. Test with a skewer—if it comes out clean, it's ready.

Meanwhile, make the glaze. Peel the zest from the lemon with a vegetable peeler. Squeeze the juice into a pan and add the zest and the honey. Add the ground cardamom seeds. Place over medium heat and simmer for 15 to 20 minutes until the syrup has slightly thickened and the zest has candied. You'll know that it has candied when the strips have become shiny and translucent and have curled up a little at the edges.

Remove the cake from the oven and let cool until you can safely take it out of the pan. Transfer to a cooling rack and place a large plate underneath to catch any drips. While the cake is still warm, skewer it all over and slowly pour the warm syrup all over the cake, making sure you go right to the edges.

Sometimes I serve this with a spoonful of yogurt.

Carrot and black pepper soda bread

My friend Serinde whips this up in no time after work—she is one of the most active people I know, and I am convinced this is what keeps her going. Carrot in bread didn't initially have my attention, but this really works.

Pumpkin seeds and carrots are the staple year-round additions, but in spring, I gently heat the yogurt and water with a handful of wild garlic, blend it together, and throw that in instead. In autumn, it's a couple of grated beets and caraway seeds. Soda bread is such an easy step into bread, and this recipe is great for first-time bread makers or to make with kids.

....

Preheat your oven to 425°F/220°F.

Put the flours, pumpkin seeds, salt, baking soda, and pepper into a big mixing bowl and mix well. In a bowl, stir the yogurt into $\frac{7}{8}$ cup/200 ml of cold water.

Add the carrots to the dry mix and, bit by bit, stir in the yogurt. Mix everything well with a fork until combined, then use your hands to bring it into a rough ball.

Grease a heavy baking tray with olive oil—or better still, if you have one, use a baking stone. Place your round of dough on the baking tray or stone and dust with a little more flour.

Make a few slashes in the top of the bread with a knife and bake in the hot oven for 40 minutes, until golden and risen.

Remove from the oven and tap the bottom of the loaf. If you get a hollow sound, it's perfect, so place it on a wire rack to cool. This is delicious warm with butter or spread with coconut oil.

MAKES 1 GOOD LOAF

1 cup plus 2 tablespoons/175 g strong bread flour

1 cup plus 2 tablespoons/175 g whole wheat or spelt flour

⅓ cup/50 g pumpkin seeds

1 teaspoon sea salt

1 teaspoon baking soda

a good grinding of coarse black pepper

⅞ cup/200 ml plain yogurt of your choice

2 carrots, peeled and grated

olive oil

Coconut vanilla loaf

This cake celebrates one of my favorite ingredients of all, the coconut. In fact almost the whole cake can be made from coconut products if you can get them—if not, I've given alternatives. Half cake, half bread, this is great for toasting when it's a few days old.

The coconut milk, coconut sugar, and coconut oil make this true coconut bread, backed up by vanilla sweetness and rounding out with almond. I like to make a loaf of this on Sunday and toast it for breakfast throughout the week. It's good spread with almond butter and a squeeze of lime or with lime or lemon marmalade.

A lot of people veer away from coconut oil and milk because they think the coconut is high in bad fats. It does contain some fat, but our bodies are able to break it down much more easily than the fat from other plant and animal sources. Our bodies need some fat, and coconuts and their milk are one of the best ways to get it.

MAKES 1 GOOD-SIZED LOAF

2 organic or free-range eggs
(or see note on chia, page 42)

⅞ cup/200 ml milk of your choice
(I use coconut, see note on page 39)

seeds from 1 vanilla pod

1 cup/150 g light spelt flour

scant 1 cup/200 g coconut sugar
(see page 275) or light brown sugar

½ teaspoon baking powder

⅔ cup/50 g dried coconut

⅔ cup/50 g almond flour

3½ tablespoons/50 g coconut oil or
butter, melted and cooled

Preheat your oven to 350°F/180°C. Butter an 8½ by 3-inch/22 by 8 cm loaf pan. Take a sheet of parchment paper just as long as the pan and lay it along the bottom of the pan and over the side. The ends of the pan will remain unlined but this is okay; you just want the paper there to help pull out the bread.

Whisk together the eggs, milk, and vanilla seeds in a bowl.

Put the flour, sugar, baking powder, dried coconut, and almond flour into a bowl and make a well in the center. Gradually stir in the egg mixture, then the melted coconut oil or butter, and mix until smooth.

Pour the mixture into the pan and bake for about 50 minutes, until a skewer inserted in the center comes out clean. Cool in the pan for a few minutes and then turn onto a rack and let cool.

Never superseeded loaf

Taking a loaf of your very own out of the oven is a pretty special moment. I've included this recipe because it's a damn good loaf of bread but also because, if you are anything like me, some days you just need some instant gratification.

This is my go-to bread recipe. I use half white bread flour and half brown bread flour, but in the United States, you'll probably have to use regular bread flour. This is deeply seeded, wholly fulfilling, and really, really easy. I've learned a huge amount about bread over the last couple of years working with my friend Tom Herbert. What Tom doesn't know about bread is not worth knowing, and some of his expertise has definitely rubbed off.

Remember this golden rule for making bread: don't be scared of wet dough. As my friend Tom would say, "The wetter the better." Keep kneading and try to flour your hands and the surface as little as possible. Have faith—it will all come together.

....

Measure out 1½ cups/350 ml of tepid water (you should be able to stick a finger in it without it feeling too hot). As a rule, I find weighing is more accurate than using a measuring cup. Now stir the yeast and honey or syrup into the water.

Next, put the flours, oats, seeds, and salt into a big mixing bowl, mix well, and stir in the water using a fork until you have a big pasty mess. Cover the bowl with a clean kitchen towel and leave for a few minutes to allow the yeast to start working.

After a couple of minutes, take the dough out of the bowl and turn it out onto a clean surface. The dough will be wet and messy, which is how it

MAKES 1 DECENT-SIZED LOAF

½ teaspoon dry yeast

1 tablespoon honey or agave syrup

1¼ cup/200 g white bread flour

½ cup/50 g oats

2 tablespoons/25 g golden flaxseeds

2 tablespoons/25 g poppy seeds

1 teaspoon sea salt

CONTINUED

should be—you can add the tiniest bit of flour from time to time as you go, but don't be tempted to add too much.

Knead until the dough becomes smooth, then put it back into the bowl, cover with the kitchen towel again, and put it in a warmish place, such as near a radiator (I put mine beside the oven, turned to a very low temperature) for an hour to an hour and a half. By the time you come back, it should have doubled in size. The length of time this takes will depend on the humidity and the type of flour you use.

Take it out of the bowl, knead for 30 seconds and then shape the dough into a flat oval and put it on an oiled baking tray. Cover with the towel again and let rise once more for 40 minutes or so.

Preheat your oven to 475°F/240°C.

After 40 minutes, slash the top with a knife and dust with a little whole wheat flour. Half fill another deep baking tray with boiling water and place on the bottom of your oven. This will create steam as the loaf bakes and help give your bread a lovely crust and texture.

Now bake the loaf in the oven for 30 to 35 minutes, until golden all over. To check if your bread is ready, lift it up and tap on the bottom. If it sounds hollow, like a drum, it's good to go. Cool on a rack so the bottom keeps its lovely crust.

Seeded Yorkshire pudding

One of the things we British do best is a Sunday dinner. My Sunday dinners have and always will focus around one thing—the Yorkshire pudding. I am from a really big family—my dad is number nine of twelve children, and I have thirty cousins, a brother, and a sister. So Sunday dinners at my grandmother's were quite something. Dinner was in shifts, and as the littlest, we always got to go first, which filled my heart with joy because it was a guarantee of one of my mother's Yorkshires (which I am still sure are the best I've ever had).

So here, aged six, the obsession started. I have tried every Yorkshire recipe that's going. I even ventured across the pond and dabbled in the world of popovers (which, by the way, is a great name). Popovers are the American Yorkshires made from egg whites whisked to oblivion to give a lighter and somewhat crisper result. But I like my Yorkshires to have a bit of heft— crispy and light on the outside, doughy chewiness on the inside. I have added some toasted seeds here for texture and flavor, which lifts this from an add-on to the main event.

There are five commandments of Yorkshire puddings: (1) Don't be scared of heat: preheat your oven to maximum; heat is your friend here. (2) Try to rest your batter for at least 15 minutes. It's key. (3) Be sure to preheat your oil in the oven until smoking hot. (4) Make sure you heat the muffin pan on the stove top while pouring in your batter. (5) Don't open the door until the cooking time is up or the Yorkshires will deflate.

....

First preheat your oven to as hot as it will go. Next, mix the flour, toasted seeds, salt, and pepper in a bowl. Pour your milk–water mix into a cup.

Crack the eggs into the bowl of flour, pour in a little of the milk mixture, and beat well until you have gotten rid of most of the lumps. Continue

MAKES 12 TOWERING YORKSHIRE PUDDINGS

1¼ cup/200 g unbleached all-purpose flour

2 tablespoons toasted poppy seeds

2 tablespoons toasted sesame seeds

1 teaspoon sea salt

1 good grinding of black pepper

1 cup/250 ml milk, topped up to 1¼ cup/300 ml with water

4 organic or free-range eggs

12 teaspoons rapeseed oil or peanut oil

CONTINUED

to beat in the rest of the milk mixture bit by bit until you have a smooth batter about the consistency of heavy cream. Now let your batter rest for at least 15 minutes.

Once your batter is ready, pour it into a large pitcher with a spout. Put about 1 teaspoon of oil into each of the cups in a 12-cup muffin pan and pop it into the oven for a couple of minutes, until the fat is smoking.

Now turn two of the burners on your stove top to medium and put the pitcher of batter next to the stove. Very carefully but quickly, take the hot muffin pan out of the oven and shut the door. Put the muffin pan on the heat and quickly but carefully pour the batter into each cup until it is about ¼ inch/2 cm from the top.

Put the pan back into the oven, shut the door, and set the timer for 12 minutes. Do not be tempted to open the door too soon – they WILL fall and fail. Check through the oven glass at 12 minutes, and if they are risen like little towers and nicely golden, take them out. If not, leave them in without opening the oven for another few minutes, keeping an eye on them.

I like to eat these with a spoonful of horseradish and some roasted beets for a simple dinner—or for the full works, see the roast dinner ideas on page 228.

To make Yorkshires the main event
- Use the batter to make one large Yorkshire pudding.
- Add a tablespoon of horseradish in the batter and pieces of cooked beets.
- Add little bits of roasted squash and a few sage leaves.
- Crumble 3½ ounces/100 g Lancashire or white cheddar cheese into the batter and add some some red onions and a little chopped rosemary.
- Make sure any cooked extras are hot when you add them, or your Yorkshires won't rise properly.

things to drink

These are drinks to which it's worth raising your glass. All too often drinks are forgotten about, just bought in a bottle, and often packed with sugar, with little imagination. To me, drinks offer all sorts of opportunities to add color, flavor, and vibrancy— even if it's just dropping a few slices of lemon, lime, and cucumber into a pitcher of tap water, or blending up an ice-cold watermelon with a squeeze of honey and lime and pouring it over sparkling water for a homemade *agua fresca*. Whether gently spiking afternoon coffee with heady cardamom or making hot chocolate that makes your insides smile, drinks deserve a little more attention and love. Here is my take on the hot, the cold, the healthy, the boozy, and the endless summer of lemonades.

endless lemonades · elderflower cordial · white peach cordial · strawberry sherbet rehydrator · supernova elderflower champagne · rosado de verano · blood orange and agave margaritas · four o'clock hot chocolate · cardamom and honey turkish coffee

Endless lemonades

We'd all like an endless summer. I make these throughout summer and into autumn, trying to stretch out the season as long as I can.

I keep a bottle in the fridge for sipping. When I am in Los Angeles, I go to a lemonade bar that has at least ten different homemade flavors, and I am like a kid in a candy store.

It's so easy to make lemonade, and using agave syrup makes it even easier as there is no need to make a syrup. If you can't get agave syrup, ½ cup/125 g of sugar bubbled until dissolved in ½ cup/125 ml of hot water will do—just pull back on the added water a little at the end.

When I have a party I like to make a few flavors and line up the candy-colored lemonades in glass bottles for people to pick and choose. They make a really good base for a great cocktail—just add some booze, fruit, and a couple of sprigs of mint or basil.

....

Slice 1 of your lemons and put it into a big pan with the juice of the other 5 (about ⅞ cup/125 ml of juice). Pour in the agave syrup and scant ½ cup/ 100 ml of water and bring to a boil. Mix well, then turn off the heat and allow to cool completely. Add the water.

Pour over ice and more lemon slices.

Watermelon
Instead of ice-cold water, add 1 pound/500 g of blended seeded watermelon and 2 cups/500 ml of cold water.

EACH RECIPE MAKES ABOUT 1 QUART/1 L

6 unwaxed lemons
½ cup/125 ml agave syrup
1 quart/1 L ice-cold water (plain or sparkling)

 CONTINUED

Lemongrass and chile

· Put 2 sticks of lemongrass and a red chile into the agave syrup. Leave to infuse as it cools and then discard the lemongrass and chile. Add the ice-cold water in the same way—once the agave cools.

Blackberry and lime

· Use unwaxed limes instead of lemons—you may need a few more limes to make up the same amount of juice. Instead of the quart of ice-cold water, use 9 ounces/250 g of blackberries blended with 3¼ cups/750 ml of water.

Blueberry and mint

· Instead of the 1 quart/1 L of ice-cold water, add 9 ounces/250 g of blueberries blended with a few sprigs of fresh mint and 3¼ cups/750 ml of water.

Honey and lavender

· Use honey in place of agave syrup. Add a few heads of culinary lavender to the syrup as it infuses, making sure you strain them out before adding 1 quart/1 L of ice-cold water.

Goji and ginger

· Soak 4 tablespoons of goji berries in water for an hour. Blend them with scant ½ cup/100 ml of water and a grated thumb-size piece of fresh ginger, and add this to the lemonade with 1 quart/1 L of ice-cold water.

Rooibos iced tea

· Add 2 bags of rooibos tea to the syrup and allow to infuse as it cools. Discard before adding 1 quart/1 L of ice-cold water.

Elderflower cordial

Whoever first immersed these floaty little blooms in a hot bath of sugary water was inspired.

Make a big batch, and it'll last you all year. Try freezing half cordial and half water in ice-cube trays and plonking them into a gin and tonic. You can even add a few of the blooms, if you have any left over, for a really pretty drink.

Gently shake the elderflowers to get rid of any lingering little creatures.

Put the sugar into a large pan with 1½ quarts/1½ L of boiling water and bring to a boil. Simmer for a couple of minutes until all the sugar has dissolved and then take off the heat.

Cut the lemons into quarters and place in a sterilized large bowl or bucket with the elderflowers. Pour over the warm syrup, cover with a clean kitchen towel, and let steep somewhere cool and dark for 24 hours.

The next day, strain your cordial using a sieve lined with muslin. Pour into sterilized bottles (see page 334), screw the lids on tightly, and store in a cool place until ready to serve.

This will keep in a cool place for up to a year.

MAKES ABOUT 2 QUARTS/2 L

50 heads of elderflowers

3⅓ pounds/1½ kg unrefined superfine sugar

2 unwaxed lemons

White peach cordial

Win friends: make bellinis all year round—well, almost.

I use white peaches if I can get them as I love the pale peachy color they give, but yellow peaches will work too. Just make sure they are ripe and sweet.

....

Place the pitted peaches into a blender, skin and all, and blend in batches until you have puréed them all.

Put the purée into a pan with the sugar, lemon juice, and vanilla and bring to a simmer. Simmer over low heat for 20 minutes, until custardy and thick, then pour into sterilized bottles or jars (see page 334), screw on the tops, and keep in a cool dry place for up to a month, until your next dose of merriment.

MAKES ABOUT 1 QUART/1 L

2¼ pounds/1 kg white peaches, halved and destoned

1¼ cup/250 g unrefined superfine sugar

juice of 1 lemon

seeds from 2 vanilla pods

Strawberry sherbet rehydrator

This is my version of a rehydration drink. Salt, natural sweetness, and lemon hit all the spots my body needs after a trip to the gym or a surf in the Welsh seas.

The salt and honey do the job of rehydrating the lemon, and the strawberries bring it together into an ice-cold sherbety glassful.

In the winter I make this without the strawberries—it won't be as sherbety but it's still really good, and this way there is no need for a blender—I just use a big pitcher.

....

First boil ¼ cup/50 ml of water. Get the pitcher from your blender, add the honey, lemon juice, salt, and the boiling water and then blend carefully for 30 seconds—it will be very hot.

Now add the strawberries and blend, then add 2 cups plus 2 tablespoons/500 ml of ice-cold water and blend again.

Pour over ice and drink.

MAKES 2 BIG GLASSES (DOUBLE THE RECIPE FOR A PITCHER)

2 heaping tablespoons best honey

juice of 2 to 3 lemons

a good pinch of sea salt

a handful of ripe strawberries, washed and hulled

Supernova elderflower champagne

The natural yeast in elderflowers, if left to its own devices, will bubble and fizz into elderflower champagne in a couple of weeks. Homemade champagne with an elderflower kick, for the cost of a bag of sugar and a couple of lemons—what could be better?

The amount of yeast in your elderflowers will depend on when in the short season they are picked and if the sun has been shining, so to help, I add a little pinch of store-bought dry yeast.

Sturdy glass bottles with a hinge top or good thick plastic screwtop bottles are a must—the fizz produces CO_2, so good strong bottles will stop the corks from popping early. For a note on how to sterilize your bottles and equipment, see page 334.

Gently shake the elderflower heads to get rid of any bits or bugs, and place in a bucket. Use a speed-peeler to peel strips of zest off your lemons and put them into your bucket with the lemon juice. Add the sugar and vinegar. Add 1 gallon/4 L of hot water, stir to dissolve the sugar, then add 1 gallon/ 4 L of cold water.

Cover the mixture with a cloth and leave to ferment for 24 hours in a warm place. After 24 hours, check to see if the fermentation process has started. There will be some bubbles on the top of the mixture—if it hasn't started bubbling yet, add a tiny pinch of yeast and, either way, leave the mixture for another 48 hours again, covered with the cloth.

Once your mixture has had its final 48 hours, strain it through a sieve lined with muslin into a squeaky clean bottle. Then pour into sterilized bottles and fix the lids on tightly so that none of the little bubbles can escape. Leave in a cool place for at least 2 weeks before sampling. It'll be best if you can wait at least a month for the flavor to develop. The champagne should keep like this for as long as a year. Serve chilled, in tall champagne flutes.

MAKES ABOUT 2 GALLONS/8 L

50 elderflower heads

6 unwaxed lemons

2½ pounds/1.1 kg unrefined superfine sugar

2 tablespoons white wine vinegar

a pinch of dry yeast

YOU WILL ALSO NEED

a large, very clean bucket or bowl for fermenting

a large piece of muslin or a clean thin kitchen towel

sterilized bottles to hold 2 gallons/ 8 L of champagne

Rosado de verano

I've spent many summers sipping this super summery drink on grassy roadsides in Barcelona. The Spanish call this super relaxed streetside drinking *botellón*—everyone brings a bottle, glasses, and some ice, and it's as simple as that.

This is often made with red wine, which works just as well, and store-bought lemonade, and I have even seen this mixed up with cola. This dusky rose version is my take on the perfect summertime drink. See page 321 for picture.

MAKES 1½ QUARTS/1½ L

1 bottle of decent rosé (nothing too expensive), cold

3¼ cups/750 ml sparkling water

⅔ cup/150 ml agave syrup

1 unwaxed lemon, sliced

1 unwaxed lime, sliced

Put everything into a pitcher with lots of ice and give it a good stir. Then drink it outside in the sunshine or on a warm summer evening.

Blood orange and agave margaritas

This could be my favorite drink of all time—bright pink, zippy with lime, and finishing off with a sweet agave kick. I like it over ice, but for a slushy frozen version, blend it with a couple of handfuls of ice in your blender.

Regular oranges will work if blood oranges aren't around. This is great for parties, as it can all be mixed in advance and poured over ice as needed—just double or triple the recipe as you need to. Tacky colorful cocktail umbrellas are encouraged.

MAKES A DECENT JUG, TO SERVE 4

2 cups/500 ml blood orange juice (about 5 blood oranges)

juice of 2 limes

2 tablespoons agave syrup

scant ½ cup/100 ml triple sec or cointreau

⅔ cup/150 ml good tequila

1 unwaxed lime, sliced

Put the blood orange and lime juices into a pitcher, then add the agave syrup and the booze, and mix.

Fill four glasses with lots of ice and pour the margaritas over the ice. Finish with a slice of lime.

Four o'clock hot chocolate

This is what kept me going through one of the coldest winters I can remember. It is a hot chocolate that calms, enlivens, and uplifts, all in one mug. It brims with deliciousness, is packed full of goodness, and is guaranteed to hit the sweet spot and bring back your joy when the four o'clock lull hits.

SERVES 2

2 cups/500 ml milk of your choice (I use almond milk)

1 tablespoon chamomile flowers or a chamomile teabag

2 tablespoons cocoa (raw cocoa is best)

optional: 1 teaspoon of maca powder (see page 25)

sea salt

a good pinch of ground cinnamon

2 tablespoons honey

Put the milk into a pan with the chamomile flowers or teabag and heat gently (if you are using nut milk, be careful not to heat it too much; just gently warm it). Once warmed, turn off the heat and allow it to sit and steep for a few minutes.

Remove the flowers or teabag and whisk in the cocoa, maca, sea salt, and cinnamon.

Sweeten with the honey, pour into cups, and enjoy.

Cardamom and honey Turkish coffee

I love cardamom and I love coffee, so this is heaven. This is a coffee for the afternoon and it deserves a slice of cake—the pistachio and elderflower cordial cake (page 304) is especially good.

This is my cheat's version. Real Turkish coffee is boiled in a little contraption called an *ibrik*, and the coffee is ground so fine that it settles on the bottom of the cup. I make this version using a French press.

MAKES COFFEE FOR 2

2 heaping tablespoons decent ground coffee

6 cardamom pods, bashed

honey or unrefined brown sugar, to sweeten

Put the coffee and cardamom pods into a French press and cover with 1⅔ cups/400 ml of boiling water. Let sit for 3 minutes, stirring a few times as it sits, then plunge and pour into cups, sweetening with honey or brown sugar as needed.

Serve in little cups, with a slice of pistachio and elderflower cordial cake.

jam, chutney, stock, and other useful stuff

Goodness comes in jars and bottles, especially ones with handwritten labels. I will happily buy most of the things in this chapter from the store. But sometimes, when I have a day with a little more time or it's raining and I don't feel like going outside, I like making things that need canning. Preserving the summer's rosy-cheeked apricots to pile onto hot buttered toast on a gray January day is so satisfying. These recipes take a little attention to detail and a bit of patience, but a line of sparkling jars of crimson summer strawberry jam will be worth the hard work, tenfold.

first-sign-of-summer jam · rosy-cheeked apricot jam · spiced nectarine and bay leaf chutney · nuts · super-quick homemade chili sauce · caramelized roasted vegetable gravy · very lazy vegetable stock · homemade vegetable stock powder

First-sign-of-summer jam

I love the first signs of summer and the warmer days when sweet little strawberries start to pop up and you know the season is truly on its way. This vivid pink jam is amazingly beautiful. It usually shows up in my house slathered on some buttered sourdough for breakfast, but it is equally happy stirred into yogurt or on top of some rice pudding.

I make this when rhubarb is around, when the first early summer strawberries are starting to ripen. I love to make it in late summer too, with the last of the season's strawberries and plums in place of the rhubarb. By regular jam-making standards, I only use a tiny bit of sugar here, so the texture is thinner than a heavy-set jam, which is how I like it. It keeps the red color and the freshness of the fruit—if you like a more firmly set jam, add a little extra sugar and cook for a bit longer.

For this jam, it's best to pick roses from a garden where you know pesticides are not used. Most florists will be able to point you toward somewhere you can buy unsprayed roses too.

A note on sterilizing jars: rather than boiling jars to sterilize them, warm them in the oven while you are working. Heat the oven to 275°F/140°C. The jars should be in there for 10 minutes minimum but can stay in longer. When your jam or chutney is ready and still hot, protecting your hands with an oven glove, carefully ladle it into the hot jars. This process will be sufficient to seal the jars safely—and it eliminates boring boiling and washing. The hottest cycle on your dishwasher will do the trick too, but just make sure you fill the jars while they are still hot.

....

Gently pull the petals off the roses and carefully run them under cold water. (No need to do this if you're using dried petals.) Set aside. Put a saucer in the freezer for checking the jam later.

MAKES ABOUT 2 QUARTS/2 L

6 unsprayed red roses or a handful of edible dried rose petals

2¼ pounds/1 kg strawberries, hulled and quartered

2¼ pounds/1 kg rhubarb, trimmed and cut into ¾-inch/2 cm lengths

1⅓ cup/300 g unrefined superfine sugar

1 unwaxed lemon, quartered

the juice of 2 lemons

4 tablespoons rosewater

Put the strawberries, rhubarb, sugar, quartered lemon, and lemon juice into a large pan, place over low heat, and allow the sugar to dissolve slowly. Once all the sugar has dissolved, increase the heat and bring to a boil, then simmer for 30 minutes, skimming off any white foam that rises to the top.

After 30 minutes, check the jam by spooning a little onto the saucer from your freezer. If it wrinkles when you push it with your finger, it's ready. If not, keep cooking for a few minutes at a time and check again. Remember to put your saucer back in the freezer in the meantime.

Once you are happy with the set of your jam, turn off the heat and stir in the rose petals and rosewater.

Allow the jam to cool a little, then, while still warm, spoon into sterilized jars. Immediately screw the lids on and set them aside to cool, and then label them and store them in a cool place until you are in need of some jarred sunshine.

Rosy-cheeked apricot jam

This is the best jam I have ever made. It is summer in a jar. Break it out on a gray January day and make everyone smile and think of summer. It is more in the French style than British traditional set apricot jam, somewhere between a jam and a compote, with a softer set and less sugar, keeping the freshness of the fruit intact.

Place the apricot halves and sugar into your biggest pan and squeeze over the juice of the lemons. Score the vanilla pod, scrape out the seeds, and add both pod and seeds to the pan. Give everything a good stir and let steep for 2 hours.

Once the apricots have had 2 hours steeping, and the sugar has dissolved and the fruit has softened, put the pan over low heat and bring to a simmer. Keep simmering for 25 minutes, stirring all the time to stop the jam from scorching. You can skim off any foam that rises to the top as you go.

After 25 minutes the jam should have thickened, and it will thicken further as it cools. To check how it will set, you can use the saucer test (see pages 334 and 335). Once the jam is cooled but still warm, spoon into sterilized jars and seal immediately. Stored in a cool place, this will keep for a year.

MAKES 4 TO 5 JARS

3⅓ pounds/1½ kg ripe blushing apricots, washed and halved

2¼ cup/500 g unrefined superfine sugar

juice of 2 lemons

1 vanilla pod

Spiced nectarine and bay leaf chutney

This is my version of mango chutney. I make it in late summer when blushing nectarines are filling the markets, but peaches would work just as well.

I eat this dotted on top of mature Cheddar (Lancashire Bomber goes particularly well, if you can find it), or generously spooned on to the side of a plate of rice and dal.

....

Chop the nectarines into small pieces, about the size of a fava bean. In a mortar and pestle, pound the fennel seeds and cilantro seeds until they are cracked.

Heat a little olive oil in a large pan. Add the chopped chiles and the crushed spices and stir for a minute until they heat up. Now add the chopped nectarines, sugar, bay leaves, and vinegar and bring to a slow simmer over low heat.

Cook for 20 to 30 minutes, until you have a deep red and orange syrupy chutney. Remember that it will set a little as it cools.

Spoon into sterilized jars (see page 334) and keep in the fridge or in a cool place for a couple of weeks until you need some sun and spice.

MAKES 1½ QUARTS/1½ L OR ABOUT 3 (1-PINT) JARS

4½ pounds/2 kg nectarines, washed and pitted

1 tablespoon fennel seeds

1 tablespoon cilantro seeds

olive oil

2 red chiles, seeded and finely sliced

2¾ cup/600 g unrefined superfine sugar

4 bay leaves

⅔ cup/150 ml white wine vinegar

NUTS

Nuts find their way into most of my cooking. Whether it's a slick of almond butter topped with banana and a sprinkle of cinnamon on toast or a handful of toasted pistachios blended into a pesto (page 176) with some grassy herbs to spoon on to roasted vegetables or almond flour stirred into a cake batter or ground to make my favorite almond and vanilla milk (page 341), nuts are fundamental in my cooking.

Nuts are full of healthy fats, which are needed by our bodies and good for our hearts. They are rich in vitamin E, minerals, and fiber. Walnuts even contain omega-3s.

I buy unsalted nuts and store them in jars in the fridge, as they keep longer. I try to eat them soaked and raw, as that way you get the maximum nutrients, but if I'm toasting them, I do them in little batches as I need them as toasted nuts go rancid much more quickly. Always use nuts within a couple of months. Fresh nuts taste best.

SOAKING NUTS

Why soak nuts? Nuts are essentially seeds that haven't been germinated. Soaked nuts are actually germinating seeds that are starting to grow into a plant. Unsoaked nuts contain enzyme inhibitors bestowed on them by Mother Nature, which stops them growing into plants but may make them harder to digest. Once we soak them in water, the nut begins to germinate, allowing its natural enzymes to work and all the other nutrients to skyrocket. If you don't have time to soak nuts overnight that's okay; just soak them for a few minutes to soften them. But if you are able to do an overnight soaking, it will help the nuts do their job the best way they can. I soak a handful of nuts before I go to bed at night for snacking and cooking the next day.

NUT BUTTER

I am a big fan of nut butters. I eat them on toast in the morning, spread them on pancakes, and spoon them into dressings and sauces. Making them yourself will be much cheaper than buying, if you get your hands on a big bulk bag of nuts.

TO MAKE YOUR OWN JAR OF RAW NUT BUTTER

•

Put about 7 ounces/200 g of nuts (pistachios, cashews, almonds, hazelnuts, macadamia nuts) into a food processor and grind for 1 to 2 minutes until you have a coarse powder. Scrape down the sides of the mixer and grind again until you have a smoothish paste. Put into a jar and keep in the fridge for up to 2 weeks. If your nut butter is a little dry, add a couple of tablespoons of peanut or rapeseed oil to moisten it. For a toasted nut butter with a deeper taste, toast your nuts at 400°F/200°C for 4 to 5 minutes until just starting to color. Cool, then follow the recipe above.

You can add a little honey, agave nectar, or maple syrup to sweeten your nut butter if you like, or a pinch of sea salt, cinnamon, or vanilla for extra depth.

NUT BUTTER ON TOAST

•

Top toast with almond butter, maple syrup, a pinch of cinnamon, and a sprinkle of sea salt.

•

Spread toast with a slick of coconut oil, peanut butter, and a little honey and sprinkle with coconut.

•

Top toast with pecan butter, sliced banana, honey, and a pinch of sea salt.

•

Mix hazelnut butter with a little raw cocoa and spread on toast for a healthy Nutella.

•

Top toast with macadamia nut butter, slices of avocado, honey, and a sprinkle of sea salt.

NUT MILK
You will need: 1 cup
of nuts, 1 quart/1 L of
water, and a muslin cloth.
Oh . . . and a blender.

↓

CASHEWS · BRAZIL NUTS · ALMONDS ·
PISTACHIOS · WALNUTS ·
HAZELNUTS · MACADAMIA NUTS ·
SUNFLOWER SEEDS · PUMPKIN SEEDS ·
SESAME SEEDS · HEMP SEEDS

→

1

Soak the nuts in cold water overnight
or for at least 8 hours.

2

Drain and rinse the nuts and put into
a blender with 1 quart/1 L of water.

3

Blend until you have a thin cloudy
mixture (careful not to splash).

4

Put the muslin cloth over the mouth
of a pitcher and pour the milk
through—squeeze out every last
drop of moisture.

5

Pour the milk into a bottle and keep in
the fridge—it is good for 3 to 4 days.

6

Sit back and feel satisfied that you have
made your very own milk.

Super-quick homemade chili sauce

This salsa is for drizzling on anything and everything, with a sure fire chipotle-chile-molasses-brown-sugar-and-fresh-vegetable hit. I use it to pep up morning eggs, to finish off my tomato soup, or as the crowning glory for black bean tacos (page 170).

This is a one-size-fits-all sauce and is loosely based on Lizano, a fiery condiment that sits next to the salt and pepper on every table in Central America.

....

Heat a little olive oil in a pan and fry the onion and carrot for 5 minutes, until soft. Add the stock and all the other ingredients except for the lemon juice. Simmer briskly for 5 minutes, until slightly thickened.

Allow to cool a little, then put into a blender and blend until smooth. Add the lemon juice, then taste, season, and balance the flavors, adding a little more lemon, chipotle, or salt if needed.

This will keep in the fridge for a few weeks or in a sterilized bottle or jar for longer.

MAKES ABOUT 1 CUP/250 ML

olive oil

1 small onion, peeled and finely chopped

½ a carrot, peeled and finely chopped

1 cup/250 ml good vegetable stock

1 tablespoon ground cumin

3 tablespoons brown sugar

1 tablespoon cider vinegar

1 teaspoon sea salt

1 tablespoon chipotle paste, or to taste

juice of ½ a lemon

Caramelized roasted vegetable gravy

This is a gravy to be proud of. Sweetness from the roasted vegetables is backed up by a little freshness from the cider. This works on roasted vegetables, Yorkshire pudding, sausage and mashed potatoes, and pot pies. I make this every year for Christmas and for all my Sunday roasts. It can be easily made a day ahead, and any leftovers freeze well.

Preheat the oven to 425°F/220°C.

Place the vegetables in a large roasting pan and scatter over the herbs. Season and then drizzle over a little olive oil. Roast in the oven for 45 minutes, until the vegetables are sweet, soft, and golden. Remove from the oven and allow to cool a little.

Using a potato masher, mash the vegetables in the roasting pan, then place the pan on the stove top over medium heat. Add the flour and stir well for a couple of minutes, until it has cooked through.

Pour in the cider and stock, bring to a simmer, then cook for 10 minutes, stirring occasionally to get all the sticky bits from the bottom of the pan.

After 10 minutes, remove from the heat and strain the gravy into a gravy boat, pressing down on all the vegetables and herbs with a spoon to get all the flavor out. Keep in the fridge until needed. Reheat with a little extra hot water or vegetable stock.

MAKES 1¾ CUPS/400 ML

2 leeks, roughly chopped

2 stalks of celery, roughly chopped

4 carrots, roughly chopped

2 whole cloves of garlic, skins left on

2 sprigs of fresh rosemary

2 sprigs of fresh thyme

2 bay leaves

sea salt and freshly ground black pepper

olive oil

2 tablespoons all-purpose flour

2 cups/500 ml cider

⅞ cup/200 ml vegetable stock

Very lazy vegetable stock

I happily admit that more often than not, I use store-bought bouillon powder or a good organic vegetable stock cube rather than making my own stock.

That is, I did until I came up with this idea. I almost feel bad calling it a recipe, as it's so easy—chopping vegetables and boiling water is as hard as it gets.

You'll need two big 1-quart/1 L preserving jars that will fit into your fridge. Don't feel tied to the amounts of vegetables below—the great thing about stock is that you can use up all the trimmings and odds and ends you have in the fridge. Just work to the same ratio, half-filling your quart jars with vegetables.

....

Fill up the kettle and bring to a boil. Divide the chopped vegetables and other ingredients between your two 1-quart/1 L jars. Fill the jars with the just-boiled water, leaving 1 inch/2 cm or so headroom at the top—each jar should hold about 3¼ cups/750 ml. Screw the lids on and leave in a safe place to cool down.

When cool, strain immediately for a light vegetable stock or put into the fridge for 12 hours and then strain for a more full-bodied stock.

Once strained, pour the stock back into the jars and store in the fridge, where it will keep for up to a week.

MAKES 2 QUARTS/2 L

2 carrots, roughly chopped

1 red onion, cut into wedges

1 leek, cut into rounds

2 stalks of celery, roughly chopped

2 bay leaves, crushed

a small bunch of fresh thyme

1 teaspoon sea salt

a few black peppercorns

Homemade vegetable stock powder

This is one of those recipes that leaves you asking yourself why it has never occurred to you to do it before. This homemade vegetable stock powder is less salty than the store-bought stuff and you can much more clearly taste the flavor of the vegetables.

The basis of this recipe is borrowed from my brilliant friend Heidi Swanson of 101cookbooks.com. This is a really useful recipe for vegans and for people who are avoiding gluten, as it can be hard to find dairy-free and gluten-free stock cubes and powder.

....

Pulse the vegetables and garlic in a food processor until they are finely diced. Add the parsley and celery leaves and pulse a few more times. Now add the salt and pulse until you have a fine paste (it will still be quite wet).

Store in an airtight container in the freezer until needed. Because of all the salt, this will remain quite powdery when frozen, so you can spoon it straight from the freezer. I use 1 teaspoon to 1 tablespoon per quart of water, depending on what I am making.

**MAKES ABOUT
16 OUNCES/500 G**

2 leeks, washed and roughly
chopped

4 carrots, well scrubbed
and chopped

4 stalks of celery, washed and
roughly chopped

1 head of fennel, washed and
roughly chopped

3 cloves garlic, peeled

a small bunch of fresh parsley

a handful of celery leaves,
from the inside of the celery

tablespoons/20 g fine sea salt

Index

Acknowledgments

Writing this book has been the joy of my life, and a roller coaster of emotions. This book belongs to many people.

First to John, my kind and gentle Welshman. You put your life on hold to help me make this book. Your kindness, utter selflessness, saintly patience, and unwavering belief make my heart swell. I am so happily bound to you. This is for you.

Since I was very small I have known I am lucky to be part of my family, the Joneses. Roger and Geraldine, the greatest parents that there are. Your endless support and love goes with me everywhere, I am in awe. Laura, my sister, from our days as little girls to writing this book, I look to you for everything, my constant support, you have held my hand through this book and my life. All we do together. You are my hero. To Owen, my brother, you blaze a trail for what you believe is right with courage and loyalty and you are truly yourself in everything you do. I strive to be as brave, as bright, and as funny.

Louise Haines, thank you for your humbling belief in me and my food, and for allowing this book and me the freedom to evolve, to be published by you and Fourth Estate is a dream. Georgia Mason, an utterly brilliant, patient, kind, and graceful editor, you have been my sounding board and you have made this book happen in your divine and perfectly worded way, I am so grateful. Morwenna Loughman, thank you too. Michelle Kane, what a doll. Annie Lee, for sifting through my words, I felt so safe in your hands, thank you.

Brian Ferry, for the beautiful pictures and incredible attention to detail and damn hard work on dark January days. I have long admired your work from afar and it was a dream to have you take these pictures. Sandra Zellmer, for the incredible design, patience, and exquisitely organized and calm manner, you are wonderful.

To my literary agent Felicity Blunt for being my confidante, backing me up, dealing with the occasional curveball.

Some dear friends have been central to making this book. Ceri Tallett, your help with my words has made this book much better. Thanks for your ceaseless kindness and dogged belief in me. Liz McMullan, and your brilliant brain, I know you've got my back, I've got yours my friend, grazie mille. Emily Ezekiel, your endless encouragement, ridiculously good cooking, friendship, and honesty have lifted me higher than I ever could have gone without it, there is so much more to come, babe. Jess Lea Wilson, Anglesey's finest, thank you for everything.

There have been countless cooks who have inspired me along the way. Jamie Oliver, for starting the ball rolling, for being repeatedly so good you leave all the others at the starting line. Ginny Rolfe, for your nurturing; Georgina Hayden, for squealing encouragement; Steve Pooley and Asher Wyborn, for the early days; and all my JO family. Tom and Henry Herbert, for culinary adventures. Sophie Dahl, for your unwavering support. Heidi Swanson, for constant inspiration and kindness. And all the cooks I've never met whose blogs, books, and pictures fill up my days.

To the kind people who helped test these recipes, I am forever grateful: Emily Taylor, Pip Spence, Christina Mackenzie, Stella Lahaine, Sian Tallett, Olenka Lawrenson, Hannah Cameron MacKenna, Ken Gavin, Nick and Anna Probert-Boyd.

To Jo at Brickett Davda, for your incredibly beautiful plates. All at David Mellor, for allowing me to use some of your carefully chosen and beautifully crafted pieces. Labour and Wait, for a bounty of wonderful things including the most incredible coffee pot. The Conran shop, for your kind loans. Holly's house, for your beautiful furnishings. Nukuku, for your generosity. And to the Lacquer Chest, Gretchen, Agnes, Ewan and Merle, for allowing me to step into your beauty-filled rooms and lose myself in one of the most special places I know.

To my Stoke Newington greengrocers; for helping me carry endless boxes of vegetables to my car, to Leila's Shop; for the most exquisite produce and allowing us to take some pictures in your beautifully crafted shop.

Matt "Muscles" Russell, for being a kind soul; Jules May, for the loan of his camera; Andy Ford, for his keen eye; and Jon P, for looking so good in an apron; to Alex Grimes, for her stories and some great cooking; to Serinde and Rhod, for their soda bread.

To countless other family and friends who have been at the sidelines over the years. To the Joneses, far and wide, our endless and brilliant family is a joy, if I named you all we'd be here forever. My friends Lizzie Prior, Priya and Bayju Thakar, Mersedeh Safa, Charlotte Coleman and JMC, Lucy White, Zoe Allen, The Dales—Roger, Sian, Phil, Liz and Scott, Holly O, Jon Abbey and The Holdens, and last but by absolutely no means least, my surrogate sister, Crystal Malachias, you are all the best of the best.